FEARLESS MEN
AND
FABULOUS WOMEN

A Reporter's Memoir from Alaska & the Yukon

✦ ✦ ✦

STANTON H. PATTY

EPICENTER PRESS

With love, to two of the unstoppable women in my life—

my dear wife, Mabs,

and my mother, Kathryn Stanton Patty

✦ ✦ ✦

Epicenter Press is a regional press founded in Alaska whose interests include but are not limited to the arts, history, environment, and diverse cultures and lifestyles of the Pacific Northwest and high latitudes. We seek both the traditional and innovative in publishing nonfiction books, and contemporary art and photography gift books.

Publisher: Kent Sturgis
Acquisitions Editor: Lael Morgan
Editor: Don Graydon
Cover and book design: Elizabeth Watson, Watson Graphics
Cover photograph: Troy Wayrynen, Vancouver (Wash.) *Columbian*
Proofreader: Sherrill Carlson
Printer: Transcontinental Printing
Illustration page 19: This is one of the cheerful sketches that my wife, Mabs, included in my lunch sacks for many years when I was on the staff of *The Seattle Times.*

Library of Congress Control Number: 2004103953
ISBN 0-9745014-0-9

Booksellers: This title is available from major wholesalers. Retail discounts are available from our trade distributor, Graphic Arts Center Publishing Co., PO Box 10306, Portland, OR 97210.

PRINTED IN CANADA

First Edition
First Printing, April 2004

10 9 8 7 6 5 4 3 2 1

To order single copies of FEARLESS MEN & FABULOUS WOMEN, mail $17.95 plus $6.95 for shipping and handling (WA residents add $2.20 state sales tax) to: Epicenter Press, PO Box 82368, Kenmore, WA 98028.

Discover exciting ALASKA BOOK ADVENTURES! Visit our online Alaska bookstore at www.EpicenterPress.com or call our 24-hour, toll-free hotline at 800-950-6663. Visit our online gallery featuring one of Alaska's favorite artists, Jon Van Zyle, www.JonVanZyle.com.

CONTENTS

Arctic Ocea

Barrow

Wainwright

Icy
Cape

Point
Lay

Umiat

Chukchi   Sea

Point
Hope

Colville   River

B R O O K S   R A N G E

ARCTIC

CIRCLE

Big
Diomede
Island

Kotzebue

*Kotzebue
Sound*

Kobuk   River

Koyukuk   River

RUSSIA

Noatak River

Little
Diomede
Island

Seward
Peninsula

A L A S K A

Bering

Nome

Koyukuk

Yukon   River

Tanan

St. Lawrence
Island

Norton   Sound

M
O
U
N
T
A
I
N
S

Nati
and

St. Michael

Innoko   River

Mt

*Yukon
River*

St. Matthew
Island

K
U
S
K
O
K
W
I
M

Kuskokwim   River

A
L
A
S
K
A

Nunivak
Island

S

*Bering
Sea*

*Kuskokwim
Bay*

Mulchatna River

Iliamna L.

*McNeil
River*

Nushagak   River

Cook

Pacific   Ocean

*Bristol
Bay*

Afognak

St.Paul
Island

Kot

Pribilof   Islands

Kodiak
Island

St. George
Island

Peninsula

MILES

| 0 | 100 | 200 | 300 |

KILOMETERS

| 0 | 100 | 200 | 300 |

Alaska

Unimak
Island

Shumagin
Islands

CONTINUED ON MAP INSET

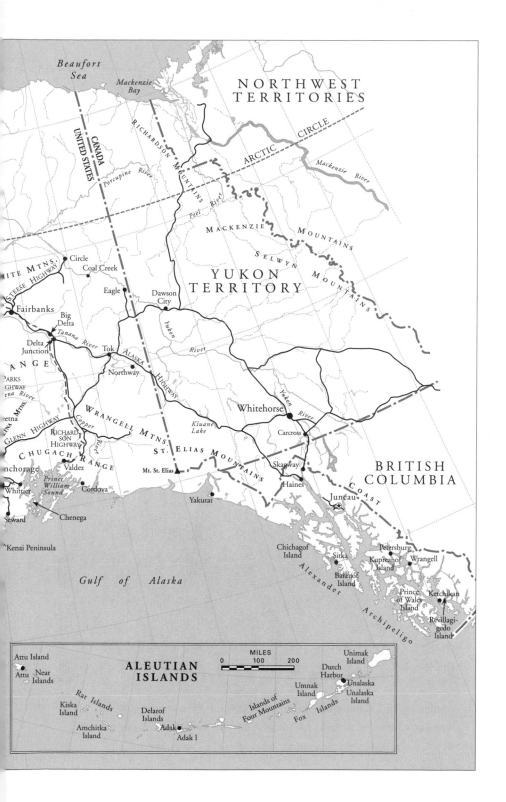

Visitors join in a blanket-tossing exhibition in the Eskimo community of Barrow, with the ice-flecked Arctic Ocean for a backdrop. The so-called blanket, sort of an arctic trampoline, is fashioned from the hide of a bearded seal.

ACKNOWLEDGMENTS

NOBODY EVER DESCRIBED me as speechless. But I am truly humbled as I remember the friends and colleagues who have enriched my life—and who helped bring this book to life.

The starting point was a conversation in April 2002 with Jacquie Witherrite, an Alaska Airlines friend, during a flight from Boston to Seattle. We were seated in the economy section of a Boeing 737 when Jacquie switched on the overhead reading lights and suggested we have a "candlelight dinner" and talk about Alaska. "You're always telling stories, now write a book," she said. "I don't want to hear any excuses such as, 'I don't have time.' Get to work."

Write a book? Maybe. I'd think about it.

Shortly after came a phone call from Kent Sturgis, publisher of Epicenter Press. "You should write a book about your experiences in covering Alaska," he said. "You aren't getting any younger."

That did it!

I signed a contract with Kent and went to work.

"It's about time," Jacquie said when she heard the news.

She gets one of the first copies.

And now my deepest gratitude goes to the following:

To the late Bob and Lori Giersdorf, who carried us along on their magic carpet for more than thirty years to explore Alaska and the rest of this fascinating world. They were family to Mabs and me. To Ray and Betty Kusler, pioneers in Alaska's visitor industry, friends for life. To Roberta Graham for opening doors for me in Alaska and the Yukon that led to memorable news stories—and to her sidekick, Craig Medred, for giving Robbie time to pal around with me in the North Country. That gal knows great people—and great wine. To His Beatitude, Metropolitan Theodosius, of the Russian Orthodox Church in America, for friendship and gentle guidance for this sometimes Episcopalian wanderer.

To June Allen, one of Alaska's best journalists, for smart story suggestions. To Bob DeArmond, one of Alaska's best historians, for tolerating my attempts at writing about Alaska history—and correcting my errors. To Dick and Patti Garvin for showing me horizons in Alaska that I might have missed.

To Dave Fremming, publisher of the late lamented *Alaskan Southeaster* magazine, for sharing his vast knowledge. To Mary Knodel, Nancy McGuire, and Howard Farley, in Nome. To Jim Walsh, of Seattle, whose pioneer parents in Nome helped to shape Alaska. To the late Al Johnson, of the Alaska-Yukon Pioneers, for careful attention to gold-rush history. To Doug Beckstead, a National Park Service historian, who records gold-mining history on the Yukon River creeks where I spent my childhood summers. To Max Brewer, arctic scientist and wise counselor to eager reporters who can be taught to avoid leaping to foolish conclusions. To Roberta Sheldon, author and valued friend, in Talkeetna. To Don Church, a retired Alaska state trooper, who guided me through his Aleutians precinct.

To those who lead the hospitality industry across Alaska. Chuck West, forever "Mr. Alaska" to his admirers. Patti Mackey, Len Laurance, and Nathan Jackson, in Ketchikan. Steve Hites, Tina Cyr, Gary Danielson, Dennis Corrington, and Buckwheat Donahue, in Skagway. Arne Olsson and the Heinmiller family, in Haines. Michelle Blackwell and the late Joe Ashby, in Sitka. Gretchen Lake, Karen Lundquist, and the Binkley family, in Fairbanks. Sharon Gaiptman and Linda Mickle, of the Alaska Marine Highway System, in Juneau. Brad (Twenty-Six Glaciers) Phillips and Al Parrish, in Anchorage. Jerre Fuqua at Cruise West. Chris von Imhof at Alyeska. Gloria Ohmer, in Petersburg. Jim Johnson, Dave Palmer, Lou Cancelmi, Jack Evans, Jack Walsh, Danna Maros, and many others at Alaska Airlines. Pam Foreman and Phil and Kay Anderson, in Kodiak. Dick and Joyce Galleher, former Nome residents.

In the Yukon, the late Alan Innes-Taylor, riverboat purser, Mountie, historian, and good friend. For access to the Yukon and all of Canada, Monica Campbell-Hoppe, of the Canadian Tourism Commission.

To Jerry Nerland, of Anchorage and Fairbanks, treasured friend since we were in grade school in Fairbanks. Rarely a day goes by that I don't receive a batch of newspaper clippings from Jerry for my Alaska files.

Many of those I want to thank are gone now—including Henry MacLeod, Mel Sayre, and Lane Smith, *Seattle Times* editors who gave me wonderful story opportunities and always found ways to improve my copy.

And to my late parents, Ernest and Kathryn Patty: thanks for conceiving me in Alaska and then blazing my life's path with class, truth, and great love.

ACKNOWLEDGMENTS

To those colleagues who gave of their time to read these chapters as the yarns emerged from my cranky computer—Hill Williams, Tom Koenninger, and Janet Cleaveland. Sometimes their suggestions displeased me, but they were right every time. Writers need editors. I am grateful for their help.

To our children, whose concerts, ball games, and graduations I missed while wandering the world: thanks Kay, Stan Jr., and Ginna. Now our great kids have nuggets of their own—Christine, Heather, Michael, Kathy, Shawn, and Grant.

Thanks also to Matthew Lowe for his whimsical illustrations. Matt is married to our adventurous granddaughter, Christine.

And, most of all, to my dear wife of more than fifty-seven years, for her love and inspiration. Mabs has given me the hours and the space to write this book. But now it's getting to be time, she says, for me to resume taking out the garbage and walking the dog. Agreed.

I have done my best to report accurately on happenings in Alaska and the Yukon. I relied on files and notebooks that Mabs has helped preserve over more than five decades of her letting me be a reporter on the loose. If there are mistakes, they are mine alone.

Thanks again, Jacquie, for the "candlelight dinner" conversation. And thanks, Kent, for the push.

I don't feel any older.

Cheers!

A playful humpback whale breaches in Frederick Sound, near Petersburg, in Southeastern Alaska.

DREAMS DO COME TRUE

THE STORY BEGINS on a ridge above the Yukon River.

At:

N 65° 17' 14.668"

W 143° 18' 47.487"

It was the kind of summer day Alaskans love—bright sunshine, but not too warm. Birdsongs. Fresh, green smells of moss and spruce. Butterflies, and just enough breeze to discourage pesky mosquitoes.

The Yukon makes a lazy curve there, one hundred miles or so northeast of Fairbanks. There are no towns or villages in the area, just a couple of old gold mines.

Canada's Yukon Territory, with the fabled Klondike goldfields, is just a few miles upriver. We kids never knew there was a political boundary between Alaska and the Yukon.

The year was 1940. Japanese warplanes had not yet bombed Pearl Harbor. There were no Russian sputniks, no men on the moon. Geologists were searching the northland for gold, not oil. Statehood for Alaska still was a distant dream.

I hiked alone that day to the summit of the seven-mile-long road that connected the Coal Creek and Woodchopper mining camps. The view from there still grabs at my heart. Just below, to the north, ramparts of the Yukon River turn a soft purple in the afternoon light. They are tall cliffs of rock and clay, creased by centuries of wind and rain. They remind me of the stone pillars that frame Egypt's ancient temples.

My father, who was managing the gold-mining operations at Coal Creek and Woodchopper, told me to watch for bears when roaming this wild country. Good advice. But this day I had some serious thinking to do.

I leaned my .30-06 rifle against a tree and rested on a mossy cushion to watch the glow of lavender light across the Yukon.

What was I going to do with the rest of my life?

I longed to see oceans and the great buildings of the world: the pyramids of Egypt, the Taj Mahal, the Parthenon, the Eiffel Tower, and China's Great Wall. But I knew even then, at the age of fourteen, that I couldn't leave Alaska, my beloved North Country, for long.

My favorite boyhood author was Richard Halliburton, an adventurer with a talent for telling mostly true tales about his wanderings. He wrote in his 1937 *Book of Marvels* about paying a toll to swim lengths of the Panama Canal. And how he explored the mysterious Inca ruins of Machu Picchu in faraway Peru.

Halliburton also told of a visit to Agra, site of India's Taj Mahal, a glorious, white-marble tomb built for a queen by her broken-hearted husband.

"As the guards came forward to drive out all visitors, I was standing in the dark shadow of a tree," he wrote. "I was so much under the spell of the Taj, I didn't, I couldn't, show myself to them . . . and the guards passed on. In a moment more the great gates boomed shut. I was locked inside."

Creeping past a sleeping sentry, the author decided to go for a swim among the lotus blossoms in a pool beside the Taj.

"The moon was well up in the sky," he recalled. "I was all alone, more peacefully alone than I have ever been. The whole garden—my garden— seemed truly enchanted. I meant no harm. . . ."

Did it really happen this way?

Maybe Halliburton embellished his reports now and then. Nevertheless, his colorful yarns set me to dreaming about world wonders.

Maybe I could climb aboard magic carpets, too.

The five Pattys at their home in Fairbanks in the early 1930s. They are (from left) Stanton H. Patty (the author), Ernest N. Patty Jr., Kathryn Patty, Ernest N. Patty, and Dale F. Patty. STANTON PATTY COLLECTION

That's it. I'll be a writer.

I'll turn out for high school football in the fall. And I'll keep tooting my trumpet in the school band and pretend that I can play like Harry James. I'll study more geography and history. And then I'll become a writer. Yes, that's what I'll do.

I left my favorite place by the Yukon River that day, sure of my direction.

That is how it happened. And later all my daydreams came true.

I'm the luckiest guy I know.

I was born in Alaska, to pioneering parents, when Alaska was young. Fairbanks, my hometown, had only 1,555 residents in 1926. Juneau, the capital, with a population of more than 3,000, was Alaska's big city back then. Anchorage, then mostly a railroad town, wouldn't blossom into Alaska's largest city until World War II.

Our Fairbanks neighbors were bush pilots, dog mushers, gold miners, teachers, and artists.

Alaska, for kids, was all about wide-open spaces and wilderness adventures. I spent my summers in mining camps, where big placer dredges, rumbling like landlocked dreadnoughts, tore gold from the frozen ground.

The Patty family's home at Sixth Avenue and Cowles Street in Fairbanks, in about 1938. My father, Ernest Patty, designed the house with a sloping roof to shed snow, and included a music room for my mother's piano. STANTON PATTY COLLECTION.

It was fun telling teachers and classmates what I did on my summer vacations:

"We flew out to the mines in bush planes, drove a bulldozer there, and after work some nights we went hunting for caribou and moose. Then we helped collect the gold from the dredges. Oh, you should see the shiny bars of gold that come out of the molds in the gold room. . . ."

We had a garden behind our home at Sixth and Cowles in Fairbanks. Potatoes, lettuce, cauliflower, cabbage, radishes, even a few strawberries. The crops prospered under the summertime midnight sun. Some of our trophy-size cabbages won blue ribbons at the Tanana Valley Fair.

But fresh produce was a precious commodity in winter. For special dinner parties, my mother would buy an overpriced head of lettuce that had been air-shipped from Seattle the previous day. Guests understood that the "air-mail lettuce" was to be admired, not eaten. They consumed only the Jell-O or other toppings. Then the still-crisp lettuce leaves were washed and passed to another Fairbanks hostess for another party.

Winters in frigid Fairbanks could be miserable for a lad with a newspaper route. Many a dark and snowy night, I wanted to ditch my bundle of *Fairbanks Daily News-Miner* editions and hurry home. One night I did just that. Customers began telephoning: "Where's the newspaper?"

My short-fused father rousted me from the dinner table and ordered me back into the blizzard to complete my rounds. It never happened again.

Part of my route was along the red-light section of Fourth Avenue known as The Line—until my mother did some mental mapping. She called Charlie Settlemier, the *News-Miner* editor, and requested that my route be changed immediately, and it was.

That made me curious about those ladies who always paid their subscriptions on time and wore housecoats or bathrobes when they answered their doors. Older boys in the neighborhood were eager to provide the answers.

That checkered stint with the *News-Miner* was the start of a career in journalism that has covered more than fifty years.

My parents came to Alaska in 1922. Dad had been hired as dean of mines for the brand-new Alaska Agricultural College and School of Mines. The hilltop college, just outside Fairbanks, later would become the University of Alaska. And in the 1950s my father became its third president.

I was born into academia, but soon to "go astray," as my father put it, by deciding early on to be a newspaperman.

"I don't understand it," said my father, the mining engineer/educator. "You could have chosen something that pays better."

"But it's a respectable calling," I responded.

"Calling?" he asked. "Maybe that's a bit strong, don't you think?"

"Well, it's calling me."

"There's no hope for you then," Dad said with a smile. "You must have been born with sand in your shoes."

If that means a hunger to go vagabonding all over the world, it's an accurate description. I'm still at it.

Dad and I had a sort of showdown many years later at the University of Alaska.

I had traveled to the campus for an interview with Dr. Christian T. Elvey, then director of the university's Geophysical Institute. Scientists there were studying the aurora borealis—the northern lights—to learn about how the solar storms that generate the heavenly lights also disrupt radio communications here on earth. Military authorities wanted to know more. So did I.

When the interview ended, I walked to the administration building to visit with my father. He was furious.

"Why didn't you clear that interview with me?" he demanded.

"With all due respect, Dad, I don't work for you. I am here for the *Seattle Times.*"

He leaned back in his chair and laughed.

"By golly, you're right," he said.

Publications have been paying me to travel to some of the most exciting places on the planet since my first cub-reporting job in 1949.

First, five learning years with the *Longview Daily News,* a small newspaper in southwestern Washington state. Then thirty-four years with the *Seattle Times.*

It was during the *Seattle Times* years that I was witness to the pageant of Alaska's recent history: the fight for statehood, the Good Friday earthquake in 1964, the Fairbanks flood of 1967, the campaign for settlement of the Alaska natives' aboriginal land claims, construction of the trans-Alaska oil pipeline from Prudhoe Bay in the Arctic to Valdez, and the *Exxon Valdez* oil spill in 1989.

And now, in "retirement," I'm a freelance travel writer and photographer for newspapers around the country. I go by Stan, rather than Stanton, much of the time these days. But when my mother was alive, that name appeared only once in print. Mom called my city editor after spotting a Stan Patty byline in the *Seattle Times.* "That isn't his name," she told city editor Henry MacLeod. "It is Stanton, not Stan." Stanton, you see, was my mother's maiden name.

Henry was wearing a big grin when he approached my desk after being scolded by my mother.

"Your mommy called," he said. "I got the message."

As for retirement? It lasted only three weeks after I left the *Seattle Times* in 1988. The writing itch was unceasing. Besides, I wanted a reason to go "home" and write more about Alaska. No matter where I travel, my heart remains in Alaska, to me the most beautiful place in the world.

Of course, I'm partial.

But then I have seen most of the world, including the Panama Canal, Machu Picchu, and the Taj Mahal of Richard Halliburton's moonlight swim. So I have a substantial database for comparing destinations.

Alaska always wins.

A salmon troller at anchor casts a foggy-morning reflection in Bartlett Cove, near the entrance to Glacier Bay National Park.

Wherever I go, I carry with me images of a land so grand that surely there cannot be any other place as glorious.

I think about a spring day in Southeastern Alaska's Frederick Sound, when a playful humpback whale vaulted for almost half an hour for passengers aboard a little sightseeing boat called the *Heron*.

"Why is the whale doing that?" a traveler asked.

"I'd like to think he's just having a good time," said Scott Hursey, the skipper.

I'd like to think that, too.

And never could I forget an evening in Glacier Bay National Park. Six of us, friends forever, had gathered to watch a sunset. Icy peaks of the Fairweather Range were tinted purple by the lowering sun. Suddenly, as if cued by a motion-picture director, a bald eagle swooped down, spread its talons to catch a salmon, and flew off into the sunset.

"It can't get any better than this," said a companion.

Well, maybe.

One morning, when I was flying home from an assignment in Europe, a friend arranged for me to join the flight crew in the cockpit of a Boeing 747.

It was my birthday. My friend Dick Garvin, a fellow Alaskan, thought I would enjoy the view as the jetliner soared over the Yukon River and Fairbanks.

I looked down on Alaska—where my parents broke trail for future generations, where a brother died while piloting his airplane in stormy weather, where lifetime friendships were forged, where my dreams began.

There were tears in my eyes. And I didn't care who noticed.

Alaska. I'm part of it. It's part of me.

As I said, I'm the luckiest guy I know.

THE ALASKA BEAT

I TOLD FRIENDS that I was in exile.

There I was in Seattle, with a great job as a staff reporter at the *Seattle Times*. But my heart was in Alaska.

"So, why don't you move back to Alaska?" friends asked.

"Because I'll never get a better job than this in Alaska, and my wife and three little kids are happy here in Seattle."

"So, what are you going to do about it?"

"I'm not sure."

I was so homesick for Alaska that I watched planes fly north until they were out of sight. I could close my eyes and follow their route: along the western edge of British Columbia, across Dixon Entrance into Alaskan skies, then by Ketchikan, Wrangell, Petersburg, Juneau, Sitka, Yakutat, and Cordova before turning across Prince William Sound to Anchorage—and on north to Fairbanks, my hometown.

Our dog, Czar, a lovable malamute from Nome, seemed to be homesick too. He'd point his nose into the north wind (when it wasn't raining in Seattle) and sort of sigh. Well, it sounded like a sigh.

"We'll figure out something, Czar."

These were my salad days at the *Times*. I was learning from great teachers such as Henry MacLeod, the brilliant city editor (nobody called him Hank), and Mel Sayre, an assistant city editor with a hot temper and a well-hidden heart of gold.

The newsroom was staffed with some of the best specialists in the newspaper game—Hill Williams, the smooth-writing science reporter; Bob Twiss, the aerospace editor who drove Boeing executives dizzy with his pipelines into their secret chambers; Lane Smith, the gentle, cool-headed religion editor who was able to cut through reams of material to show reporters what mattered most for readers; Jay Wells, the maritime editor; Paul Staples, the labor editor; Dick Moody, a crack police reporter; Johnny Reddin, an Irish storyteller who wrote copy so delightful that it should have been set to music; Alan Pratt, master of the witty editorial cartoon.

One of Pratt's gems offered a solution to the controversy over where to build another bridge across Seattle's Lake Washington. Since nobody could agree on the route, Pratt suggested building it from one end of the lake to the other. Bravo!

One day I had an offer from a national insurance company to move to the Midwest and become its public-relations director. The salary would be almost three times what I was drawing at the *Times*.

I didn't want to go, but the kids needed new shoes—they always needed new shoes. Stan Jr. could demolish a pair of patrol boots in a couple of weeks. Daughters Kay and Ginna always wondered why we couldn't buy them pretty clothes like their rich school chums.

Before making the job decision, I decided to have a chat with Mel Sayre. Mel had a home on Whidbey Island, but stayed weekdays at a small house in the north end of Seattle. I called and asked if I could drop by for a visit. My wife, Mabs, went along, but at the last moment decided to stay in the car while Mel and I talked.

I found the crusty editor sitting at a table with a bottle of Jim Beam. We poured some hefty helpings, then, timidly, I told Mel about the offer from the insurance company.

"Well, of course, you should do what's best for your family," he said.

And then, turning on the Mel magic, he added: "But how could you leave the *Times*? You're not the public-relations type. You're a reporter."

**Mount McKinley, North America's highest mountain, is mirrored in Wonder
Lake deep inside Denali National Park**

We had another drink or two. Mel began reciting the history of journalism, almost from the invention of the printing press. He covered the traditions of journalism ("We are all that stand between the public and corrupt politicians, you know") and then listed the big stories we had covered together.

Mel and I both had tears in our eyes when I said good night and returned to the car.

"You're not leaving, are you?" Mabs asked.

"No."

"Mel did a number on you, didn't he?"

"Not really."

"Tell me another."

A few days later, I put an arm around Czar and told him, "Well, Czar, old boy, maybe there's a way."

I went to Mel, on newsroom time this time, and proposed that we begin consistent coverage of Alaska news.

"Convince me," he said.

I told him that important things were happening in Alaska. There were reports of a major oil hunt on the North Slope, up in the Arctic, by Prudhoe

Bay. Meanwhile, Alaska's native peoples were organizing in hopes of winning a settlement of their long-standing aboriginal land claims. And the fishing industry was in tough negotiations with Japan over salmon and halibut harvests in the North Pacific Ocean and the Bering Sea.

Besides, I reminded Mel, Seattle and Alaska had a long history of being tied together by economic events,

"Remember the Klondike gold rush?"

"Hell, yes," Mel replied.

"It was big, Mel. The steamer Portland reached Seattle July 17, 1897, with almost two tons of gold from the Klondike. The rush was on! It was a stampede. Thousands of gold-seekers came here, to Seattle, to buy supplies, then went on to the Klondike. The mayor of Seattle quit and joined the stampeders. So did several *Seattle Times* reporters."

"The Klondike is not in Alaska," Mel said.

"True, but Seattle prospered because of the gold rush—and most of the gold-seekers had to travel through Alaska to get to the Klondike in Canada's Yukon Territory."

Mel scowled. His expression reminded me of someone with stomach pains.

"I'll have a talk with Henry and see what he thinks," Mel said. "Now, get back to work. We have a paper to get out."

About a week later, there was a note from Mel, scrawled on a half sheet of copy paper.

"We'll give it a try," he wrote. "When do you want to go to Alaska?"

I gave Czar a hug that evening.

"I'm going home, old boy," I told him.

There was just one catch. Mel told me there wasn't much of a budget for my Alaska travels.

"We can give you a cash advance of about three hundred dollars, that's all," he said.

"Fair enough," I said.

Let's see—three hundred dollars should just about buy the air ticket. There wouldn't be much left for lodging and meals. No problem. Stan Jr. doesn't really need another pair of patrol boots yet.

"I've never seen you so happy," Mabs said. "Have a great time up north. We'll be fine."

Mabs covered home plate for me for more than three decades while I roamed Alaska and most of the rest of the world for the *Times*. On many trips I opened my suitcase to find cheerful stick drawings by Mabs. She isn't a great artist, but she's a wonderful wife.

"The marriage has lasted only because you've been away most of that time," daughter Kay says.

I wrote a rather brassy first column in the *Times* to introduce our Alaska coverage.

"This is Alaska's time in history," I told readers. "It will be a fascinating adventure to chronicle Alaska's development in the years ahead. A land of promise and excitement."

One of the first stories I covered on that first trip home was about Don Sheldon, the legendary bush pilot of Mount McKinley.

Sheldon's story seems a good way to begin this book of Alaska-Yukon yarns.

I hope you enjoy them.

CHAPTER 1

ALASKA'S EAGLE

TALKEETNA, ALASKA—The little ski plane was wrapped in a wild world of ice and rock.

Ahead, Mount McKinley soared into the clouds—defiant, yet alluring. We were off for a day of sightseeing with Don Sheldon, Alaska's best-known bush pilot.

For more than twenty years, the daring birdman flew single-engine light planes through the treacherous canyons and cliffs of McKinley. He made ski landings on the crevasse-laced mountainside as casually as you might coast into a supermarket parking lot. There were days when he did this a half-dozen times.

But there was nothing flamboyant or reckless about Don Sheldon. His caution was meticulous. His humility approached shyness. His love of life and family was filled with warmth.

"This is tough country," he told friends. "If you don't do everything to the best of your ability, look out or you'll be leaving your aircraft around to decorate the peaks. And you have to be a little lucky, too."

It was February 1967. Sheldon was hunched over the wheel of his Cessna

Don and Roberta Sheldon enjoy playtime with their ten-month-old daughter, Holly, at their home in Talkeetna, in 1967.

180, searching ahead through the frosty windshield. His fingers formed a gentle, almost affectionate, touch on the controls. Smile lines branched from the corners of his eyes. The massive bulk of Mount McKinley was just ahead.

"Well, by golly," Sheldon said in his cowboy twang. "Let's go take a look."

Gaping chasms opened below the wings. Granite spires, like knife blades, reached out for the plane. Sheer granite walls, scoured clean by fierce winds, rose for thousands of feet above us. The plane rocked with sickening motions.

Sheldon lifted a wing to clear a razor-sharp ridge. Then he banked sharply to squeeze through a narrow canyon

It was a terrifying moment. My breathing was shallow. My palms were clammy. The only sound was the whine of the engine.

Finally, as if pushed by a catapult, the Cessna shot into the open above Kahiltna Glacier. The landing zone—the crevasse-pocked glacier—was in sight. But the glacier was a blinding glare, white with a frosting of fresh snow.

Sheldon squinted down at the tilted glacier. Crevasses dropped into dark-blue infinity. To the left was the shimmering bulk of Mount Foraker. Off the other wingtip was Mount Russell, another of McKinley's lofty neighbors.

"There was a terrific avalanche on Russell when I was up here yesterday," Sheldon said as we circled above the glacier. "It filled the whole area with snow and 'smoke,' like a bomb burst spreading out."

Sheldon lined up for the landing, dived, glided and touched down softly on the plane's aluminum skis. We had landed—uphill—on the glacier, on a slope of 15 degrees, at an elevation of 8,100 feet. When it was over, the landing seemed almost routine.

Welcome to Mount McKinley!

"Well, let's get out and have a look around." Sheldon said cheerfully.

It was a bright, cold winter day, a day to applaud ceiling-unlimited scenery from our vantage point on Alaska's rooftop.

"This mountain is the highest point on the North American continent—20,310 feet," Sheldon noted. "Shucks, it's probably the highest mountain in the world. McKinley's base starts almost at sea level. Those mountains over in the Himalayas start at 20,000 feet and then go up."

Little did we know that in a few days Sheldon would be involved in a tragedy here on Kahiltna Glacier. He would be summoned to fly out the corpse of a French climber who had tumbled into one of those deadly crevasses.

But this was a day to wander the Alaskan skies with Alaska's eagle, Don Sheldon.

Admirers said the virtuoso pilot "owned" Mount McKinley with his daring mercy missions for stranded mountaineers. Sheldon made no such assertion.

"Sometimes the weather on the mountain is like a wild woman," he said. "Then the best thing to do is to leave it alone."

Don Sheldon is gone now. Cancer took his life in 1975, at age fifty-three.

Gone, too, is the romantic era of trailblazing bush pilots such as Carl Ben Eielson, Bob Reeve, Noel Wien, Harold Gillam, and Joe Crosson.

Those early-day pilots were Alaska's cowboys. Every schoolchild in the frontier territory knew their names. If their photographs had been printed on collectors' cards, we would have treasured them like Babe Ruth and Joe DiMaggio keepsakes.

Able pilots still fly around Mount McKinley and other monarchs of the Alaska Range. But today's band of birdmen challenges the Alaskan skies almost in anonymity.

Such was not the case with Donald Edward Sheldon.

✦ ✦ ✦

THE LEGEND OF DON SHELDON began in 1955, when he plucked eight U.S. Army scouts from the frigid whitewater of Devils Canyon in the Susitna River, not far from his flying base in Talkeetna.

The soldiers were trapped when their boat rammed hidden boulders in a stretch of rapids. They were clinging to a steep rock wall when Sheldon happened to sight them from the air. Somehow, Sheldon managed to land his lightweight Aeronca floatplane upstream from the men in the narrow gorge, then maintain control with the throttle as the plane drifted—backward— through the rapids.

Sheldon held the Aeronca in position until two of the soldiers were able to climb aboard the tiny plane. Then the pilot and his passengers floated backward for another mile and a half of Devils Canyon before spinning around and making a downriver takeoff.

Pulling off such a feat just once bordered on the miraculous. But that day Sheldon repeated the maneuver three more times, until he had rescued the last of the shivering scouts.

Later, when asked what he best remembered about the episode, the bashful pilot said: "I guess it would have to be the expression on those guys' mugs as they crawled aboard my old plane."

James Greiner, Sheldon's friend and biographer, said that during the rescues in the raging waters of Devils Canyon Sheldon "was like a man blindfolded, rolling backward toward a cliff in a car without brakes. . . ."

Colorado-born Don Sheldon drifted to Alaska in 1938. He drove a milk truck in Anchorage for a while, then headed with a friend to Talkeetna, about a hundred miles north of Anchorage. They had only enough cash for the train fare to Talkeetna.

"An old-timer took a look at us two green young fellers and offered us the use of a cabin if we could cut firewood for him. We took it," Sheldon said.

"The next morning there was a terrific noise outside our cabin. I stepped

Parka-clad Don Sheldon fuels a Cessna bush plane at his Talkeetna base as mountaineers load supplies for a 1967 winter flight to Mount McKinley.

out and there was an old bull moose. I reached for a rifle and we had our meat supply. We traded half for groceries and then we were in business."

Alaska's barnstorming bush pilots soon caught Sheldon's attention.

"I could tell at a glance that it was the best way to get around the country," he recalled. "Far better than beating yourself to death on a pair of snowshoes."

Flying lessons followed. Sheldon won his pilot's license about the time that America was pulled into World War II. He enlisted in the Army, hoping to become an aviator. But instead Uncle Sam turned him into a tail gunner with the 8th Air Force. Twice he survived crashes of B-17 bombers shot down over Europe.

"But I got in a little flying on long missions from the middle of Europe, and I had some valuable experience in high-altitude tests that paid off on Mount McKinley years later," he said.

In 1948 Sheldon bought and refurbished two military-surplus light planes down in the Lower 48 states. He sold one and flew the other to Alaska.

"Came back to stay. Been here since," he said.

Lanky, tousle-haired Don Sheldon was in a merry mood the day we went sightseeing.

"Yahoo! he yelled happily as he loped toward the Cessna in the sparkling light of a winter morning.

"Beautiful day. We'll go huckledeebuck."

Soon the little plane was winging toward Mount McKinley, only sixty air miles north from Talkeetna.

When Sheldon was in the air his radio contact back home was his pretty, young wife, Roberta. Nobody had to tell Roberta Sheldon about the risks of flying in this unforgiving North Country. Her father was Bob Reeve, the bold bush pilot who opened the stormy Aleutian Islands to aviation.

"I've never known anybody like Don," Roberta said when Sheldon was out of earshot. "He loves life so much. And he's a wonderful guy."

An Alaska bush pilot is supposed to come from central casting as a dashing, hard-driving adventurer wearing a leather flying jacket and a flirty smile. There were a few like that. But Sheldon neither smoked nor drank. His family was his main reason for living.

"I'm a lucky man," he said.

✦ ✦ ✦

EARLY ON A JANUARY MORNING in 1967 Sheldon drove to Talkeetna's little railroad station to meet some new customers. Eight eager men scrambled down from the Alaska Railroad passenger car—members of the first expedition to attempt a winter climb of Mount McKinley.

"Well, hi there," Sheldon called, thrusting out his hand to each of the newcomers.

Sheldon's assignment was to fly the climbers and their ton and a half of supplies to a base camp on Kahiltna Glacier.

"When can we get started?" the mountaineers asked.

Sheldon looked up the valley and studied Mount McKinley. There was a long, angry cloud across the summit.

"Well, not today," Sheldon said. "That cloud is snow being driven by the wind. Probably sixty miles an hour or more up there. We'll try tomorrow, if it sobers up."

Later that morning, after the climbers' gear had been trucked to Sheldon's hangar, the pilot quizzed the newcomers about their preparations.

Ahead for the adventurers lay a bitter contest on the mountain with blizzards, whiteouts and temperatures sinking to a low of 100 degrees below zero. In an emergency, it would be up to Sheldon to land his plane on the always-dangerous mountain for a rescue attempt.

Sheldon warned the climbers about lethal weather on Mount McKinley, such as the violent winds that were whipping snow plumes off the top of the mountain this day.

"I remember one time up there when I had to take off for two miles downhill," he said. "Clear-air turbulence was slamming pieces of ice and rock as big as houses off the cornices. There were awful crevasses below, but I figured I'd better keep going and get out of there right then. That was something."

Next morning, Sheldon waved to the impatient mountaineers waiting by his hangar. A rosy sunrise beamed on Mount McKinley.

"We'll go check things out," he said.

Sheldon stuffed the Cessna 180 with his first two passengers and some of the climbers' food, fuel, sleeping bags, snowshoes, and ice axes.

Atop the load was a spray of spruce boughs. Sheldon would drop the dark-green branches on the glacier before landing to help judge his depth perception on the glare-white glacier.

"We should be back in about three hours," he told Roberta.

Sheldon warmed the engine a long time. Finally, he pointed down the snowy runway, lifted off, and turned toward Mount McKinley. Shafts of sunshine ricocheted from the silvery fuselage.

I waited with Roberta Sheldon. A shortwave radio tuned to Don's aircraft frequency hummed in the background as Roberta played with their dark-haired daughter, Holly, ten months old. Don had nicknamed his daughter Blueberry.

About two hours later there was a tiny dot in the sky as a plane approached

**Don Sheldon's single-engine Cessna rests on Mount McKinley's Kahiltna
Glacier after a landing on skis. Mount Foraker, another monarch of the Alaska
Range, is in the background.**

Talkeetna. It was Sheldon. He had landed the first two men on Kahiltna
Glacier.

"The wind was really howling over our heads up there," he said. "But we
managed to get in under it."

The remaining climbers were jubilant. Before long, Sheldon was in the air
again. And again, each time buzzing over the snow-bonneted rooftops of
Talkeetna.

At 3:20 P.M. Sheldon checked in by radio.

"Roger, Roger, WEX," Roberta acknowledged, giving the call letters of
the base station.

Daylight was fading. Sunset was little more than an hour away.

Ten minutes later, Sheldon called to say he was returning to Talkeetna for
the last two passengers.

"He's trying to beat the darkness," Roberta said. "He'll do it, too."

Sheldon landed and swiftly reloaded the plane with more freight and the two passengers. The little plane shook loose from the field and bored through the darkening sky toward McKinley.

Roberta warmed Holly's dinner while listening for the radio. There was only a steady rattle of static.

Then at 5:25 P.M. Sheldon called. He had delivered the last passengers and was on his way home.

A quick flash of relief crossed Roberta's face. She lifted a spoonful of strained carrots toward the baby's puckered mouth.

A few minutes later an engine sputtered. Sheldon was back and taxiing toward his hanger. His wingtip lights winked red and green.

Stars were blazing in the black sky. Snow crunched underfoot as the weary pilot walked home.

"We got all eight of them in, and about fifteen hundred pounds of their gear," Sheldon said.

"I'm proud of you, Roberta said.

"Well, there you go," Sheldon said. "It was nothing."

Holly screamed with joy when she sighted her father.

"Hiya, Blueberry," he said.

Roberta studied her husband's tired eyes.

In a husky voice and with a fist drawn back in mock anger, she asked, "Was it dangerous up there?"

"Naw," Sheldon said.

"OK, then, go feed the chickens," Roberta said, handing Sheldon a bucket of chicken feed.

The pilot shuffled out the door, toward the henhouse.

"Those chickens, they're Roberta's pets," he said.

Less than two days later, Don Sheldon and I would return to Kahiltna Glacier on a sad mission.

One of the winter climbers—Jacques Batkin, from France—was dead. His companions said Batkin had tumbled into a hidden crevasse on Kahiltna Glacier.

"That glacier is a chamber of horrors," Sheldon said. "There are bottomless crevasses disguised by windblown snow."

Now it was up to Sheldon to return to the glacier to remove Batkin's body.

'It has to be done," he said.

A steady snowfall was showering Talkeetna.

"The weather must be having a fit up there on the mountain," Sheldon said.

Somehow, Sheldon made another ski landing on the glacier, and with Ray Genet, one of the surviving climbers, loaded Batkin's body into the Cessna.

"We'll go on up the mountain," Genet said, with tears in his eyes. "Jacques would not want us to turn back."

Sheldon returned to Talkeetna. We carried Batkin's remains, now wrapped in a sleeping bag, into Sheldon's ice-cold sheet-metal hangar.

"This is tough country," Sheldon said.

The expedition did push on. Three of the seven surviving climbers reached the top of Mount McKinley. On the way, they reported a wind-chill temperature of minus 148 degrees. They suffered hunger, frostbite, and exhaustion. Their conquest of Mount McKinley was an epic chapter in the history of mountaineering.

One of those who made it all the way to the roof of McKinley was Ray Genet.

Genet was unforgettable. His buddies nicknamed him Pirate.

With a fierce expression and bushy, black beard coated with ice, he looked like he owned the whole darned mountain. There was a wonderful confidence in Genet's voice. He seemed like a man electrified, a storm about to be unleashed.

October 2, 1979.

The unthinkable happened. Ray Genet died on Mount Everest. They said he froze to death. His body is still there.

Don Sheldon wasn't around to hear the news. The great airman made his last flight January 26, 1975, when he lost his battle with cancer.

Left behind were his widow, Roberta, and their three children, Holly, Kate, and Robert.

To the end, Sheldon told friends that he would survive the disease and return to fly Mount McKinley.

"Disregard the terrifying rumors about my health," he told me a month before his death.

They buried Don Sheldon in Talkeetna's tiny cemetery, by the airport where he flew his many mercy missions. On his grave marker are these words:

Mount McKinley, 20,320 feet high, crowns the Alaska Range in a view from the cockpit of Don Sheldon's bush plane.

"He wagered with the wind and won. His wife and children loved him."

I want to remember Don for the day we returned from a rock-and-roll flight to blustery Mount McKinley. He looked back at the mountain, broke into laughter, and said:

"It's one helluva pile of rock, isn't it?"

It sure is.

CHAPTER 2

BELLE OF THE YUKON

DAWSON CITY, YUKON TERRITORY—There really was a Klondike Kate.

I met her in 1948. She was every inch a belle, even at age seventy-one. Tall and handsome, with hair the color of antique silver and eyes as blue as the northern sky. She had a smile that would melt snow. Her cheerful laughter trilled like a songbird in spring.

Kate was visiting my father, a longtime friend, when we met. She wanted some business advice about her mining claims. Dad was a good source. He was managing a group of gold mines in Alaska and across the border in Canada's Yukon Territory.

"Well, that's good enough," Kate told Dad as we entered the room.

And then she turned toward my wife, Mabs, and me and grinned. We must have been staring. We were in the presence of Klondike Kate, the superstar of the great gold rush to the Yukon.

That long-ago stampede was madness on a grand scale. More than one hundred thousand men and women set out for Dawson City and the Klondike goldfields in 1897 and '98. Perhaps fifty thousand arrived, but only three hundred or so found enough gold to call themselves rich—and most of those lost their pokes to women such as Klondike Kate.

Kate stood and looked at us with a smile.

"Your father and I knew the Yukon when it was the most exciting place on earth," she said. "I'm sorry you missed it."

With that, she swept out of the office, head high, as if exiting stage left in a theater crowded with admirers.

"Always on stage," my father said with a laugh.

Then he grew serious.

"You must always treat Kate with respect," he said. "She was a dance-hall girl, yes, and doesn't mind talking about it. But she never was a prostitute. She is a fine woman."

Klondike Kate. Vivacious and lovely. She was the toast of the Klondike when gold was king and she was its queen. Yet, she had a life of romance and heartbreak as poignant as that of any character in literature.

Kate has been dead since 1957. But her legend lives on today as travelers roam the dusty streets of old Dawson City and hear about how the miners found "nuggets the size of your fist" and threw them at the feet of Klondike Kate and other damsels of Dawson.

Kate held the spotlight until the day she departed this world, never denying that she had been a dance-hall queen in a gaudy time, but hurt terribly by much of the trash that was written about her. Untrue stories persisted that Kate was little better than a Dawson City prostitute. I still hear such slander when friends ask about her. It reminds me of the kind of tabloid garbage on view at supermarket checkout counters.

The truth (told without so much as a blush) was contained in a treasure trove of Kate's keepsakes that I browsed in 1973, when her stepson, Willard Van Duren, telephoned me at the *Seattle Times*. Van Duren was wondering what to do with musty boxes and trunks of things Kate had stored over the years.

The inventory included fancy gowns from the Klondike years, her high-button dancing shoes, ostrich plumes, fragments of Kate's handwritten memoirs, correspondence with famous friends—including Marjorie Rambeau, the actress, and Rex Beach, the gold-rush author—letters from some of the men in her life, a suitcase stuffed with fancy evening purses, hundreds of old photographs, an unpublished try at sentimental poetry.

Van Duren told me he wasn't sure what he would do with the cache.

I had the impression that he would welcome a feature story in the *Times,* hoping the publicity would fetch some hefty bids from collectors.

As things turned out, Van Duren did arrange to sell many of his stepmother's things to museums in Whitehorse, the Yukon capital. No doubt eager collectors acquired some of the choice items, but, if so, they aren't letting it be known.

I was able to borrow a few of the documents and make copies.

And my wife, Mabs, has two of those lovely evening purses—fashioned of mesh, with lacy links of enameled metal. One contains Kate's rosewood rouge box. There's also a book of matches printed with the words Kate always added by her autograph: "Mush on and smile."

"Kate's purses are coming back in style," Mabs says. "We'll go out some evening with one of them and I'll show off a little while you tell stories about Klondike Kate."

It's a deal.

Van Duren said he had known Kate for many years before she and his late father, William L. Van Duren, were married in 1948. That was Kate's third marriage.

"She was a great lady—a very gracious and intelligent person," Kate's stepson recalled.

"Aunt Kate (that was what close friends and down-on-their-luck old-timers called her in later years) didn't talk much about her early life when we were together," Van Duren added. "My guess is that was because of her pain over the way she had been treated by Alexander Pantages, the theater man."

But we are getting ahead of the story . . .

✦ ✦ ✦

Who was the lady known as Klondike Kate?

She was born Kathleen Eloisa Rockwell in 1877, in Junction City, Kansas, just west of Topeka. Her mother called her Kathleen or Katie, never Kate. Klondikers didn't know her at first as Klondike Kate. That label came later, but nobody remembers who gave her the nickname.

Kate's parents were divorced when she was a child. Her mother, Martha, later married Judge F. A. Bettis, a colorful lawyer, and in 1882 or so the family moved to Spokane, Washington. Like the offspring of other prominent families, Kate was sent away to a series of private schools for several years.

"While I was in school the big crash [the financial panic of 1893] came," Kate wrote in the memoirs found by her stepson. "Our home was sold and my father [Judge Bettis] and Mother separated."

Soon after, Kate and her mother left from Seattle for New York aboard a four-masted sailing vessel.

"Around the Horn," Kate recalled. (There was no Panama Canal in those days).

"We reached New York almost broke—we had $83 between us," Kate wrote. "There was nothing we knew how to do—and I had to figure a way to make a living for both of us. We were desperate."

One day, Kate answered a newspaper advertisement for chorus girls. It was the start of her career in show business.

She joined a road company, but a week later found herself stranded in Pittsburgh.

"There the company went broke—flopped. . . . another girl and myself went into a church that day. I remember, and prayed for some way to get back to New York. Then she thought of sneaking into a boxcar and stealing a ride back."

The two young women did climb into an empty railroad boxcar, but were discovered by the train crew.

"I guess we looked like a forlorn pair of kiddies," Kate said in the memoirs. "We told them our story and they allowed us to remain in the car. We got to New York all right, but we were both broke.

"When I arrived home Mother was frantic. She had the neighborhood aroused and the police had been searching for me. She didn't want me to go on the stage after that, but I had had a taste of the freedom of the chorus girl's life, and was determined to see more of it.

"Dancing was as natural to me as walking," she said. "My feet were just made for music."

And so Kate joined a five-a-day dance troupe on Coney Island.

"Quite a respectable place. . . . The show would have been closed if we had dared to appear bare legged as the girls do today."

After a year in New York, Kate returned to Seattle to take another dance-hall job. It was not the vaudeville role she had expected.

"I found it was a place where you had to get men to buy drinks from the bar, as well as to work in the show," she said. "I didn't want to work there, but

I owed for my ticket cost. The older girls taught me how to ditch the liquor so I didn't have to drink much and so I stayed on."

The year was 1898—and "everyone was talking Klondike," Kate wrote.

"I wanted to go!"

And go she did. But it took two harrowing journeys to reach the Yukon's city of gold.

The first time she teamed with other entertainers and climbed over Chilkoot Pass (still a strenuous ascent for hikers today) to Lake Bennett, British Columbia. There her companions decided to return to civilization. Kate stayed on, alone.

"Nothing daunted me," she said. "I went to work in a little dance hall there. I was the entire show."

Later she pushed on toward Dawson City, still hundreds of miles away. Then came the challenge of navigating Whitehorse Rapids, a barrier of raging whitewater. Most passengers on Klondike-bound rafts and scows were ordered by the North West Mounted Police to walk around the rapids. Klondike Kate decided to ride.

She disguised herself in men's clothing, and at the last moment jumped aboard a scow heading into the churning waters.

"I made a run for it and I was aboard," she said. "I turned and laughed at the Mountie. The last I heard he was muttering something about getting off that scow 'in the name of the Queen.' I waved at him and into that inferno of seething, foaming water we went, one of the greatest thrills of my life."

There was a letter waiting for Kate when she arrived in Whitehorse. It was an invitation to join a big show troupe that was being formed to entertain in Dawson City. Kate returned to Seattle to sign up with the Savoy Theatrical Company.

And so it was that Kate finally reached the Klondike.

This is what she wrote of the Dawson City over which she reigned:

"There were three large dance halls there, every one with a bunch of pretty girls. You had to be or the men wouldn't dance or buy drinks.

"The men came in dressed in the work clothes, but the girls had to be 'On Parade' all the time. I paid as high as $1,500 for a dress made in Paris.

"Money was nothing but something to spend. Each dance cost a dollar . . . and after every dance the man went to the bar with his girl and bought a drink. I have danced as many as 183 dances in one night.

Klondike Kate carried a torch for dapper Alexander Pantages during gold-rush times in Dawson City.
STANTON PATTY COLLECTION

"There weren't many fights up there, as you would suppose there would have been. The men, roughly dressed as they were, never had much trouble. They were fair and honest and I never knew one of them to go back on a pal.

"One reason, I believe, for that was it took a good man or woman to get through to Dawson back then.

"Those dance halls up there almost in the shade of the North Pole were picturesque. . . . The illumination was from big oil lamps. Big round stoves that got us hot when you shoved four-foot lengths of wood into them provided the heat when it was cold and snowing outside. Memories come to me now—the wind howling outside, the aurora flashing in the north . . . like the dance of life, now bright, now falling and fading away.

"That first year in Dawson was, I think, the happiest in my life. For I never dreamed of what years of sorrow and remorse lay ahead of me."

It was during her glory days in Dawson City that Kate met and fell in love with Alexander Pantages, a dashing, young immigrant from Greece who was working as a bartender at the Orpheum Theater. One night Kate went to the Orpheum to see a production of *Camille*.

"I was sitting in one of the boxes—you know how you'll feel eyes on you, and finally you turn directly to them," Kate said. "I looked down at the bar and directly into his eyes."

Kate and Pantages became sweethearts and for two years, as she confided to my father, they "cabined together" in Dawson City.

Later, as the Klondike gold rush ebbed, they moved to Seattle, where Kate said she loaned Pantages the money to open the Crystal Theater at Second Avenue and Madison Street. That was the beginning of a theater empire for Pantages that eventually was worth a reported $24 million.

Pantages never repaid the loan to Kate—and in 1905 married another woman, a talented violinist by the name of Lois Mendenhall.

Kate also married later, but never stopped carrying a torch for Pantages. Among her possessions was a photograph of a middle-aged Pantages, framed with wistful poems and song lyrics. One is titled "Forgetting."

"I held no bitterness," Kate wrote in her secret memoirs. "That's one thing I know nothing of, revenge or hate."

The wealthy Pantages went on trial in Los Angeles in 1929 on a charge of criminal assault involving a seventeen-year-old female dancer. Kate was present at the trial, but was not called to testify. The court noted her presence and described her as the person who staked Pantages in his days of poverty. The jury found Pantages guilty, but two years later he won a new trial and was cleared. Nevertheless, the case ruined Pantages. He died in 1936 at the age of sixty-four from hardening of the arteries. His estate had dwindled almost to nothing by that time.

After being set adrift by Pantages, Kate lived awhile longer in Seattle and at a lodge she named Idlours on nearby Hood Canal. Then she moved to the high-desert area of central Oregon, an area she loved, where she spent most of the rest of her life. At various times Kate operated a ranch, a boarding house, a lunch counter, and a nursing home there.

And she was a regular at meetings of the Alaska-Yukon Pioneers for many years. Most of the old-timers who knew her are gone. Now their sons, daughters, and grandchildren gather for annual reunions and talk about "old times, good times" in the North Country. I'm proud to be one of them.

✦ ✦ ✦

A KNEE INJURY forced Kate to give up her stage career when she was a young woman. She even told of scrubbing floors for a living in what she called "the dark days."

Dressed in a fancy gown, this is how Klondike Kate appeared for Dawson City dance-hall audiences in 1900, at the peak of the Klondike gold rush.

Johnny Matson, a Yukon miner, who wooed and won Klondike Kate, rests at his cabin on Matson Creek. STANTON PATTY COLLECTION

"But I never let misfortunes defeat me," Kate told an interviewer. "When things looked blackest, I'd go out and find someone who was worse off and help them. In doing that, my own troubles didn't seem so hopeless."

Kate's first marriage, in 1915, in Prineville, Oregon, was to Floyd Warner, a handsome young cowboy. It was a poor match. Terse entries in Kate's diaries in 1919 tell part of the story.

"Left Floyd," she wrote on September 4.

"Served divorce papers on Floyd," she wrote five days later.

Nowhere in Kate's papers is an explanation of what caused the breakup. It was one chapter of her life that Klondike Kate closed forever.

A fairy-tale love that flickered in a Klondike stampeder's heart for thirty-three years finally brought happiness to Kate in July 1933 when she married a Yukon gold miner by the name of Johnny Matson.

My father knew both Kate and Matson, and told of spending time with the couple in Dawson City.

"I first saw them in September, 1944," Dad wrote in *North Country Challenge,* his own book of memoirs. "They were an incongruous couple. Johnny had come down the Yukon on the last riverboat of the season and Kate had met him at the dock. They were walking up Front Street in Dawson, Johnny carrying his battered suitcase with a corner of clothing peeking out; Kate a head taller, looking down with a companionable smile on the weather-beaten man tagging along beside her."

The love of Johnny Matson for Klondike Kate began on Christmas Eve of 1900 in Dawson City, when the dance-hall girls presented a special show for the far-from-home miners. Kate made a grand entrance in a flowing, white gown, wearing a crown of lighted candles in her red-gold hair. Matson, one of those lonely miners in the audience, fell in love with Kate that night, but lacked the courage to tell her so.

"She looked like an angel," Matson told my father years later.

Kate told Dad that she was not even aware of Matson's existence that night, but remembered the Christmas show.

"I had a terrible time getting the candle grease out of my hair," she said.

Many years after that Klondike Christmas, when Matson still was mining in the Yukon, he happened on a newspaper feature story about the girl of his dreams, who had fallen on hard times down in Oregon. He worked up the courage to write Kate and let her know that she had not been forgotten.

But the letter was not mailed for almost a year. The closest post office was in Dawson City, almost one hundred miles from Matson's mining claim. It would be months before his annual trek to Dawson City to buy winter supplies.

Kate, alone, too, and living then in a shack near Bend, Oregon, read Matson's letter—and responded with several letters of her own. They arranged to meet at the 1933 International Sourdough Reunion in Vancouver, British Columbia.

A few days later, they were married—in Vancouver, Washington.

"They came to Dawson on their honeymoon," my father said. "Kate wanted to spend the approaching winter with Johnny at his camp. But it was no setting for this gregarious woman and Johnny knew it. He arranged that she should return to Oregon and they would meet every other summer at Dawson."

One summer Dad decided to have a look at Matson's claim as a possible gold-dredging prospect. He met Kate in Dawson City's Arcade Cafe and offered to carry a letter to Matson. Kate's eyes, he recalled, lighted up with gratitude.

"She picked up a menu, scribbled something on it, and handed it to me with a smile," Dad said.

On the menu she had written: "Mush on and smile. Klondike Kate. Win or lose, a Sourdough never squawks." It was her way of saying thank you.

I have that menu with Kate's unique autograph. The Arcade was serving moose steak, caribou cutlets, leg of grizzly bear cub, and arctic grayling that evening.

The next day Dad set off for Matson Creek with two brothers, Joe and John Sestak, Matson's close friends. It was a formidable trip: fifty miles up the Yukon River by motorboat, ten more miles up the Sixty-Mile River, then a twenty-seven-mile hike over swamps and hills to Matson's claim.

Dad and the Sestaks were the first people Matson had seen in ten months.

The first night, after the supper dishes had been washed, Matson opened Kate's letter from Dawson City and spent a long time reading and rereading it. The only sound was the ticking of a big alarm clock on the kitchen table.

"Kate is a fine woman," Matson said. "She's had a hard life. Pantages treated her like a dog. It is God's will that I be the one to protect and provide for her."

My father recalled: "My heart went out to this simple man. He was happy in his dream."

Dad and the Sestak brothers left the next morning. Matson, a stooped, little man, waved a farewell.

"We would be the last people he would ever see," my father said.

In 1946, Matson's annual letter to Kate failed to arrive at Kate's home in Oregon. Joe Sestak went to investigate. He found Matson, who was eighty-three, dead in a trail shelter a few miles from his cabin. He may have been on his way to Dawson City to wait for Kate.

Death, said the authorities who later investigated, probably was due to natural causes. As investigators reached the cabin, a wolverine scurried into

Klondike Kate and Johnny Matson pose for a wedding photograph after their 1933 wedding in Vancouver, Washington. STANTON PATTY COLLECTION

the woods. Matson's body was half out of the window of the cabin, where the wolverine had dragged it.

And so the man who married Klondike Kate was buried in a grave by the gold creek that bears his name.

"Johnny was a wonderful man," said Kate, with tears in her eyes.

At the close of her memoirs is a short story she wrote about a quiet, little man who "stood there all alone" in the corner of a dance hall while gamblers rolled dice, and whisky glasses clinked on the bar.

"Dream Girl," she titled the story.

It told about a Christmas Eve and a miner who never had spoken to the girl of his dreams, nor she to him.

"But this was Christmas Eve and maybe, just maybe, she'd look at him and perhaps she'd smile," Kate wrote in "Dream Girl."

"She glanced at the little chap standing there alone, turned to her courtiers and said, 'Wait, he looks so lonely I'm going over and say Hello to him.' He just stood there waiting and hoping as he had done so often. . . .

"'Want to dance?'

"He stood, smiled and said, 'No thanks. I don't dance.'"

There seems no doubt that Klondike Kate was the dream girl in the sketch and Johnny Matson was her admirer.

Better than anything else, perhaps, these few lines of "fiction" tell how much Kate admired the man who waited those thirty-three years to tell her of his love.

◆ ◆ ◆

ONE OF THE PERSONS Kate notified of Matson's death—by telegram from Dawson City—was William L. Van Duren, a family friend of many years. A longtime public accountant in Oregon, he first met Kate in the 1920s when he was keeping books for her little cafe.

Kate and Van Duren, a widower, were married in April 1948 in Vancouver, Washington, across the Columbia River from Portland, Oregon.

The *Columbian,* Vancouver's daily newspaper, reported that Kate looked "pretty as a picture" at the ceremony in the Clark County Courthouse. Witnesses included Police Chief James Fleming and Mrs. Fleming, of neighboring Portland.

The *Columbian* writer reported that Kate's eyes "still fill with tears when she talks about her Johnny (Matson)" and pointed out that the marten fur piece she was wearing was a gift from "my Johnny."

Then, the wedding ceremony over, she stepped outside to greet her public.

"Spontaneous applause met her and the crowd burst into a rendition of 'K-K-K Katy, Beautiful Katy.' Bowing on all sides the Yukon belle and her husband left the courthouse amid a shower of rice," said the *Columbian*.

Kate and Van Duren had almost nine pleasant years together. Then on the morning of February 21, 1957, at their home in Sweet Home, Oregon, Van Duren found the onetime queen of the Klondike dead in her bed at age eighty.

Her ashes were spread by aircraft over the desert countryside she loved between Bend and Burns, Oregon.

Van Duren died the following year in Everett, Washington, at the age of eighty-one.

Kate, who remembered having pokes of gold thrown at her feet in Dawson City's dance halls, died virtually without funds. The many lean years after the gold rush and then medical bills in her sunset years had sluiced away her earnings.

Even her last few gold nuggets, some stitched into a necklace, were stolen by a bunco artist who promised to place them in a bank box for safekeeping.

Kate left a little poem she called "My Will."

And all that I can leave you
Are memories of the past—
The dreams we dreamed together
That were too sweet to last.

To the ones who bandied gossip,
Tore my heart with two-edged words,
I leave my full forgiveness
To combat the bitter words.

"What a gal!" a newspaper writer said of Kate after her death.
She would have loved that epitaph.

CHAPTER 3

THE BIG STORY

ANCHORAGE—What is the biggest story you ever covered in Alaska?"

I get that question often from readers and colleagues.

It wasn't the Good Friday Earthquake in 1964 or the *Exxon Valdez* oil spill in 1989.

It was the crusade that Alaska's native peoples waged to win a decent settlement of their aboriginal land claims.

Their campaign surged through Alaska, toppling an incumbent governor and a popular former governor—then on through the board rooms of Big Oil, and finally to Congress and the White House.

The stakes were huge:

- The future of Alaska's eighty thousand Eskimos, Indians, and Aleuts— at that time among the poorest people in the United States.
- The proposed oil pipeline from the arctic oil field at Prudhoe Bay south to Valdez on Prince William Sound.
- The unfinished dreams of the young, cash-strapped state of Alaska.

In the end, there was this equation: no land-claims settlement = no oil pipeline.

It wasn't so much an ultimatum as it was smart strategy on the part of native leaders.

Oil—billions of barrels of oil—had been discovered in 1968 at Prudhoe Bay on the North Slope. Oil companies holding the rich leases at Prudhoe Bay wanted to move their treasure to market. They proposed a pipeline to the ice-free port of Valdez, and ordered eight hundred miles of four-foot-diameter steel pipe from fabricators in Japan.

A done deal?

Not so fast, the natives said.

The oil companies required rights-of-way across Alaska to build their pipeline. Native organizations said the route would cross lands over which they had had dominion for more than ten thousand years.

Checkmate.

Meanwhile, because of environmental concerns, the federal government had imposed a "land freeze" to halt development on public lands in Alaska.

I was in Alaska frequently for the *Seattle Times* to cover the land-claims battle—and later, construction of the oil pipeline. But I was able to report only the major developments as they occurred. That's the way the news business works.

"Keep your story to no more than twelve hundred words," editors instructed.

Frustrating. I wanted to write more.

Jack Roderick, a longtime resources expert on the Alaska scene, did. He wrote a book in 1997, titled *Crude Dreams* (Epicenter Press), in which he describes the land claims/pipeline drama in fine detail.

How I envy Roderick's vast knowledge of the petroleum industry and his ability to craft long-range visions for Alaska! His book adds the grace notes of history that connect events, big and little.

For example, Roderick recalls how in 1966 the natives punished Democrat William A. (Bill) Egan—Alaska's first elected governor after statehood in 1959—when Egan failed to fully support their land claims. The natives backed the Republican nominee, Walter J. Hickel, who won the governor's race. Hickel had told native leaders he would back their land claims if they would not stand in the way of the state's plans for oil leasing at Prudhoe

Bay. Later, as secretary of the interior in the Nixon administration, Hickel kept his promise.

There was more.

In 1970, Bill Egan was returned to the governor's office. This time he defeated Governor Keith Miller, the Republican incumbent, Hickel's successor, who was opposed to a generous allocation of lands for the natives.

Meanwhile, the oil companies decided they'd better back the Alaska natives in their battle to win a land-claims settlement.

It was a strange alliance.

Roderick describes it this way:

"Desperate to secure a pipeline right-of-way—and aware that the land-claims issue was standing in the way—pipeline owner-companies directed their Washington lobbyists to vigorously support some kind of Native land settlement. . . . these lobbyists were keeping track of the pipeline permitting process and trying to convince Congress that a settlement of the [land] claims issue would be good both for the nation and for the oil industry."

No settlement = no pipeline.

A United States Senate staffer noted that members of Congress from oil-producing states "as a matter of course don't tend to vote with natives or Indians." But in this case, they would conclude: "If the oil industry says it's OK, maybe it's the right way to go."

On December 14, 1971, Congress passed the Alaska Native Claims Settlement Act.

The historic legislation granted Alaska natives almost $1 billion in cash and 40 million acres of land—more than 10 percent of Alaska's land area.

The act also created twelve regional, for-profit corporations in Alaska, based mostly on ethnic groupings across the frontier state. It also provided for the formation of more than two hundred village corporations. At last report, the regional and village corporations had total assets of almost $3 billion from investments ranging from resort hotels to telecommunications.

Alaska natives = Alaska's newest capitalists.

✦ ✦ ✦

ON DECEMBER 18, President Richard M. Nixon signed the native-claims act into law.

Charles (Charlie) Edwardsen Jr., in 1977—a vocal and articulate fighter in the campaign for the Alaska native land claims settlement.

A few days later the Interior Department established a hundred-foot-wide corridor from Prudhoe Bay to Valdez for the trans-Alaska oil pipeline.

Now it was a done deal.

There was jubilation across Alaska. There also was cruel cynicism.

I was having dinner at the Baranof Hotel in Juneau when the land-claims settlement was announced. Two "Ugly Alaskans" were chatting at a nearby table.

"Don't worry about the natives getting all that money from Congress," one said. "We'll get it back when they piss it away, as they always do when they're drinking. We'll supply the booze."

Oh, yeah?

These guys didn't know Howard Rock, Emil Notti, Willie Hensley, Byron Mallott, Joe Upicksoun, Eben Hopson, Charlie (Etok) Edwardsen Jr., and other warriors of the land-claims struggle.

Charlie Edwardsen, an angry young Eskimo from Barrow, sometimes was so cantankerous that it seemed he talked only in bullhorn shouts. An interview with Charlie was like a tussle with a cranky polar bear. But in calmer moments, he was an articulate spokesman for Alaska's natives.

**Howard Rock, in 1972—
the Eskimo editor who
gave Alaska natives a
strong voice in the battle
for settlement of their
land claims.**

During a U.S. Senate hearing he asked the best question I heard during the land-claims brawl:

"How can white men sell our land when they don't own it?"

Edwardsen was referring to the state of Alaska's sale of North Slope leases to the oil companies—a transaction that netted the state more than $900 million.

"Robbery," Charlie called the lease sale.

The same could have been said about the sale of Alaska to the United States by czarist Russia in 1867.

Alaska was sold without the consent of Alaska's native peoples. They received none of the proceeds. This was their land. They were here first.

Russia didn't discover Alaska. The natives already knew where it was.

I was reared in an Alaskan home where tolerance was taught at an early age.

I have a photograph of my mother with a group of Athabascan Indian children from Eagle village. The scene was a summertime gold-mining camp by the Yukon River. Mom gathered the kids around her on a mound of gravel left behind by the gold dredge and read aloud stories about a world far beyond Eagle.

Among the favorites were *The Wizard of Oz* and *Tom Sawyer.* And *Robin Hood.*

"These are wonderful young people," she told me. "I wish they had better schools."

We heard stories—true stories—about how native children were punished for speaking their native languages in some federal Bureau of Indian Affairs village schools. Sometimes the pupils were spanked; sometimes their mouths were doused with soap and water.

"Speak English!" they were told by government teachers.

But there also were kindly teachers who loved the native children and introduced them to great music and art.

My mother, a librarian by training, who could have been one of those inspired teachers, played the piano, beautifully. Hoagy Carmichael's "Stardust," for me; Claude Debussy's "Clair de Lune," for my dad.

Missing from her stack of sheet music was a popular tune of the time in Alaska, "Squaws Along the Yukon."

"Awful," she said of the song. "I don't ever want to hear the word 'squaws' in this house."

Later, when my father became president of the University of Alaska, he created strong, new programs for native students.

Why wasn't this done earlier?

Maybe it took awhile for some of us to realize that the natives are fellow Alaskans.

"Please don't make us into tourist curiosities," Dominic Thomas, a King Island Eskimo folk dancer, begged me one day at Nome. "We are people, too, just like you."

I read the other day that the University of Alaska had won recognition from the National Science Foundation and major business corporations for a curriculum that is guiding native students through four to five years of tough engineering and science studies.

No surprise there. They are people just like us.

But I stray from my story—the big story.

✦ ✦ ✦

I HADN'T HEARD about the campaign for native land claims until October 18, 1969.

Representatives of native organizations from throughout Alaska were meeting that day in Anchorage. Eskimos, Athabascans, Tlingit and Haida Indians, Aleuts—meeting together for perhaps the first time in Alaska's history. Some of the delegates had been traveling for days from their remote villages to attend the conference called by the Cook Inlet Native Association.

I was in the lobby of the Anchorage Westward Hotel when Emil Notti hurried from the meeting room and handed me four clipped-together sheets of yellow legal-tablet paper. They contained his notes from the meeting.

"You'd better have a look at this," Notti said. "It's going to be a big story."

Notti, then president of the Cook Inlet Native Association, called for the meeting of native leaders after hearing rumors that the federal Bureau of Indian Affairs was drafting a "final solution" to the long-dormant land claims of Alaska natives.

"It dawned on me that the natives should have something to say about it, some voice in the matter," said the shy, soft-spoken Athabascan from the Yukon River village of Koyukuk.

"I wrote letters to every native spokesman I knew to invite them to a meeting here in Anchorage. I thought maybe we would have maybe fifteen people at the meeting—but we got three hundred!"

The delegates voted during the Anchorage meeting to form the Alaska Federation of Natives—and join forces to win a fair settlement of their land claims.

For once, there was unity in the widely scattered native community— stretching from Ketchikan in Southeastern Alaska to Bethel in Western Alaska and north to Barrow in the high Arctic.

"We have a big job ahead," Notti said.

Why did Emil Notti decide to make this fight?

"I didn't think the natives were getting a fair shake," he said.

Then Notti talked emotionally about a typical native breadwinner who leaves his home village to look for work in Anchorage.

"He arrives with his last hundred dollars, if that much," Notti said. "He doesn't know where he is going to sleep tonight. He doesn't know how to find a job. He stands around on Fourth Avenue [the tavern district] with nothing to do. He's lost. . . . "

Notti also believed it was "cruel and wrong" for native children to be torn from their families to attend distant government boarding schools.

"This happens just when the child is old enough to begin learning things

Emil Notti, in 1973—early crusader for a congressional settlement of the land claims of Alaska's native peoples.

from his parents," Notti said. "About then he would be taking notice of how to trap, how to hunt, and things like that.

"Sending him away to school is breaking the family ties. Then, when he gets out of school, he's not really equipped to make a living in the white man's world—and having been away so much he can't make a living in the village, either, because he doesn't know how to survive there.

"He's missed all those years. He doesn't fit in either world."

Notti's eyes filled with tears as we talked.

"I know this is so," he said. "It happened to me. I left home at age eleven and never went back."

Notti later was elected president of the native federation—a position he didn't seek.

"There are lots of people around who could do it better," he said.

But he was ready to battle for settlement of the native claims.

"This is something that has to be done," he said. "We are going to see it through."

Today, thanks to Emil Notti and the other native leaders, there are state-supported schools in most of Alaska's native communities. Native youngsters no longer have to leave home to attend BIA boarding schools in the Lower 48 states. And, at last, they are being encouraged to preserve their native languages.

Notti gives much of the credit to the late Howard Rock, the Eskimo editor of *Tundra Times*, a statewide native newspaper.

"It was Howard who got hold of my letter calling for the Anchorage meeting and really gave it headlines," Notti said. "That's what generated the excitement."

✦ ✦ ✦

HOWARD ROCK—maybe my best journalism teacher.

To know this humble man was to discover the true heart of Alaska.

He was born Howard Weyahok, in Point Hope, an ancient village on the shore of the Chukchi Sea. He had no plans to become a newspaperman. But fortunately for Alaska he edged into journalism at the time he was needed most by his fellow natives.

Years before the land-claims fight began, Rock had left Alaska to study art at the University of Washington in Seattle. When he ran short of money there, he found time to design ivory curios for Seattle jewelers.

In 1961, Rock decided to return to Point Hope. Back home, he found his people worried about Project Chariot, an Atomic Energy Commission plan to use nuclear blasts to carve a harbor on the arctic coast.

The AEC proposed to detonate several nuclear devices at Cape Thompson, not far from Point Hope, in a test described as "geographical engineering." The agency promised that radioactivity would be held "to the lowest possible level."

Sadly, some Alaskan newspapers and chambers of commerce quickly endorsed the project as good for the economy.

But villagers in the Arctic were worried. How would their children be affected by the radioactive fallout? What about contamination in the food chain of the wildlife they hunted for food?

"They didn't know how to go about protesting to various people," Rock said. "They wanted me to help them write letters and so on."

Also voicing opposition to Project Chariot at that time were Olaus Murie of the Wilderness Society, Barry Commoner of the American Association for

Howard Rock works at his typewriter in the Tundra Times office in Fairbanks, in 1968.

the Advancement of Science, and other environmental leaders. Murie, a long-time field biologist in Alaska, ridiculed Project Chariot as "this atomic play-thing."

Visiting at Point Hope that year—and equally concerned—was Henry Forbes, Alaska policy chairman of the Association on American Indian Affairs, and Laverne Madigan, the association's executive secretary.

During a meeting in Point Hope, Rock suggested that native councils in the Arctic get together and consider publishing a newsletter to warn villagers about the "bomb threat." Later, some of the Eskimo leaders did meet, at Barrow, and discussed the possibility of publishing a small newspaper.

Forbes telephoned Rock from his home in Milton, Massachusetts, to say he would provide financial backing for such a newspaper, on one condition: that Howard Rock be the editor.

"I gave several reasons for not doing it," Rock recalled. "I had never been a newsman. But then I agreed to do it, reluctantly."

The new newspaper, founded in 1962, was named *Tundra Times*. It was

Snug in a down parka and fur hat, I visited a North Slope oil well in the winter of 1975. STANTON PATTY COLLECTION

owned by a native corporation—the Eskimo, Indian, Aleut Publishing Company. Howard Rock was elected president and editor.

Tundra Times led the fight against Project Chariot—and in 1962 the project was canceled, quietly, by the AEC.

Alaska's natives were finding their voice.

Now the stage was set for the land-claims fight.

"At first, it was kind of discouraging," Rock said as the land-claims campaign began. "Then, one by one, the native leaders started speaking up. The paper was able to show them that we do have a voice and that people will listen to us. Now the people are holding their heads higher."

Many times during the land-claims years, I would take my cues from Howard Rock.

"You're doing fine," he would say. "But don't get too close to your story."

That was Rock's style. Always calm, never strident. Determined, but not impassioned. Fair, never extreme.

"Keep doing what you're doing," he said. "We trust you to tell the truth."

At the top of page 1 in every edition of *Tundra Times* was this line: "Speak the absolute truth."

Many honors came to Rock after the native land-claims settlement. He was named Alaskan of the Year and received an honorary doctorate in humane letters from the University of Alaska. He also was nominated for a Pulitzer Prize.

But none of this changed him

"I didn't do these things alone," he said. "

The last time I saw Rock was on a raw winter afternoon in Fairbanks. Working late, as usual, in his cluttered office, the Eskimo editor was pasting up pages for that week's edition of the newspaper.

Rock was dying of cancer. He had lost weight. You could see flashes of pain cross his face. Then he would erase the agony with a cheerful smile.

I'll lick it," he said of the cancer. "The only problem is that I get a little tired this late in the day."

"In that case," I suggested, "let's go have a beer."

We adjourned to Tommy's Elbow Room, down Second Avenue from the *Tundra Times* newsroom. Rock ordered a bourbon and water. Then, deep in thought, he talked about the early days of the *Tundra Times* venture and the long struggle to win the historic land-claims settlement.

He never said so, but history will record that Rock, perhaps more than anyone else, was responsible for that victory. There were times when his was about the only muted voice in the native-versus-nonnative (and sometimes native-against-native) storm that threatened to tear apart the young state. *Tundra Times* and Howard Rock welded together sometimes militant factions for the battle—and, in the end, earned the plaudits of their foes.

Rock gave the natives dignity and purpose. And he gave nonnatives a lesson in decency and tolerance.

"The fight was right," he said that winter evening in Fairbanks. "But I never wanted to create any animosity, and I hope I didn't."

He smiled.

"You know," he teased, "I'm still not a newsman. But I'm trying all the time."

We ordered another round. Rock grew quiet. He shivered in his black overcoat—and stared into space, almost as if, in his mind, he was home in Point Hope.

It was time for me to head for the airport for a flight to Anchorage.

"Goodbye, old friend," I said, patting Rock on a shoulder and leaving him alone with his thoughts. I knew it was the last time we would meet. My eyes were filled with tears as I walked into the night.

Howard Rock, the greatest Alaskan I have known, died April 20, 1976, at the age of sixty-four, in Bassett Army Hospital on the outskirts of Fairbanks.

But first he made his final deadline for *Tundra Times.*

The late Tom Snapp, editor of the *Pioneer All-Alaska Weekly,* was one of Rock's closest friends. He said Rock was near collapse as the gallant editor put the finishing touches to his last edition.

"He sat there at his desk with just a few close friends until about 9 P.M.," Snapp said. "It was as if he was just too weak to move.

"The next day he was hospitalized. There was little the doctors could do for him then. At first he refused painkillers, knowing they would interfere with his ability to converse with friends. Then they were administered, and shortly before midnight he passed away."

"His death has taken a giant from among us," said Governor Jay Hammond. "No one can fill the void he leaves."

Rock's last editorial was a message of love and hope for his Eskimo people.

"In the Inuit (Eskimo) world within the Deep Arctic," he wrote, "you

A visitor photographs a section of the trans-Alaska oil pipeline near the Yukon River. The 800-mile-long pipeline extends from the Prudhoe Bay oil field in the Arctic to the port of Valdez on Prince William Sound.

have learned to live in great harmony with your varied environments. In order to do that, you have had to traverse difficult paths. . . .

"Go forth with good plans for yourselves and those who will come after you. Humanity or humanitarianism within yourselves will enhance your convictions.

"Stay close to your God. Also—always remember your ancestors."

They took Rock home to Point Hope to be buried with his people.

The funeral was held in Point Hope's little Episcopal Church. Then his coffin was placed on a sled and towed by snowmobile to the village cemetery. There, as the temperature hovered around zero, Howard Rock was lowered into his resting place, a grave carved from the arctic permafrost.

It happened that shortly after Rock's remains arrived in Point Hope, villagers landed the first bowhead whale of the season.

"He brought us joy, instead of sadness," villagers said.

Lael Morgan, a gifted author who worked with Rock for several years, wrote:

"It was as if he entered the Pearly Gates and said, 'Send those folks a whale.'"

An upbeat ending. Howard would have liked that.

✦ ✦ ✦

THE NATIVES WON their land-claims settlement. The oil companies got their pipeline. The state of Alaska still is receiving oil royalties from the bountiful North Slope.

It's a done deal. Or is it?

Jack Roderick, who chronicled the oil/land-claims drama in *Crude Dreams,* wonders about that, too.

"The oil people will explore in the state for decades to come because vast new reserves remain to be discovered," he writes. "With the money will come more of the challenges and the upheaval that have both plagued and enriched all of us who call Alaska home, and that will follow our children and our children after them.

"Can you blame us if we have mixed feelings about the storehouse of natural resources that is ours?"

It's still a big story.

CHAPTER 4

JERKED TO JESUS

FAIRBANKS—Did he—or didn't he?

I chuckle every time I walk by the grave of W. F. (Wrong Font) Thompson in the Clay Street Cemetery. The pioneer editor may have written the most outrageous newspaper headline in the history of Alaska journalism.

It happened (or didn't happen) on April 15, 1921, when one Mailo Segura was hanged in downtown Fairbanks for the murder of J. E. Riley.

Legend has it that Thompson, then editor of the *Fairbanks Daily News-Miner,* penned this headline about the public execution:

JERKED TO JESUS

Thompson denied it. But several Fairbanks residents, including Frank Young, a deputy U.S. marshal assigned to the hanging detail, said the horrific headline did appear that afternoon in the *News-Miner.* So did some of the newspaper's staffers.

We'll never know for sure. No copies of the infamous headline exist. Instead, there is an account of the hanging with this headline:

THE WAGES OF SIN ARE NEVER REDUCED

The late Paul Solka Jr., a longtime *News-Miner* writer and historian, said there was "sound evidence" that Thompson did write the gruesome headline—but it may have been used for only part of the day's press run, then replaced with the less objectionable "Wages of Sin" headline.

Frank Young also remembered that Fairbanks clergymen objected vigorously to the "Jerked to Jesus" version. I grew up knowing Young. He was a kindly, soft-spoken man of his word.

Paul Solka said Duke Stubbs, a *News-Miner* printer and sometimes writer, apparently witnessed a scolding Thompson received from an angry delegation consisting of a Presbyterian minister, a Roman Catholic priest, and an Episcopal rector.

According to Stubbs, Thompson fully expected repercussions over the "Jerked to Jesus" headline and pretended to be busy when the clergymen stormed into the newspaper office "practically three abreast."

Stubbs said Thompson greeted them with, "Well, gentlemen, I don't believe I've ever seen the three of you together before. It must be a matter of grave concern which confronts you. Can I be of help?"

The clerics told the editor "in no uncertain terms" they considered the "Jerked to Jesus" headline of the previous day to be in blasphemous bad taste. Thompson, Stubbs said, feigned surprise, then launched into this explanation of the craft of headline writing:

"A headline writer faces several problems: his head must summarize the matter appearing beneath; he is limited to a set number of letters, words, and lines.

"Now let's take the head to which you object. . . . I think we all agree that the man died when a sudden wrench of the rope broke his neck. Now 'jerk' is a synonym for 'wrench' but it's shorter and often preferred by headline writers. It seems to me the headline states only the facts of the case: Segura died by a sudden jerk of the rope which broke his neck, and his soul winged its way to Jesus. I can see nothing wrong with the headline. It neither understates nor overstates the facts."

"Without further ado," Stubbs recalled, the clergymen "turned on their heels and departed."

Did it really happen this way?

Dermot Cole, a longtime *News-Miner* columnist, described "Jerked to Jesus" as "the most famous headline that ever did or did not appear in the pages of the *Daily News-Miner.*"

Cole then quoted a denial issued by Thompson a year or so after the furor.

"If anything like that ever happened in this paper we have no recollection of it and it must have been some joking printer or reporter in this office who slipped that heading over on the newspaper of this town," Thompson wrote.

However, Cole noted, Thompson some years before had written a headline for an execution that occurred outside Alaska—JERKED TO ETERNITY it said. That one still can be found in the archives.

Thompson never was one to waste a colorful phrase.

"He loved to write," said Paul Solka.

"I was with him a lot of years, and many times watched him," Solka recalled. "As he wrote a story you could see, all over him, that he was enjoying what he was doing. He would pound that old typewriter, pretty good for a hunt-and-peck man, and smile as though every moment was the happiest one he had ever experienced."

The truth of the "Jerked to Jesus" matter went to the grave with William Fentress Thompson on January 6, 1926. Pneumonia took his life in Fairbanks at age sixty-two. Fairbanks stores and professional offices closed for an hour on the day of the funeral to honor the one-of-a-kind editor.

W. F. Thompson was known as Wrong Font, a nickname derived from his initials. (Wrong font—usually expressed as "wf"—is a proofreader's symbol for the wrong size or face of type in a news story.)

Sometimes Thompson also referred to himself as Wandering Foot.

For sure, he was a drifter, stopping off in Arizona, Utah, Texas, California, Washington state, British Columbia, and Canada's Klondike before settling down in Fairbanks about 1906.

But details of his early newspapering days are sketchy. His life, Thompson said, "was not for publication."

And he added: "I attribute my longevity to having always—against great opposition—lived my life in my own way."

The last sanctuary for individual journalism died with Thompson, the *News-Miner* mourned.

Well, maybe not.

✦ ✦ ✦

IN 1957, a lovable rascal by the name of Albro B. Gregory boarded an Alaska Airlines plane in Seattle.

The Nome Nugget building on a bright winter day.

"Where does this plane go?" he asked a flight attendant.

"Fairbanks," she replied.

"Good enough."

In Fairbanks, Gregory soon found a job on the *News-Miner*. Then he roamed Alaska, working for the *Ketchikan Daily News,* the *Juneau Empire,* and the *Petersburg Press* and maybe a few other publications before landing in the old gold-rush town of Nome.

I first met Albro Gregory in 1968 in Petersburg, where I was giving a talk about international-fisheries problems for an audience of halibut fishermen. Gregory was there to cover the meeting for the *Petersburg Press.*

Now, please understand that my dear friend Albro never claimed to be a teetotaler. He was maybe the best newspaperman who ever wrote about Alaska—and now and then enjoyed a dram of Chivas Regal.

So, there I was at the microphone in the Sons of Norway Hall. Gregory was seated at the rear of the stage, rocking back and forth in a metal folding chair. Suddenly, there was a crash. He had fallen off the platform

Moments later, he was by my side, his left hand covering the microphone.

"Stan," he said, "do me a favor. Come into the office in the morning and write a story about your speech. OK?"

I did, and the story appeared under Gregory's byline. It was, as I remember, a pretty good speech, at least in print.

June Allen, today one of Alaska's finest writers, was a devoted colleague.

"Albro gave me my first job, with the Ketchikan paper back in '64, bless his heart," June said. "It was the best training in the world for writing.

"Albro's charm, I think, was that he remained a child. Not childish, but childlike. The world was fun to him and he enjoyed every minute of it!

"Felt-tip pens came out in the mid-1960s, and Albro just loved anything new like that. He was always in the office by 5 A.M., when he tore the copy off the teletype and draped those coils of perforated tape on hooks along the wall. Then he did the sports. By the time I got there at 8 A.M. he was editing local copy to get it ready for the Linotype guys.

"As soon as he heard me in the outer office, he'd call, 'June Bug. Can you give me a hand here?'"

Before long Albro would signal June that it was time to go shopping for a new felt-tip pen.

"We'd go down to the drugstore and get some pens, and then he'd giggle, he really giggled!" June recalled. "And we'd head into the New Deal bar next door and have a beer and then go back to work."

Shortly after his stint in Petersburg, Gregory moved on to Nome and became editor and publisher of the *Nome Nugget*. It was there that the fun really began.

History records that an earlier *Nome Nugget* editor had rushed to the pulpit of a local church to announce that he was the new editor and was asking for God's help to do his job in the rowdy gold town.

"Well," said Gregory, "I haven't made such a plea yet. But you never know . . ."

The freewheeling editor began by waging a campaign against those outsiders who would thrust newfangled things like paved sidewalks and streets on Nome. Such foolishness, he wrote, would surely spoil Nome for the tourists.

"It seems to me that if we here in Nome want to wade through mud sometimes and get dust blown in our eyes at other times, it should be our own damned business," he thundered in a page 2 editorial. "Next, they'll be telling us to wear white shirts and ties to the office, just like in Anchorage."

If paving were to proceed, Gregory said, the way to counter it was to get the politicians to approve an urban-renewal program—"and extract enough cash from that to put down board sidewalks to hide the concrete."

Was Nome ready for Albro Baggely Gregory's brand of frontier journalism?

"I love this paper," he said.

"This is Alaska's oldest surviving newspaper. The *Nugget* has been published continuously since 1901, except for a brief spell in 1934, when a fire—caused by an overturned booze still—wiped out most of the town."

With his bushy, nicotine-stained beard and wool shirt, Gregory was the picture of a sourdough. Some said he looked like Santa Claus; others thought there was a resemblance to Ernest Hemingway.

I remember him as a sometimes playful, sometimes cantankerous, crack reporter.

Early one morning in November 1974, when I was a reporter for the *Seattle Times*, there was an Associated Press bulletin about Nome being battered and flooded by the worst storm in the town's history.

"Phone someone in Nome and get the story," the city editor said.

I placed a call to Gregory at the *Nome Nugget*.

"You got me just in time," he joked. "I haven't even had a drink yet."

I knew that Gregory had been a respected wire-service reporter in Washington, D.C., New York, and Chicago before moving to Alaska. This day he would dictate crisp, detailed notes to me as if he were still working for United Press.

"Here we go," he said.

"The wind went up to 69 knots, blowing from the south-southwest. I went down the street, toward City Hall. I could hear the roar of the sea. I hesitated. A wall of water came through the alley—my God—all the debris with it. Logs were hitting the side of the City Hall and rolling across the street. I waded through. That was just the start of the night. . . . "

This was Gregory at his best. We had the story.

When I visited Nome the next year, Albro was complaining about how someone had planted "a damned parking meter right in front of my newspaper office."

Several weeks earlier, there was a city-government proposal to install revenue-getting parking meters on Front Street. Gregory was furious, and fought the idea with a series of editorials.

In Anchorage, Mayor George Sullivan, one of Gregory's good friends, got wind of the fiery editor's displeasure and conspired with city officials in Nome to play a joke on him. They decided to place Nome's first and only parking meter directly in front of the *Nome Nugget*. The installers

Albro Gregory, editor of the Nome Nugget, smiles as he greets visitors to the newspaper office in 1969.

struck while Gregory was across the street at his favorite saloon, the Breakers.

"When he came out, there was the meter," says Nancy McGuire, the present editor-publisher of the *Nugget*. "All he did was to scratch his head and look at it."

Gregory took me on a "tour" of the parking meter and grinned.

"I love this town," he said. "We are the last frontier of the last frontier."

There were times, in print, when Gregory's words could be as burning as acid in an open sore. And other times when he could be as funny as any stand-up comedian.

Old-timers in Nome still remember his "Peace at Christmastime" editorial in 1972.

"This is the time of Christmas," he began. "This is a time when joy should take over and bitchiness come to a sudden, jolting halt."

Then, a few paragraphs later, he began an attack on someone he identified only as a "stupid individual" who had signed the name of a close friend of Gregory's to a nasty letter to the editor.

"If I ever get my hands on the bastard who did this awful thing, I believe I might take a paint brush to him where it would do the most good," Gregory vowed.

Merry Christmas, indeed!

Gregory enjoyed tangling with preachers who tried (without success) to reform Nome. One clergyman complained that houses of ill repute were operating in Nome.

"I told him he was wrong," Gregory wrote. "Professional girls would starve to death here because of the abundance of the free kind."

Another day, Gregory published a front-page bulletin that informed readers:

"Word has been received from a reliable source in Cairo, Egypt, that on or about June 27 Nome is to receive the first bactrian that has ever been shipped to Alaska. Watch the paper for details."

Bactrian?

Nomeites had to turn to their Funk & Wagnall's to solve that one. And Gregory was just kidding, anyhow.

(Bactrian—a type of camel.)

Nome rests on a bed of permafrost, permanently frozen ground, by the Bering Sea. Problem was that when heat radiated from some of the old buildings, the permafrost melted in places, tilting furnishings like tipsy revelers. Such was the case at the *Nome Nugget* in Gregory's day. The typesetting machine had to be chained down so it wouldn't slide across the wobbly, sloping floor. And in spring, when the permafrost at Nome's Belmont Point Cemetery melted sufficiently, it was possible to resume burials of the deceased in the icy earth after long winters of storing corpses-in-waiting.

That put Gregory in mind of a yarn about an early-times prospector whose wife was buried on a sandspit out toward the edge of town.

This is how Gregory wrote the story:

"Some years later, during what is referred to as the 'Great Storm of 1913,' many graves were washed out and caskets floated around until they were grounded.

"The prospector, whose cabin stood on pilings not far away, awakened that night to the pounding of something against the stilts. He looked out and saw a casket. So he waded in and secured the coffin to one of the pilings with a rope. Next morning the storm abated. The miner went out and opened the coffin he had tied up and there lay his long-dead wife.

"By golly, Martha," he was quoted as saying, "Y' look like y' always did, except your hair is a little bit longer."

June 1980. Albro Gregory was getting ready to leave his beloved Nome.

No, the crusty editor was not being chased out of town—although that had been threatened a few times.

He had decided to retire and move to Fairbanks with his new wife, the former Jane Konicki, a regional representative for the Social Security Administration.

They met the summer before when Jane visited the *Nugget* on routine business. The wedding took place across the street at the Breakers, the place Gregory called "my other office." Can-can girls greeted the couple as they entered the bar. The wedding cake was topped with Chivas Regal miniatures.

"I'll settle down and write my memoirs," Gregory said.

June 2 was proclaimed Albro Gregory Day in Nome, with a grand farewell dinner at the Fort Davis Roadhouse. I had flown to Nome, at Gregory's request, to be the keynote speaker at his retirement banquet.

"Let's hoist a few and talk," he said when he met me at the airport.

"Damn, I feel humble," he said. "I've loved this newspaper like she was a beautiful, naked woman. And, by golly, I've had fun."

The fun wasn't over yet.

Gregory had published a retirement edition that proved to be a shocker. There was a photo of Albro on page 1, with the middle digit of his right hand in the vertical position.

"Albro says Goodbye to Leo!" was the headline.

The caption: "Words are not enough to express Albro's feelings for the Mayor as he waves goodbye to the Mayor."

Mayor Leo Rasmussen and Albro had been feuding for years. Newcomers to the *Nugget* staff were instructed to be sure that any photographs of Rasmussen be taken from behind the mayor. "Get his bald spot," Gregory ordered.

Mayor Rasmussen exploded with rage when he saw the special edition with Gregory's "salute."

For reasons he never explained, Gregory changed his mind later in the day and replated page 1 with a benign photo of his smiling self. So there were two retirement editions that day. I have both in my files.

It was a great party. A police car, siren screaming, delivered Gregory to the Roadhouse. We all had prime ribs and a glass or two of spirits. I rose and said some nice things about my old friend.

And then Mr. and Mrs. Gregory took up residence in Fairbanks, where Albro planned to write those memoirs.

They never were written. Albro B. Gregory died January 15, 1987, at age seventy-six, of a heart ailment.

Next morning there was a note from the *Seattle Times* telephone operator on my desk: "Mr. Gregory passed away."

The fun was over.

CHAPTER 5

EARTHQUAKE!

ANCHORAGE—The chill of a snowy evening was settling over Alaska on March 27, 1964—Good Friday. The time was 5:36 P.M.

First there was a shudder, then a savage, grinding roll.

In the terrible shaking that followed, mountains swayed, triggering avalanches of rock and ice. Highways became rolling, writhing ribbons. Homes and stores collapsed. Bridges and radio towers twisted and fell. Railroad tracks coiled like paper clips. Great gashes opened in the ground.

When it ended, 131 were people dead. Tidal waves—scientists call them tsunamis—claimed many of the lives, as far away as the coasts of Oregon and California.

And the snow kept falling, lightly, silently, like tears.

Alaska had suffered the most powerful earthquake in the known history of North America, with a magnitude of 9.2 (and registering 8.5 on the Richter scale in use at that time).

"The entire earth vibrated like a tuning fork," reported the United States Geological Survey.

The next morning George Carkonen, a *Seattle Times* photographer, and I

Fourth Avenue in downtown Anchorage is a scene of disaster in the aftermath of the 1964 Good Friday earthquake. GEORGE CARKONEN PHOTO FOR THE *SEATTLE TIMES*

were on the first plane into Anchorage from Seattle. It was a slow, propeller-driven Constellation of Pacific Northern Airlines.

There was no hope of landing a fast jetliner at Anchorage International Airport. The control tower had collapsed. And a million gallons of jet fuel had spilled across the runway.

"There's just been another sharp aftershock," said Captain Jerry Fay, the Connie pilot, as we neared Anchorage. "I'm not sure if we will be able to land."

Finally, Fay received clearance to land. He dived through the clouds and circled the stricken city at low level.

From the air, there seemed to be no sign of life. All we could see were jumbles of shattered buildings and heaps of snow-streaked earth plowed into furrows by the earthquake. It looked like hell turned inside out.

We didn't know then that several other communities—Seward, Valdez, Kodiak, Whittier, and native villages from Prince William Sound to Kodiak Island—also had been pounded and drowned by the earthquake. News about tragedies in the rural areas was slow to reach relief agencies. Except for the voices of a few ham radio operators, most of Southcentral Alaska was cut off from the rest of the world.

I'll never forget the cool of the flight attendant as we landed on the icy runway.

"Ladies and gentlemen," she said calmly, "this is Anchorage International Airport."

Carkonen and I hurried off the plane and hitchhiked into downtown Anchorage.

It was a grim scene. Shivering families were lined up at street-corner canteens manned by soldiers from nearby Fort Richardson. Many homes were without heat or drinking water. Gasoline was in short supply. Residents were being urged to report to emergency centers for typhoid shots.

"Hi, there," a young soldier called to passersby at Fifth Avenue and F Street. "How about a good cup of coffee?"

Nearby, rescue crews discovered a man's body under the rubble where the J.C. Penney department store had crashed. There were rumors that several shoppers had been trapped inside the building. Firefighters and police officers began crawling through the wreckage on their bellies to search for victims. The rumors turned out to be false.

Air Force Staff Sergeant Roderick Howells told us of escaping with his wife and two children from the third floor of Penney's as the building shook apart.

"I don't know how we got out of there," he said. "I guess God was with us."

"Everything started coming down. I reached for the children. Then the floor went out from under me. I caught myself on a part that didn't drop and climbed back up. The ceiling fell. A piece hit me in the back. But I found the kids again and we raced down the back stairway. There was no panic."

Lieutenant Colonel Daniel G. Rody of the Salvation Army walked from store to store, collecting groceries, baby diapers, and other necessities for the quake victims. Someone pressed a five-dollar bill into his hands.

"Bless you," the donor said.

"Bless you, Sir," Rody replied with a warm smile.

Alaska was stunned and wounded. But the pioneer spirit that built the North Country never flickered. Not even for a moment.

"Can you imagine not being able to find a drink in this town?" an old-timer asked as he surveyed the wreckage of a dozen or more saloons strung along Fourth Avenue. It was the city's first dry spell in memory.

From a ledge of earthquake-torn land, I had a chance to survey damage to the Turnagain neighborhood in Anchorage. GEORGE CARKONEN PHOTO FOR THE *SEATTLE TIMES*

Mayor George Sharrock, grim-faced and exhausted, surveyed the damage with a gaggle of federal officials who had hurried to Alaska to help.

"This is a great city—and it's going to be greater after this," Sharrock said.

Tex Bailey, an Anchorage taxi driver, told the mayor that she would drive any quitters and complainers to the airport "free of charge."

"We don't want any sissies here," she declared.

We moved on, to the fashionable Turnagain neighborhood. The scene there was pure horror. Turnagain's base of mushy earth and clay had been churned into trenches by the quake. Broken bits of beautiful homes were scattered on the edge of the sea.

Two children had vanished when the ground opened. Their father wanted to dig for them. It was no use.

"Where do you begin?" a bystander wondered to himself.

Seven persons stranded on a shrinking island in the Turnagain slide joined in a snow-water baptism as the earth swayed and crumbled around them.

Juanita Summers told of fleeing with her two children when the earth-quake began. She looked back and saw her house drop over a cliff. A chasm opened at her feet. Trees snapped. Severed power lines sizzled in the snow.

"This is the end of the world," she thought.

Soon other neighbors were gathered with the Summers family on a mush-room-shaped island of jiggling soil. There seemed to be no hope of surviving.

"Have you ever been baptized?" Mrs. Paul Caughran asked Juanita Summers.

Mothers and children knelt. Mrs. Caughran melted snow in her hands and baptized all.

The quake stopped.

"I looked up at the sky and it was blue and calm," said Juanita Summers.

Getting the first Anchorage story to the *Seattle Times* was a challenge. George Carkonen and I had found bunks at neighboring Elmendorf Air Force Base. But the only working telephones were in the communications center on Government Hill—and they were reserved for military personnel.

A young enlisted man was in charge of the phones. I was an Army enlisted man during World War II and remembered how intimidating it was to be ordered around by officers. So (forgive me, please), I snapped at the young airman: 'I'm Major Bob Reed, and I need that telephone right now.' With that, I had a telephone line for twenty minutes, long enough to dictate the story to the *Times* city desk.

Bob Reed, the Elmendorf public-information officer, was a friend. He administered a proper scolding later, but with a smile. He understood that journalists have to be "creative" when covering a story as big as the Good Friday earthquake.

"Just don't do it again," Reed instructed.

✦ ✦ ✦

MEL SAYRE, OUR CITY EDITOR, told us to find out what was happening in the rest of Alaska.

They still were burying the dead when we reached little Valdez. Only skeletons of buildings were standing in the town of one thousand residents.

"We really have nothing left," said Mayor Bruce Woodford. "But you can't keep Alaskans down for long."

Thirty Valdez residents died when the city's cargo dock disappeared in a massive underwater landslide. The victims had been crowding the Valdez waterfront for the arrival of the *Chena,* an Alaska Steamship Company freighter.

"The earth just opened up and swallowed everything," an eyewitness reported.

Captain Merrill Stewart, skipper of the *Chena,* reached the ship's bridge just as the Valdez dock fell into the swirling sea.

"I saw people running—with no place to run to," Stewart said. "It was ghastly. They were engulfed by buildings, water, mud, everything."

Then the 10,815-ton *Chena*—which had been lifted like a toy thirty feet or more by a tidal wave—dropped where the people had been standing.

"There was no sight of them," Stewart said. "That kept me awake for days."

Chena was spinning around the harbor in a deadly dance, heeling over, sliding on the muddy bottom as outgoing waves sucked water out of the bay, then crashing into rocks and broken pilings.

"We rolled wildly, from side to side, like a rag doll," Stewart said.

Somehow, the *Chena* broke free of the debris and found open water.

"It was a miracle," Stewart said.

Crew members aboard the *Chena* wore the look of death days after the tragedy.

"It was horrible," said Carson Dorney, the second engineer.

"*Chena* rolled over about 45 degrees into a big whirlpool. Three men were spinning around in the pool. Two went under right away. The other was float-ing on a piece of roofing. It swallowed him, too."

Just before the quake, crew members had tossed oranges to two children on the pier. Moments later Dorney and the others watched helplessly as the children fled.

"Some fellow picked up one of the youngsters and was pulling the other along," he said. "They all disappeared."

Dorney rode a lifeboat to shore with six Valdez longshoremen who had survived the hammering aboard the *Chena.*

"There were huge fissures," he said. "I fell into one while carrying a body I had found."

Owen Meals, a resident of Valdez since 1903, was determined to save his town. He offered to provide a new site, on firm bedrock, a few miles away. Valdez was rebuilt there, and survived.

✦ ✦ ✦

SEWARD, ACROSS PRINCE WILLIAM Sound from Valdez, was a pitiful sight. The railroad town of thirteen hundred persons had been punished by earthquake, fire, and tidal waves. At least twelve people were killed.

Seward had no choice but to bear its ordeal alone. The Alaska Railroad had been knocked out. The only highway into town was blocked by landslides and shattered bridges. There was no way to telephone in or out. Seward might as well have been on another planet.

About two hundred residents were camping in the high-school gym when we reached Seward aboard an Alaskan Air Command cargo plane. Hundreds more were taking some of their meals at the school.

"Money has no value here right now," said William C. Vincent, a Seward city councilman. "There's nothing for sale. No one has any income—not a single industry is left."

Seward's waterfront on mountain-rimmed Resurrection Bay was a crescent of destruction. Bright fires still were burning in railroad tank cars. Dozens of other overturned railcars were scattered on the beach in grotesque array. Still others vanished somewhere in the bay when wild tidal waves—thirty feet high or more—cleaved away part of the shore. No. 1828, a seventy-ton locomotive, was hoisted by a wave and tossed on its side like a child's plaything.

Huge fuel-storage tanks, blackened by fire, were shifted, still upright, from their foundations. Yet, just across the street from the tank farm, was an undamaged home.

Everything in Seward was coated with an oily, black scum from the ruptured petroleum tanks. Witnesses said it looked as if the sea was on fire as blazing fuel, spread by the waves, rushed toward the head of the harbor. Boils of muddy, debris-laden water were sighted a mile from shore.

"Pathetic," muttered George Carkonen, while lining up a photo of the mangled waterfront. Carkonen, a fearless and dedicated professional, had photographed everything from murders to aviation disasters and rarely led with his heart.

Carkonen's classic Good Friday Earthquake photographs were seen throughout the world. It almost didn't happen that way. His 4-by-5 Speed Graphic press camera, just out of a Seattle repair shop, had a light leak that he discovered only after the film had been developed. Just in case, he had decided to back up the Speed Graphic with an old, German-made camera that fit in his jacket pocket. That was the camera that recorded the great photos.

Robert Lentz, a Seward trucker, was standing nearby as Carkonen photographed. He told of watching a wall of water and fire pour over what he thought was "the whole town."

"The docks on the waterfront catapulted into the air and fell as burning wreckage," he said. "Railroad cars flew through the air. I saw one boxcar hurtle about a block.

"Boats tried to ride the crest of a tidal wave. I remember there were about fifty fishing boats in the harbor. There isn't even a skiff left now."

Ray Doyle was cruising through Seward in his car, making announcements with a loudspeaker system. His commercial radio station had been wrecked by the quake.

"I wish we could find a 100-watt transmitter," Doyle said. "Then we could go on the air and give our people news and even some music."

An Air Force officer heard Doyle's request, and said a transmitter would be flown to him as quickly as possible. Doyle smiled a thank you and continued driving down Jefferson Street with his makeshift public-address system.

Seward had been declared an All-American City just before the disaster.

"We were scheduled to receive the award this weekend," said Councilman Delmar Zentmire. "But the ceremony will have to be postponed now. We'll get to it some day. But before we do, we'll have to win it all over again."

And plucky Seward did just that. Today Seward is one of Alaska's busiest cruise-ship ports. And the Alaska Railroad is rolling daily with bumper loads of freight and passengers.

✦ ✦ ✦

NOBODY SUFFERED MORE than the Aleut villagers of Chenega, at the western end of Prince William Sound. A tidal wave towering an incredible seventy feet wiped the helpless village from the face of the earth. Twenty-three of Chenega's ninety residents died.

"Everyone lost someone," said Larry Evanoff, who was away at school at the time. Evanoff lost his mother and father, aunts and uncles.

That giant wave chased a father carrying his two small daughters while a third daughter ran beside him. The father was the Reverend Nicholas Kompkoff, a Russian Orthodox priest. He told this chilling story to *Tundra Times*, an Alaska natives' newspaper:

"The day started as usual, peaceful and quiet, but there seemed to be a feeling of tension in the air. . . . At the time [of the quake] I was at the opposite end of the village from our house. As I was running home I met my wife and she asked me where our children were and I didn't have the faintest idea.

"I reached the dock. I found my three daughters and quickly took the two younger ones and started running toward higher ground with the oldest girl ahead of me. Someone yelled 'tidal wave' and I started running faster, but I was too slow. Before I realized it the water was upon us and in trying to reach for the oldest girl, I lost hold of one of the girls I was holding in my arms.

"The two girls were swept away from me immediately by the force of the water. The last word my oldest daughter uttered was 'Dad,' that was all and they were lost to me forever. I was powerless to do anything.

"The force of the water carried me past the church which was on higher ground and across a stream behind the church where I landed feet first into a snowbank. I still had my youngest daughter in my arms. . . . "

A bush pilot flew by two days later and saw that Chenega was gone.

But not forever.

In 1983 the survivors returned to build a new Chenega—they named it Chenega Bay—fifteen miles north of the vanished village.

"Home at Last" was the headline in the *Seattle Times* that day.

✦ ✦ ✦

FAR TO THE SOUTHWEST, downtown Kodiak was a junkyard of broken buildings and fishing vessels scattered on Main Street by a series of tidal waves. But a few days after the quake, fishermen were digging trenches to move several of their beached boats toward the harbor.

"We are not waiting for help to come to us," said Pat Cannon, the waterfront salvage boss.

Captain Harvey Harbaugh's seventy-five-foot *Albatross* was leading the strange boat parade. First a path was bulldozed through the soggy soil. Then *Albatross* was pushed from its dry-land perch into the trench and towed to the harbor. The next high tide refloated the fishing boat. Then workmen began digging out another fishing vessel, the *Hekla*.

More than one hundred boats were anchored in the marina on Good Friday. Only two were bobbing there the morning after the quake.

And then a week after the disaster, a wicked windstorm damaged eighteen more boats. One of those, *Marguerite,* was slammed across a rock jetty like a teeter-totter. Poking up from the blue-green water near the jetty were the masts of another boat, *Fidelity.*

All over town, bulldozers crushed and scooped debris toward blazing bonfires as residents raked ruined household items from their spongy front yards.

"We didn't lose anything that can't be replaced," said Kay Anderson, a Kodiak housewife. "The important thing is that we are alive."

The roar of the bulldozers and the growl of chain saws played a fugue with the wind and ocean waves. But they did not compose a dirge. They were the sounds of Kodiak's energy.

Show-and-tell time was laced with grim reality in Mrs. Newinger's first-grade classroom at Kodiak Elementary School. The teacher invited her twenty-three pupils to talk about their earthquake experiences.

Kay Lynn Carpenter: "I remember that a mud puddle was dancing up and down in my yard. I thought it was funny."

Matthew Keplinger: "The wall was shaking back and forth. I told my brother, Mark, to stop shaking the wall. My daddy was in his fishing boat. I was afraid he went down with the boat because he didn't come home until late."

Lori Weisser: "The houses of three of my friends in school went into the water."

Florise Coutee: "My mother told us all to go outside. She went out, too, but only had one slipper on."

Judy Richardson: "I was in the bathtub. I felt like a boat swimming."

Jean Newinger, the teacher, said a sharp aftershock jolted Kodiak a few days after the Good Friday earthquake.

"We were reading a story when it hit," she said. "The children stood up and crowded around me. Some of them held onto me very tightly. A couple of them cried."

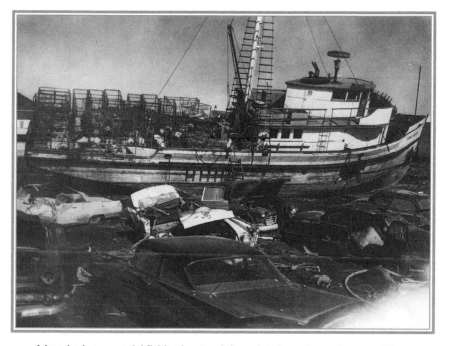

A beached commercial fishing boat and the twisted wreckage of automobiles litter a section of downtown Kodiak. The island city was hammered by a series of tidal waves during the Good Friday earthquake. GEORGE CARKONEN PHOTO FOR THE *SEATTLE TIMES*

Kodiak kids invented a new game of make-believe after the quake. They called it Earthquake and Tidal Wave. Four toddlers acted it out as their mothers watched on a wave-torn beach with a backdrop of wrecked fishing boats.

First the children had a tea party, stirring sand into paper pups.

"Now, let's pretend there is an earthquake," said Cindy Heglin, age five.

Cindy and one of her playmates, Cecile Ardinger, also five, grabbed their dolls and dashed for shelter. They returned a few moments later to "see the tidal wave come in."

"That's the way it is here," said Mrs. Harold Heglin, wife of Kodiak's fire chief. "Kids all over town are playing the game. They are the adaptable ones."

Kodiak held onto its sense of humor during the cleanup. Out at Potato Patch Lake, which had been emptied by the quake, "prospectors" were mining the lake bottom—searching for thousands of dollars worth of whiskey buried in the mud where the lakeside Beachcombers night club was flattened.

"The beachcombing is terrific," one happy finder reported.

The whole town was talking about the adventure of Skipper Bill Cuthbert and his crab boat, the *Selief.*

As the earthquake stopped, State Trooper Don Church hurried to the Kodiak police station to sound a warning on the marine-radio network. He knew that lethal tidal waves soon would follow the quake.

"Get to high ground!" Church called by radio.

Out in the harbor, Bill Cuthbert heard the message and tried to start the cranky engine of the *Selief.* No luck. He waited for the waves to strike.

"*Selief, Selief,* where are you?" Trooper Church asked as he called the roll of local fishing boats.

Cuthbert's response: "It looks like I'm back of the schoolhouse, five blocks from the harbor."

That's exactly where one of the tidal waves had tossed the *Selief.*

✦ ✦ ✦

George Carkonen and I left Alaska weeks later on a night when the northern lights were waltzing in the sky.

"We'll be OK," Anchorage friends said at the airport.

Alaska: land of snow-crowned mountains, of nameless valleys and meandering rivers, jade fiords with shining glaciers, wild sheep prancing on high cliffs, dusty gravel roads through the wilderness, slender birch trees like silver lace against the deep-blue sky—and unafraid families who love this tough country too much to leave it.

They knew that self pity and despair would only slow the process of rebuilding their young state. It had been only five years since Alaska won statehood. And less than a hundred years since Alaska was ruled by czarist Russia.

Yes, I thought to myself, Alaska will be OK.

CHAPTER 6

BROKEN DREAMS

UNALASKA ISLAND—I thought someone was going to die.

A howling wind from the Bering Sea slammed the vessel *Robert Eugene.* Frothy blue-green waves raced by the boat, shattering into high-flying spray. Empty oil drums bounced across the pier, clanging like cymbals and rolling into the sea.

"I don't like the looks of this," Rufus Choate said.

Choate, a Montana cowboy, had moved his family here to the Aleutian Islands to establish a sheep and cattle ranch. His wife, Alice. Their sons, Jim, age twenty, and Ted, age ten. Their daughter, Sue, twenty-one. Smoky, a playful sheepdog they rescued from a shelter in Seattle. And Kushka, a striped-orange cat that never strayed far from Ted. The boy lived with pain: he was afflicted with hemophilia, a severe blood disorder.

The *Robert Eugene,* a seventy-four-year-old former Seattle fireboat, was the family's floating home while the Choates worked to convert an abandoned World War II post office into a ranch house.

It was November 1964.

The *Robert Eugene,* a former Seattle fireboat, lies at anchor in Dutch Harbor after transporting the Choate family and livestock from Seattle to the Aleutians.

Jim Choate, a sinewy six-footer, his dad's mainstay, was away this day. He was crewing on a crab-fishing boat, the *Fern.*

There were two guests aboard the *Robert Eugene.* One was Wayne Mathews, who had returned here just that afternoon from dental surgery in Anchorage. Jim Choate was taking Wayne's place aboard the *Fern.* And I was bunking with the Choates while writing about their adventures for the *Seattle Times.*

We were more than two thousand miles from Seattle—almost a thousand miles west of Anchorage—in a tiny community of mostly Aleut natives.

The Aleutian Islands. Stepping stones of history—first the ancient Aleuts, then cruel fur hunters from Russia, then the terrible bombs and bullets of World War II.

And storms. Killer storms.

The *Robert Eugene* slammed against the pier. The wind was roaring like a runaway jet engine.

"I would guess that the wind is a good fifty or sixty knots, with gusts to seventy-five," Mathews said.

Rufus Choate and Mathews went outside to check on the mooring lines that held the boat to the rickety dock of a wartime submarine base. They added another safety cable, just in case.

An abandoned World War II military post office building served as a temporary home for the Rufus Choate family on Unalaska Island in the Aleutians.

"The only way the boat can get away now is to take the dock with her," Rufe said.

"It sure is invigorating out here," he added with a wry smile.

Back aboard, Choate unfurled a chart of the Aleutians and pointed to pockets along the chain of islands where the *Fern* might have found shelter from the storm.

"She's all right," he said. "There are lots of places to duck into."

Sheets of seawater flew past the *Robert Eugene*'s portholes. Fuel barrels banged down the pier.

Military units left behind hundreds of the oil drums at the close of World War II. More than ten thousand U.S. soldiers and sailors were stationed here on Unalaska Island and at neighboring Dutch Harbor after Japanese carrier planes bombed the Dutch Harbor Navy base in June 1942. Japanese soldiers moved swiftly after the bombing raids to capture two of the Aleutian islands—Attu and Kiska. United States and Canadian forces won back the islands in 1943.

Crumbling ruins of the lonely fortresses, from Quonset huts to abandoned hospitals and ammo dumps, still dot the tundra all through the Aleutians. The Choates had arranged to lease 268,000 acres of grazing land on Unalaska Island from the federal government.

Wild, wind-whipped waves race across Dutch Harbor during a storm that tests the Choate family as it attempts to establish a sheep and cattle ranch in the Aleutian Islands.

(Unalaska also is the name of the Aleut village on Unalaska Island. Dutch Harbor, today one of America's most important commercial-fishing ports, is on Amaknak Island, across a narrow channel from the village.)

With the Choates aboard the 110-foot *Robert Eugene* on the long voyage north and west from Seattle were five hundred Columbia sheep, thirty-two Hereford cattle, fifty chickens, four sows and a boar, three geese, five saddle horses, a heifer named Candy, and a milk cow they called Lucky. The animals made the trip in a maze of between-decks pens.

"We came with an ark," Rufus Choate joked.

"It was just time to move from Montana," he added. "When you can hear your neighbor's rooster crow, you know you need more space."

Young Ted was restless as the wind screamed.

"Play me a game of cribbage, please, Mom," he urged.

"I have to play a game of washing dishes first," Alice Choate said. "Besides, it's a good day for you to do your arithmetic."

Gusts wrenched at the boat. Furious waves smashed on the rocky shore by the old sub base. The storm was building. Rufe went below for a rare afternoon nap. Alice was reading and crocheting in the galley.

The darkening sky was churning with rain, snow, and sleet—all at the same time. The wind blasted off the mountains from the north, then pivoted inside the harbor and lashed at the boat from the opposite direction. They call sudden gusts of storm winds here *williwaws*.

Now the wind was shrieking at more than one hundred miles an hour. This was a williwaw.

Suddenly, about 5 P.M., there was a terrible lurch. The two-inch stern line had parted! Then three more lines broke in rapid-fire sequence. Only a cable on the bow held the swinging, rocking *Robert Eugene* from crashing onto the rocks.

Wayne Mathews, still in his traveling street clothes, ran into the blinding wind and rain and leaped to the dock with the severed stern line. He barely made it. By now Choate was on deck. He took another line from Mathews and looped it around a big cleat on the vessel's stern. Both men struggled to maintain their footing. The wind was pushing them toward the boiling sea. Stinging sleet raked their faces.

I couldn't stay on my feet, so I knelt on the deck and tried to take photographs with slow color film and a camera dripping with water. Even now, four decades later, those pale photos of Dutch Harbor's wild seas are frightening.

Half-shielding her face from the ice bullets, Alice Choate pitched in, too. She held tightly to another of the torn lines.

Mathews made another jump to the pier to recover a broken line. This time the brave fisherman dived into the darkness, landed on a pile of lumber, rolled, and slid along the slippery timbers.

"I knew I was on the dock when I hit, but I didn't know how I would get stopped," he said.

Mathews crawled behind a broken piece of the dock for protection from the screaming wind that by then was topping 125 miles an hour. Meanwhile, Rufe and Alice worked silently to fasten shreds of mooring lines to the boat. Finally, the lines held.

Alice returned to the galley and began repairing her windblown hair with a brush. An angelic smile lighted her face as she noticed her frightened son watching her.

"Play you a game of cribbage, Ted," she said cheerfully.

Choate and Mathews filled their coffee cups. Smoky, the dog, cowered under the galley table.

"That was a close call," Rufe said. "We'd have been lucky to get off alive if the boat had gone on the rocks."

"We get into the darndest predicaments," Alice said with a nervous laugh.

The two men went outside again to lash more lines to the boat. The williwaw still hammered relentlessly. Choate and Mathews decided to take turns standing watch for the rest of the night. The plan was to keep the main engine running. If all the lines failed, maybe they could maneuver the *Robert Eugene* into open water.

On the pier, oil barrels continued kiting through the night. The tired old boat surged, straining its mooring lines.

"It's dangerous out there," Mathews said.

"I'm getting used to it now." said ten-year-old Ted.

"Yes," his father said, "that's like the farmer who fed his horse sawdust. Just when the horse was getting used to it, it died."

The ordeal was not over. Just before eight o'clock there was a mighty gust that caused the *Robert Eugene* to tremble.

"There went a line!" Mathews shouted.

The men bolted out the door and saw the broken stern line hanging uselessly over the port side. A bow line also had been sawed in two.

Alice had dinner ready when they returned an hour later.

"The storm could last another week," she said, with an ear tuned to the wind.

Doors of long-deserted military buildings all across Dutch Harbor banged a ghostly cadence. There were no comforting lights of neighbors' homes. The wind shrilled another crescendo.

We were alone in the Aleutian darkness.

❖ ❖ ❖

THE WIND STILL PANTED next morning, but the worst appeared to be over.

"Well, we're still here," bleary-eyed Rufus Choate said.

Snowflakes hurtled by, almost parallel to the sea.

"Things look about normal this morning," Rufe said as he watched the horizontal snowfall.

The *Fern* still had not arrived with Jim Choate. But his parents were confident that the crab boat was tucked into a safe anchorage somewhere along the Aleutians.

A weary Alice Choate takes time out from her chores at the Choate family's sheep and cattle spread on Unalaska Island, in 1964.

There was a burst of sunshine. It was bright, like a photographer's flashbulb.

"Better look quick or you'll miss it," Alice said.

Rufe and Wayne Mathews went ashore to search for pieces of wartime cable that could be used to bolster the *Robert Eugene*'s pieced-together mooring lines.

Smoky whined to follow. Alice boosted the dog over the rail and it ran through the snow and slush to catch up to the men. There was a sweet aroma in the galley as Alice baked a lemon pie for lunch.

Two hours later the men were on the way back. They were dragging several lengths of cable, plus two discarded truck tires that would be put to use as shock absorbers between the boat and the pier in the next storm.

"We saw where last night's wind ripped the roof off an old Navy power plant," Mathews reported. "Even some big 4-by-12 trusses were torn loose and carried a long way."

Rufe finished a big slice of pie and sighed.

"Well, we have chores to do," he said.

The ranch property was a skiff ride across the choppy bay to the shore of

Unalaska Island. A little bridge—called the Bridge to the Other Side—now connects Unalaska village with Dutch Harbor. But there was only perilous open water in 1964.

We rode the skiff to the Unalaska side, then boarded Rufus's battered pickup truck and drove through the Aleut village to the ranch. Lance and Jeff Craig, from Unalaska village, new friends of the Choates, already were there to care for the animals. They had been at the ranch the day before, through the storm, working by automobile headlights.

"That was awful nice of you," Rufe said. "We were kind of busy yesterday."

Young Jeff Craig grinned. "You got here just in time," he said, turning over the milking to Rufus's experienced hands. Lucky, the cow, seemed to agree, turning its big brown eyes toward Choate.

Daylight was fading in the misty, white valley as Rufe walked to the unfinished ranch house for a gas lantern. It was like a painting, a scene from America's past, as he knelt on the rough, wooden floor of the cabin in the white glow of the lantern.

Suddenly, the air outside was still. The storm had blown itself out. The valley was quiet and lonely as the rancher hiked back to the pickup. Fresh snow crunched underfoot.

It was dark when we set out again in the skiff, heading home to the *Robert Eugene*. Rufus swiveled a flashlight to pick out the course. And then the throttle lever on the outboard motor snapped. The control must have been damaged during the storm.

Somehow, Wayne Mathews was able to operate the throttle manually while following hand signals from Rufe as the skiff skipped across the water. The top rim of a silver moon showed above a cloud. The Big Dipper, with the North Star of Alaska's beloved flag, winked overhead like a beacon.

We turned around a buoy and homed on the welcome galley lights of the *Robert Eugene*.

After dinner, the family talked far into the night about their dreams for the struggling wilderness ranch.

"You're *some* people," Mathews said. "When I think of the work you have to do . . . "

"Sure, there's lots of hard work ahead," Choate interrupted. "But I'd be working as long as I live, anyhow."

Rufe reminisced about rugged days on the Montana range, when he was a

A grim-faced Rufus Choate surveys damage to the vessel Robert Eugene during a fierce storm.

cowboy and then a rodeo hand. Once he waited alone for a week—in zero-degree weather—with a herd of cattle in his care. He ran out of food and had to burn old railroad ties to stay warm.

"I've been in tough spots lots of times," he said. "But things are going to be OK here. The sheep are doing fine right now. They have heavy coats. They grow a very good fleece up here. It should sell at a premium. This is good country."

Rufe yawned and rubbed a hand through his shaggy, silver-streaked hair.

"Jim better get here pretty soon," he said. "He can give me a haircut."

✦ ✦ ✦

NEXT MORNING THERE was a thundering crash on the deck of the *Robert Eugene*. The starboard cargo boom—a steel pole weighing almost a ton—had snapped off its gear housing. Rust on the jagged break showed that the machinery had parted long ago and was being held in place only by the weight of the boom.

"Wow!" Mathews exclaimed. "If that thing had come down in the big wind the pilothouse would have been wiped out. Now it comes down for no reason."

Rufe shook his head in wonder. His shoulders seemed to sag.

The men fashioned a sort of cradle for the crippled boom, then set out for a full day of work on the ranch.

"It's a winter day, for sure," Rufe said.

On a rise above the future ranch house, Choate unlocked heavy metal doors to a wartime ammunition-storage depot, where the family's food and other supplies were cached. The dark, tube-shaped cavern was buried far into the hillside.

"This is the grocery store," he said, shouldering hundred-pound sacks of chicken feed as if they were picnic lunches.

Later, Choate shifted the pickup into four-wheel drive and drove along a rough, cliffhanging military road to check on his sheep. Snow swirled as the truck climbed through the clouds. Then drifts blocked the high-country road.

We walked the rest of the way, to a ledge overlooking Summer Bay, where the sheep were pasturing. Stretching out below was a vast panorama of snow-fields, deep, brown valleys, and silvery streams. Summer Bay, with bands of snow-free grass for the sheep, could be seen faintly through the gauze of falling snow.

"Those sheep better have golden fleece," Rufe said.

Then Rufe decided to drive over to neighboring Captain's Bay to see if the overdue crabber, the *Fern,* had returned with his son Jim.

The *Fern* was there, after riding out winds that the crew estimated at 135 miles an hour—and an engine breakdown. Rufe and Jim exchanged calm greetings, but relief showed in the father's glistening eyes.

Wayne Mathews rejoined his crew and went to work on the *Fern*'s damaged engine. Jim hurried back to the *Robert Eugene* to see his mother.

"Well," Alice Choate said without betraying her emotions, "you did get home." Then she inspected her son and his grease-smeared clothing. "You'd better get changed for supper," she said.

Later, as Jim devoured a wedge of leftover lemon pie, Alice outlined the work ahead: the broken cargo boom, repairs for the outboard motor, a new blower for the boat's tired, soot-spraying galley stove, and more.

"Don't worry, Mom," Jim said. "We'll get them fixed."

It was a happy family scene that night after several servings of beef stew and a chocolate cake for dessert. There was a radio warning of a new storm brewing in the Aleutians, but the galley was filled with contentment.

Young Ted, suffering with hemophilia, was recovering from a sprained ankle. The youngster laughed when his father tickled a bare foot. Smoky curled on the floor, next to Jim. Kushka, the cat, napped in Alice's lap.

"I'll never see the end of this place in my lifetime," Rufe said with a far-away look in his eyes. "Maybe Jim will. I don't know . . . "

Snow tumbled softly on deck. The Aleutian night wrapped around us like a black scarf. This was how it must have been when other pioneer families loaded their belongings in covered wagons and moved west, beyond the horizon.

Rufe began reciting poetry in his easy drawl, a verse from something he called "A Cowboy's Prayer."

> I thank you, Lord, that
> I am placed so well,
> That You have made
> My freedom so complete.

A few days later, Rufe drove me to the Dutch Harbor airport. It was time to return to Seattle and write about this remarkable family. I gripped Choate's calloused right hand and held it for a time.

"Someday, I expect to be back here and find these valleys of yours crammed with sheep—and they'll all have golden fleece," I told him.

Rufe smiled. "We've made a start," he said.

◆ ◆ ◆

IT WAS THE LAST TIME I saw Rufus Choate. Less than two years later, on May 16, 1966, he fell dead of a heart attack at age fifty-three. They said the brawny rancher worked too hard, had too many worries.

Several weeks after Choate's death, the *Times* asked me to return to Unalaska and see how his family was getting along. I found Alice Choate at the cabin that was only half-finished when I was bunking with the Choates in 1964 aboard the *Robert Eugene*. It was a shining day in the Aleutians, with fat clouds brushing the mountains. The valleys were green and bursting with life.

Alice Choate had a pot of coffee on the stove. There was a jar of wildflowers on an antique table that had been one of her mother's wedding presents.

Ted, now twelve, waved at me from a wheelchair. He twisted a knee a few days before and said he was getting around mostly on crutches. His disposition was as sunny as ever.

Ted's big brother, Jim, was working as a watchman at a crab cannery on Captain's Bay, a few miles away. He returned home on weekends to help his mother.

Sue, their daughter, had married Jack Graham, a veteran mariner who helped sail the Choates to Unalaska in 1964. Sue and her husband were over on neighboring Umnak Island, salvaging equipment from a grounded freighter.

The *Robert Eugene* was for sale.

Alice Choate poured me a cup of coffee, and said she had decided to stay in this lonesome valley.

"I thought about going back to Montana after Rufe died," she said. "But this is my home now."

It was clear that the ranch had fallen on hard times. Marauding packs of village dogs had wiped out most of the family's five hundred sheep.

"We've only been able to find twenty-eight of the sheep alive," Alice said. "The dogs got the rest of them. Rufe had already decided last winter to give up on sheep here, at least for now, and concentrate instead on beef cattle. It just wasn't practical to go on with the sheep.

"The cattle are doing fine," she added. "They're fat and slick.

"I sell a little milk in the village. The people are anxious to get it and it keeps me busy. And Ted brings in extra money by selling eggs from the chickens to customers in the village. His dad turned that responsibility over to Ted when we started the ranch."

Missing from the family was Smoky, the playful sheepdog.

"He got to running and just disappeared last winter," Alice said.

But Ted still had Kushka, his cat, and a new kitty and a parakeet for company.

Alice Choate was surrounded by memories—and reminders of her adventurous husband, a capable, cheerful man who felt hemmed in by civilization down in Montana. Rufe's heavy wool jacket still hung on a hook, as if waiting for his return. His rifles were loaded and ready on a wall rack. An old boiler cut open for use as a fireplace stood in the room where Rufe used to store his gasoline and heating oil.

"Rufe loved it here," Alice said.

"We had his funeral in the Unalaska school gym. An elder of the Russian Orthodox Church in the village gave part of the eulogy. One of the teachers, an ordained Methodist minister, took part, too. The church choir of Aleut people sang two songs in their own language. It was very nice. I think Rufe would have liked it."

They buried Rufus Choate in the village cemetery here, where wild geraniums fall in purple waves and the mountains huddle in a chilly embrace. His red-granite grave marker stands out in a cluster of Russian Orthodox crosses.

Rufus E. Choate
1912-1966

"I'm just glad that Rufe got up here and got started," Alice Choate said. "This is what he wanted.

"I'm going to stay and let things kind of simmer along. You can't hurry a ranch, anyhow."

✦ ✦ ✦

I saw the Choates again in 1969.

"This is still home," Alice said.

But the gentle woman with a voice as soft as a cello looked weary. Almost alone, she had turned the gloomy military building into a cozy home. She did most of the plumbing, wiring, and painting herself.

"There's nothing remarkable about me," she insisted. "There are all sorts of people doing things like this around the country. I just want to keep Rufe's dream alive."

✦ ✦ ✦

Many years later, in 2002, I returned to Unalaska again and asked about the Choate family.

"They're not here anymore," a friend said. "They all just sort of moved away."

CHAPTER 7

ONLY IN ALASKA

BRISTOL BAY—Just about every Alaskan has a bear story.

Mine is about two guys who almost shared a sauna with a grizzly.

We were on a fishing trip to Kulik Lodge, in southwestern Alaska's Bristol Bay area—Bob and Lori Giersdorf, dear friends of mine from Seattle; my wife, Mabs; and yours truly.

The fishing was excellent. We landed our limits of rainbow trout and lake trout during a busy first day of casting flies and lures. Catch-and-release was the lodge operator's policy; it's our practice, too.

"Let's go for a sauna," Bob suggested after dinner.

There was a small sauna building on the shore of Kulik Lake, about a hundred yards down a gravel path from the main lodge. It was built of spruce logs and looked as if it might have been assembled in a hurry by some amateur carpenters.

"Sauna? Good idea, Bob."

Our wives decided to stay behind.

"It's a lovely evening for reading a good book," Lori said.

"Ditto," Mabs agreed.

Bob and I walked to the sauna, shed our clothes, and settled back to tell fish stories. Like the time in Alaska's Glacier Bay National Park when Mabs caught a 163-pound halibut—and a few minutes later Lori pulled a halibut that weighed in at 168 pounds. I got skunked that day.

"You sure did," Bob said with a laugh.

A half-hour later, we were properly pink with perspiration.

"Let's go join the ladies," I suggested.

"Wait a minute," Bob said, standing and opening the sauna door a few inches. He had heard something outside.

"Oh, oh," he said, "I think we're going to be here for a while. Better have a look."

I cracked open the door—and was eye to eye with a half-ton brown bear that appeared to be at least eight feet tall. The bear was standing and tearing at the exterior logs.

"Now what?"

"I'm not sure," Bob said.

I thought of all the bear precautions I'd read during a lifetime of roaming Alaska.

"Do not feed bears," is one of the imperatives.

I had no intention of feeding this bear.

There's a brochure published by the Alaska Department of Fish and Game that says a traveler should learn to "understand bear talk."

"Bears communicate through body posture. . . . bears will often stand and swing their heads to and fro. When bears do this, they are trying to get a better idea of what you are."

What we are? Grizzly grub, that's what.

Another bulletin from the fish and game people:

"Bears are resentful of any intrusion while feeding, and it's dangerous to crowd them."

Who's crowding whom?

By now, the grizzly or brown bear (Ursus arctos, one and the same, according to bear biologists) was doing its best to wreck the sauna.

"What do we do now?"

"Yell!" Bob said. "Maybe the girls will hear us and get help."

We began shouting. "Help! Help! Bear! Bear! Help!"

Not long before, I had covered a story about a grizzly that killed a

Fall colors tint the tundra as a grizzly prowls Denali National Park.

photographer near Cold Bay, on the Alaska Peninsula. Conclusion: Maybe bears don't like photographers. And maybe this one saw me fishing with a camera around my neck.

I had been hoping all that day to snap photos of Bristol Bay's massive grizzlies. A few hours before dinner, we were searching for bears on a hillside above the lodge. We looked down and saw two bears sauntering across the lodge grounds. By the time we returned, the bears had departed.

More pounding and slashing sounds. The grizzly was determined to join us.

I was remembering a news story about the pilot of a military observation plane who skimmed a bit too low over rugged terrain near Yakutat and disturbed a bear that was fishing for salmon. The grizzly took a swipe at the plane and caused enough damage to cause an emergency landing.

And then there was the story about a government geologist who was seen clinging to the top of a very skinny spruce tree during a bear encounter in Alaska's Brooks Range. The bear waited patiently at the base of the tree until chased off by a helicopter.

Craig Medred, outdoor writer for the *Anchorage Daily News,* says many bear problems are largely the result of human behavior.

"Knotheads," is how Medred describes tourists who feed bears in the wild and do such silly things as pursuing bears with cameras.

"There's always some idiot who has to push the envelope," he says.

Craig, all we wanted was a sauna.

Many hikers carry bells and pepper spray in Alaska—bells, so as not to surprise bears on the trail; pepper spray for what could be the last line of defense. Outdoorsmen also are told they need to be able to identify bear scat when exploring the wilderness.

A prankster friend provided this information: "Grizzly bear scat has little bells in it and smells like pepper." Thanks a lot.

Bob and I yelled until we were hoarse. The bear continued clawing at the log wall. Sometimes it sounded as if two bears were pummeling the sauna. Then we heard the blare of a vehicle horn alongside the sauna. A voice called: "It's OK now—you can come out."

A lodge caretaker had discovered our predicament and chased off the bears—there *were* two of them—with a pickup truck. Bob and I sprinted to our cabins, running barefoot over the gravel path, with nothing for coverage except our towels.

Lori and Mabs laughed when they heard the story.

"We heard you shouting," Mabs said. "But we thought you were just having fun—or that maybe you had gone for a dip in the lake and were yelling because of the cold water.

"Maybe you should go back now and collect your clothing."

✦ ✦ ✦

ADMIRALTY ISLAND—We met a man who knew how to get along with grizzlies.

He was Stan Price, custodian of the Pack Creek bear sanctuary on the northeastern side of Admiralty Island, not far from Juneau. Price was able to move casually among grizzly gatherings, with only a hemlock stick for protection.

"Better than a gun," he said. "A little tap on a bear's nose will do it."

It was the summer of 1981 when we visited Pack Creek to meet the bear man of Admiralty Island and his wife, Esther. Stan jokingly described the shy woman as "my mail-order bride."

Price, then eighty-one, had been living with bears at Pack Creek since 1954. Esther arrived several months later, after considerable back-and-forth correspondence.

"Stan spent so much money on postage that I thought I might as well marry him and save the postage," Esther said.

Esther and Stan Price pose on the deck of their floating cabin in Pack Creek's bear country.

Their home was an old cabin on a raft of logs that rose and fell with the tides. They collected drinking water from a spring most of the year—and melted snow for water in winter. The couple had no human neighbors, except for an occasional visiting bureaucrat, and that suited them just fine. The bears were their family.

"There're wonderful animals," Stan said.

Price had a favorite, an orphan cub he named Susie. He found the youngster in a close-by meadow and decided to offer it protection from marauding male grizzlies. A few years later, Susie disappeared, then returned to show Price her new cub.

And then there was Belinda.

"She was a constant companion, just like a big, curly dog," Stan said. "You could sit down and talk to her. She seemed to understand."

Belinda vanished in 1974 after almost twenty years of feasting on Pack Creek's salmon runs. Price thought a hunter killed the bear.

"I have no use for firearms," he said.

Garlands of fog draped the ever-green forest around Pack Creek the day we dropped in to meet Stan and his bears. Four grizzly sows with cubs were foraging for pink salmon near the cabin. Bald eagles soared with the wind. It was an idyllic scene.

"You really missed something this morning," Esther said. "Stan was walking down the beach, being followed by a doe and two fawns—and a bear with her cub!"

Next morning, we watched from a safe distance as a mother grizzly and two cubs appeared. The sow stopped, rested on her side, and began nursing the cubs.

Stan Price, friend of grizzlies, in 1981

Stan Price watches a mother grizzly and twin cubs fish for salmon in Pack Creek on Admiralty Island.

"That's Brownie," Price said. "She's a regular."

A few minutes later, Brownie approached within forty or fifty feet of us, turned, and splashed upstream to capture a salmon.

The close-up scene was a rare treat—and certainly not recommended for most bear encounters. It was possible in this case only because of Stan Price's relationship with the bears, and maybe because Brownie was busy feasting on salmon.

"She doesn't need a fishing license," Price said with a laugh.

Stan Price died in December 1989. He was ninety. Esther died a few months later.

And then the bureaucrats moved in. Today the sanctuary—which was Price's private preserve—is known as the Stan Price Wildlife Refuge at Pack Creek. It is managed by the U.S. Forest Service and the Alaska Department of Fish and Game. Permits are required for visits.

An armed guard is on duty during the summer months to protect visitors. He doesn't carry a hemlock stick.

Stan Price's ashes are there, too.

✦ ✦ ✦

SITKA—APRIL FOOL!

On April 1, 1974, a band of mischief-makers from Sitka executed what their ringleader called the perfect prank.

They startled Sitka residents early that morning with what appeared to be an eruption of Mount Edgecumbe, a long-dormant volcano only thirteen miles across the sea from the Southeastern Alaska community.

Clouds of heavy, black smoke rose from the 3,270-foot volcano for twenty minutes. Police and firemen were flooded with panic calls. The Coast Guard commandant at Sitka dispatched a helicopter and a whaleboat crew to check out the situation.

How could this be? Mount Edgecumbe had been asleep for hundreds of years.

The Dirty Dozen cheered.

The Dirty Dozen—a merry gang of jokesters led by one Oliver (Porky) Bikar—had spent three years planning the cataclysm.

"It was wonderful!" Porky said.

Years later, Porky wrote an article for *Alaskan Southeaster* magazine, telling in detail how the stunt was accomplished. The plan, he recalled, was to transport a hoard of rubber tires to the crater of Mount Edgecumbe, set the tires afire, and simulate a "gigantic" eruption. Clear weather was required for the caper.

"I woke on a beautiful, clear April 1, 1974 morning to see Mount Edgecumbe showing off in all its glory," Bikar recalled. "I said to my wife, Patty, 'This is it. We have got to do it today.'"

Bikar and his cohorts needed a helicopter to dump the tires on Mount Edgecumbe. But they were unable to persuade local helicopter outfits to cooperate.

"No guts." Porky said.

And so they called on Earl Walker, a helicopter operator in Petersburg, eighty-five miles away. "Walker loved the idea," Porky said.

Bikar prepared two rope slings, each about 150 feet long, then rigged about sixty tires on one line and fifty or sixty on the other. Then he gathered oily rags, cans of Sterno, diesel oil, and military-type smoke bombs.

"I'm not telling where I got those," he said of the smoke bombs.

The Dirty Dozen hooked the tire-festooned slings to the hovering helicopter, "and off we went to the mountain."

Pilot Walker dropped the tires on target, then landed so that Bikar could get on with the mischief. Porky stamped out APRIL FOOL in the snow, in letters about fifty feet high, and added black spray paint for good measure. He made sure that the message could be seen only from the air.

"I set the whole mess ablaze and then we headed back to Sitka," Bikar told *Alaskan Southeaster.* "Smoke billowed from the crater with a clear blue sky as a backdrop.

"In the meantime, the radio and police station phones were ringing off the hook.

"I found out later that the 'eruption' made the Associated Press wire service world-wide."

Cost: $850 for the helicopter time.

"Well worth it," Porky said.

In 1980, when Washington state's Mount St. Helens erupted—really erupted—Porky received an envelope from a law firm in Denver. With some trepidation he opened the envelope and found a copy of the *Denver Post* with a photo of rampaging Mount St. Helens—and this note:

Sitka's dormant Mount Edgecumbe appears to be a smoking volcano, but it's just a prank. STANTON PATTY COLLECTION

"This time you little SOB you've gone too far."

Mabs and I were in Sitka in 1976 for the annual Alaska Day parade, and we were startled witnesses of another stunt involving Porky Bikar. Swarms of spectators were gathered along Lincoln Street in downtown Sitka for the parade. It was a grand event, with entries ranging from Eskimo dancers to marching bands.

Just as a Model-T car—decorated as a parade float and driven by a smiling Porky Bikar—was abeam the Elks Club, up from the Model-T popped a topless dancer. The crowd gasped. Mothers covered their children's eyes, but it was too late.

"Porky's done it again," someone said.

Bikar was arrested and charged with "aiding and abetting indecent exposure." The mostly undressed dancer pleaded guilty to a charge of indecent exposure and left town.

"But I'm not guilty!" Porky declared.

The Dirty Dozen had struck again. This time the joke was on Porky.

✦ ✦ ✦

KODIAK—The first time I met Smokey Stover in his hometown of Kodiak, he shook my hand and reached into his shirt pocket for a half-full glass of Scotch whiskey.

"Don't you get a lot of shirts wet that way?" I asked.

"Not at all," he said. "When I go shopping, all I have to remember is to pick items off the top shelves."

Paul H. (Smokey) Stover was one those wonderful characters who make Alaska so much fun.

As president of the Kodiak Disposal Company, Smokey was Kodiak's major junk dealer. His place of business covered eight acres of wrecked automobiles and assorted trash. Not exactly a highlight of Kodiak's scenic tours.

"You can see it's a dump," Smokey said with pride.

The social event of any week was the Friday lunch that Smokey hosted at the dump. The guest list usually included local politicians and curious tourists. The menu featured clam chowder, as only Smokey could prepare it.

The Dump Diner began when Smokey dug too many clams—about five hundred pounds of clams—at his gillnet-fishing site on nearby Raspberry Island.

"I wondered what to do with all those clams—and decided to invite a few friends to the dump for chowder.

"No charge. All I ask is that the guests bring some Scotch once in a while."

Smokey said he wanted to "bring a little class" to the Dump Diner by leading discussions of world events. "I'll be the moderator," he said.

The agenda at one meeting included these items:

"Topic: The United States should get the $7.2 million back from Russia that the U.S. paid for Alaska. It's quite obvious that Russia swindled our country into buying land that it didn't own."

"U.S.A. Events: Absolutely nothing new, different, unusual or even any political improvements."

"Menu: Scotch and water and clam chowder, as usual."

Smokey told his guests that he wouldn't be taking sides during an upcoming election to choose a new governor for Alaska.

"There's no sense in getting all excited," he said. "Four candidates are running and there's a darned good chance that one of them will be elected. The time you get worried is when nobody will take the job."

Smokey also announced that he had written the United States postmaster-general to apply for the job of postmaster in Kodiak. It was all in jest, but I'll bet the postmaster-general read the letter.

This is what Smokey wrote:

"I presently run the local junk yard, so naturally can put your junk mail in the right place.

"As (retired) general foreman of the Alaska Road Commission, I know how to get along with fellow government employees: Never criticize them for being late to work, how they dress, for taking sick leave during the busy season, or bringing spiked coffee in their lunch boxes.

"I will only require a small, unfurnished office with an outside exit. I seldom hang around my office all day when I can be building good relations at one of our local taverns.

"I am anxious to get back into a civil-service job. It seems that in my private business, I only pay taxes, licenses and good wages to support everyone but me."

Smokey didn't get the job.

"Sorry about that," I told him.

"Oh, well," he said, "I'm working on another project. It has to do with my gillnet site over at Onion Bay. Population: eight—my family. I'm the mayor and city manager there. That cuts down on expenses.

"We're organizing the Onion Bay Golf and Country Club. There will be a one-hole golf course. You really don't need eighteeen holes. You can always go back eighteen times and keep shooting.

Smokey died in June 1994 in Kodiak at age seventy-two.

Paul (Smokey) Stover, an Alaskan since 1942, enjoyed playing the clown.

"But he also had a serious side," said a Kodiak friend. "He did a lot of good for this town with the Boy Scouts and other civic activities. He was one of a kind."

For sure.

I still have my membership card for the Onion Bay Golf and Country Club. The serial number is 000001.

"I'm honored," I told Smokey.

Later, on checking, I found that every member had the same number.

All of his friends were Number One with Smokey.

✦ ✦ ✦

KETCHIKAN—June Allen, one of my favorite Alaska writers, tells a story about Dammit the donkey, a work animal that spent its retirement years in Ketchikan.

Dammit actually was a burro, but June said Ketchikan folks never quibbled about technicalities.

The saga of Dammit was related to June by the late Bob Ellis, one of Alaska's legendary bush pilots, and Norma Anderson, former postmaster in the town of Craig, on Prince of Wales Island.

It happened some time in the 1940s. Ellis received an order to fly a donkey over to Craig. The critter was due to arrive from Seattle aboard an Alaska Steamship Company vessel.

"Well, when the donkey arrived, 600 pounds of him, including crate, Bob realized his original plan to transport the animal wasn't going to fly," June wrote.

The donkey (burro, that is) would have to go by a mailboat, which made a weekly run from Ketchikan to Craig. Unfortunately, the weather during the week the donkey arrived was especially bad and the mailboat trip had to be canceled.

"That left Bob to care for the donkey," June reported. "He took Dammit home with him and housed him in the basement."

The Ellises decided to throw a party. Bob bet his guests that he could produce a donkey. They scoffed. Then Dammit was led upstairs from the basement. Ellis joyfully collected on the wagers. But then Dammit refused to descend the steps.

"He wasn't willing to learn a new skill," June said.

Finally, the mailboat delivered Dammit to Craig, where the animal would have a career as a freight hauler for an enterprising old-timer by the name of Bailey Sanderfer.

"The whole town was excited, and when the whistle announced the arrival of the mailboat that carried Dammit . . . it turned into a sort of holiday," June said. "Old Bailey Sanderfer had a cart ready for his new dray animal and the town, which Bob [Ellis] said probably had never even seen a horse, much less a donkey [or a burro], was ready to celebrate."

Norma Anderson, the postmaster, said Craig didn't need much of an excuse to celebrate.

"I remember once that someone said it was his brother's birthday, so we threw a big party," Norma recalled. "The brother was in California, so he didn't know about it, but it didn't matter."

One day Dammit's owner staged a rodeo, with Dammit as the featured act.

"Apparently Dammit performed well because they took him to a bar and bought him a beer," June said.

Dammit dutifully put in his time on the job. But when trucks came to Craig his services no longer were needed. The *Ketchikan Daily News* announced that Dammit had returned to Ketchikan aboard the mailboat *Dart* to join the Lawrence (Kit) Carson family.

Dammit, June said, stayed out of trouble most of the time he was with the Carsons. But his braying at what June called "ungodly hours" may have caused a scuffle that made the police blotter.

The *Daily News* of May 5, 1951, reported that Carson had filed a complaint against one Wesley Miller, who was alleged to have fired a shotgun at Dammit.

"Carson says he then threw Miller into the bay and ended the argument," said the *Daily News*. "According to reports, the donkey was not seriously injured."

Later, Dammit was moved to a grassy area at Wolf Point.

"The men built a corral for him and housed him in a tool shed," June said. "Passing fishermen would call out to the donkey and Dammit would bray his return greetings."

Came a day when Dammit was feeling poorly.

"The town responded by collecting food to tempt the animal," June Allen wrote. "During a longshoremen's strike, when only beer and tombstones could be unloaded, Mrs. H. P. Hansen bought the last bale of hay from a local dairy for Dammit. A bakery gave all its old bread to him. The cut grass from the Federal Building and other lawns was donated for the ailing burro.

"When he came down with pneumonia they sat up with Dammit all night and doctored him with whiskey. But they were unable to save him.

"Dammit the Donkey was buried near Last Chance campground on the old Ward Lake Road. And thus ended an entertaining chapter in the story of Ketchikan."

Only in Alaska . . .

CHAPTER 8

ON THE ICE

POINT HOPE—There is a whaling village on the far-northwest coast of Alaska that scientists say may be the oldest continuously inhabited community in the western hemisphere. Ancient Eskimos, who had no written language, called it by a name that sounds like Tikiraq.

Tikiraq—meaning "index finger" in Eskimo—describes how the wind-whipped village site pokes like a bony finger into the Chukchi Sea, 130 miles north of the Arctic Circle.

Modern man, for reasons unknown, named the village Point Hope.

"We don't know for sure how old Point Hope is, but certainly much more than 2,500 years," said the late Howard Rock, founder of *Tundra Times*, the statewide newspaper for Alaska's native peoples. Point Hope was the Eskimo editor's birthplace. And now he rests forever in the frozen earth here.

I first visited Point Hope in 1964, about the time that change was beginning to catch up with the village of 350 or so Eskimos. There still were cozy, half-underground houses roofed with sod sliced from the tundra. Food was stored in ice caches dug into the permafrost that begins just inches below the tundra. There was no running water in the village. No telephones, only short-wave radio. The arrival of a mail plane was a civic occasion.

Point Hope Eskimos prepare their whaling camp on Chukchi Sea ice, in May 1965.

There was contentment then in old Point Hope. There also were vivid contrasts.

Eskimo drummers were entertaining one night in the village recreation hall. Their faces could have been carvings of dark ivory. Their circular drums, thumped from underneath with single sticks, were covered with the taut skins of whale livers. The drumbeat pulsed and pounded. The drummers began chanting in unison. Their wives, garbed in fur mukluks and parkas, caught the tempo and began dancing, swaying and shuffling, in a ballet as old as time. One of the dancers had a baby stuffed far down in the back of her parka. Better than a backpack.

Jimmy Killigvuk, age seventy-three, a village elder, stepped out front to lead a hunting song. His eyes burned with bright fire.

"Before I go hunting," said the old man, "I sing a hunting song for a whale. Then I meet the whale. It is quiet. I kill him. After the kill, my wife comes out on the ice and boils the meat in fresh water. . . . "

The drums thundered.

Boom! Boom! Boom! Boom!

And then it was over.

"Now for some American dancing," announced the Reverend Keith Lawton, the village's Episcopal missionary, as the sweating drummers packed their instruments. Vinyl recordings dropped onto a phonograph turntable. First, "Stupid Cupid," a noisy rock-and-roll tune. Then Elvis Presley's "Hound Dog." Eskimo youngsters began gyrating with movements that looked a lot those of my dancing teenagers back home.

"Sure, we know the Twist," said one of the young dancers. "Some of the older kids brought it back when they left Point Hope to go to school."

For sure, things were changing in this village that was old before Christ was born.

"Come again," Keith Lawton said when it was time for me to depart.

"I will. And when I do, I hope to go whale hunting with one of the Eskimo whaling crews."

"It may be possible. We'll see," the missionary said.

✦ ✦ ✦

IT WAS MAY 1965 when I returned to Point Hope. The little ski plane from Kotzebue bounced to a landing in deep snow. Summer still was a long way off here. Eskimo families clustered around the plane, eager for mail and a look at visitors.

The Reverend Keith Lawton stepped out of the crowd and shook my hand.

"Welcome back," he said with a big smile.

Lawton was a figure from central casting in his heavy fur parka. Handsome and athletic, the thirty-four-year-old missionary was both friend and shepherd to his Eskimo flock. He lived in their world. He hauled ice for drinking water by dog team from a frozen freshwater lagoon eight miles away. He traveled alone with his Siberian huskies to take the word of God to other tiny villages along the arctic coast. When store-bought food was in short supply, Lawton and his red-haired wife, Jackie, set the table with caribou and whale meat.

They loved this village and its gentle people.

"I think this is the most wonderful experience of our lives," said Jackie Lawton.

I was here in hopes of joining a hunt for the bowhead whale—*agvik,* in the Inupiat Eskimo language. But first, permission had to be arranged. Lawton had offered by mail to open negotiations with one of the Eskimo whaling captains.

Amos Lane, a Point Hope whaling captain, tests his harpoon-like darting gun during a hunt for bowhead whales.

"It will be a ticklish matter," he cautioned as we plodded through the snow to the St. Thomas Mission home. "They won't want you to be in their way—to hurt their chances of landing a whale.

"Whaling is serious business with these people. Not only for food, but because it is an important part of their heritage. Anyhow, we'll give it a try."

A cold wind stung our faces. The temperature was about zero. The little village was half-buried under springtime snowdrifts. I stamped the snow off my boots and went into the mission house to visit with Jackie Lawton and their children—seven-year-old Ian Scott, five-year-old John Mark, and Adrian, who was just a year and a half old.

Lawton went to present my request to Amos Lane, a top whaling captain.

Later, Jackie and I walked across the village to the native store. Tail-wagging puppies from the Lawtons' pack followed. Jackie shooed them back. Along the way, children waved and shouted her name.

"After you have been here awhile, they will call you by name, too," she said.

John Oktollik, a whaling captain and village elder, ran the store. A few days before, Oktollik's crew had harpooned the first bowhead of the season, a thirty-foot giant. Figure about a ton of meat to the foot for a bowhead.

ON THE ICE

There was fresh muktuk—strips of whale skin and blubber—for sale at the store, part of Oktollik's harvest. The oily muktuk, best when eaten raw, is like candy to the Eskimos. Maybe it's an acquired taste, but muktuk is one of my favorites, too.

Jackie chatted with several parka-clad Eskimo women in the store and then began hiking home with her groceries. One of the reasons the Point Hope community has been here for thousands of years, she explained, is that the village is in the path of the annual northward migration of the bowheads. Whale meat still was a village staple. These proud, self-reliant Eskimo families were not feasting with the help of food stamps.

Keith Lawton was waiting for us.

"I think you will be able to make arrangements all right with Amos Lane to go on the hunt," he said. "You are in real luck. It is a fine crew with strong paddlers. Last year Amos's crew got the first whale."

I went to meet the thirty-nine-year-old whaling captain.

Amos Lane was cordial, but reserved, as he explained what would be expected of me at his hunting camp out on the Chukchi Sea ice. We shook hands on it. Then his eyes smiled for the first time.

"We leave tonight—take plenty of warm clothes," he said.

✦ ✦ ✦

THE DOGSLED HURTLED across the white desert of the frozen sea. Suddenly, the sled careened wildly—bouncing, rocking, and slamming against hummocks of ice. Then it overturned, and I was sent rolling like a snowball.

Bruised and breathless, I struggled to stand. I was about to ask Amos Lane why he was driving so darned fast. And then I saw a smile on his leathery face.

"You flipped the sled on purpose, didn't you" I asked.

At first he didn't answer. The smile grew wider.

"Yep," he said.

"Why?"

"We wanted to see if you could handle the spill without losing your temper. We have to know if we can put up with you for a week out at the hunting camp."

"Fair enough."

We could see other whaling crews moving westerly on twisting paths through jumbles of ice boulders. The mushers fought to find passages through the maddening maze. Arctic travelers call such ice formations pressure ridges. They are scattered chunks of ice, some as big as houses, pushed onto the shore ice by storm winds and powerful currents.

Frosty dogs were tugging sleds carrying the Eskimo skin boats called umiaks. The twenty-four-foot-long whaling boats are covered with the skins of ugruk, the bearded seal, stretched over driftwood frames. All of the crews were searching for leads (rhymes with "beads"), streaks of open water in the sea ice. When bowhead whales are on the move they surface for air in a lead, perhaps long enough for a harpoon strike.

Keith Lawton, the Point Hope missionary, was leading the way with his own team of fleet sled dogs. He wore a .44-caliber revolver and a hunting knife on his belt.

It was the season of long daylight in the Arctic. The sun still was in the sky at 9 P.M., flashing stripes of fiery red across the ice. In the shadows, the snow and ice were tinted a soft blue.

Lawton stopped his team.

"We'll have to walk the rest of the way," he shouted. "The ice is too thin, too dangerous, from here on."

We trudged through the deep snow in silence. The dogs followed. Then, as we rounded a pinnacle of ice, we sighted a lead where Amos's crew had made camp. We had traveled more than two miles from the village.

The tired dogs burrowed into the snow. The whalers used their hunting knives to shape a wall of ice blocks for a windbreak. Then a canvas shelter for the cook tent was anchored to suitcase-size ice blocks.

There was no time to waste. Amos and his men climbed into the umiak and took their assigned places. The missionary joined them. They were gripping paddles, waiting for their captain's signal to push off into the lead at the first sign of a whale.

There wasn't a sound. Quiet is important in the hunt.

Now the sun was only a smudge of rouge on the western horizon, over toward Siberia.

There was a blast of air near us! A shiny bowhead was on the surface. Swiftly, our umiak was off in pursuit. The whale sounded, dived, as if sensing danger.

The chase went on for more than an hour. The crew paddled three miles up the lead before stopping to rest. There was no way to tell where the leviathan would surface next. Our umiak never was close enough for the harpooner in the bow to attempt a strike.

You have to be almost atop a bowhead to make the kill. Some bold crews steer their skin boats right onto thrashing whales.

"All we got this time was exercise," Keith Lawton said as we returned to camp. "But there will be another chance."

Younger members of the crew were waiting with hot tea and crackers for the hunters. Nineteen-year-old Daisy Tuzroyluk, the camp cook, melted snow for water and fed chunks of whale blubber into a crude stove for fuel. The strong-smelling whale oil sizzled. The stove, I saw, has been fashioned from a discarded oil drum.

Then Daisy cooked strips of polar bear meat. It tastes good only when you are very hungry.

"Eskimos are real meat-eaters," Amos said with a grin as he bit into his portion.

I had taken along a case of Army C-rations—just in case. I never opened it. Maybe I was ashamed to eat "white man's food" in the presence of the fearless Eskimos. Besides, I found myself liking most of the camp fare.

It was one o'clock in the morning. A gunshot broke the stillness. Amos's brother, Jacob, had killed a fifteen-hundred-pound beluga whale with a single bullet at one hundred yards. Good shooting.

Our umiak moved into the lead again to retrieve the white whale and tow it to camp. The hunters dragged the carcass out of the sea with ropes stretched across their backs and shoulders, then cut into the steaming meat with long-handled knives and lances. Soon the snow was drenched with blood in the arctic twilight.

Afterward, some of the whalers kept watch for bowheads. Others slept on caribou skins in the open. An hour later there was another shot. A beluga had been hit, but sank instantly. Nothing was said.

Another shot. This time Amos was the marksman. A second beluga was hauled to camp for butchering.

Amos decided to send a sled into the village for supplies. Eager huskies lunged and howled with anticipation as they waited to be hitched. It was four o'clock in the morning. The bright sun burned blinding reflections into the snow.

By now, the lead had widened—from a crack in the sea ice to a channel four hundred yards across—with the help of a friendly breeze and a swift current. Conditions were ideal for whaling. Lookouts on ice towers atop the pressure ridges scanned the lead. The temperature was about 5 below.

In the cook tent, Daisy was napping on a dogsled that had been moved inside for a bed.

I crawled into my sleeping bag and dozed off with the soft voices of the Eskimo hunters talking their mysterious language in the background.

✦ ✦ ✦

I WOKE TO A SUDDEN weather change. A fierce wind was howling out of the northeast. Wind blasts shook the cook tent. The ocean current was running like a river. Our lead, now just a streak of open water, was threatening to close.

The Eskimo hunters were hunched under a sheet of canvas.

"Water is too rough right now—too risky for my men," Amos said. The whaling captain had not slept all night.

There was an explosion just north of our camp.

"Sounds like a darting gun [harpoon]," Amos said. "Somebody has hit a whale. I hope they can get it in."

The darting gun, the Eskimos' hard-thrown hunting weapon, is a nineteenth-century device. Attached to a wooden shaft is a brass tube fitted with a bullet-shaped projectile called a bomb. Ahead of the tube is a barbed harpoon tip. First the harpoon is driven into the bowhead. Then a trigger trips and shoots the projectile deep into the whale, where it explodes. It takes a strong man to hurl the thirty-pound spear.

Through binoculars we could see a poke—an inflated seal skin—bobbing in the water about a mile away. The float marked the harpoon strike.

Whaling camps like ours were strung out for several miles along the lead. Amos wanted to help the other crew land the bowhead, but realized it was impossible to paddle against the surging current.

"Can't do it," he said. "We wait here."

All boats participating in a kill receive shares of muktuk and meat according to a formula worked out generations ago.

The blizzard was worsening. Exposed flesh numbed within minutes. Amos was wondering whether to break camp and return to the village, four

A lone Eskimo whale hunter stands atop an ice pinnacle to search for signs of whales.

miles across the treacherous ice. There also was a danger that the ice could part between our camp and Point Hope, stranding us on our ice raft.

"We go," Amos decided.

The men collapsed the trembling tent and stowed their gear in the umiak for the return trip. Three dog teams were ready for the journey home. Amos, with his crack team of fourteen huskies, would pull the heavy umiak. Henry Nashookpuk, with a lighter load, would go ahead with his team to break trail. I went with Henry.

The dogs turned into the blinding snow, picking a trail through jagged ice boulders of a pressure ridge. Somehow, the valiant huskies knew where to go

Paddlers of a Point Hope whaling crew maneuver their fragile umiak through the ice-choked Chukchi Sea.

in the white wilderness. Snow pellets were like needles against our faces. Now frostbite was a hazard.

Behind us, Amos and several of his men were on foot, pushing the umiak through deep snow to help the dogs. The boat looked as if it were heaving through ocean surf.

Henry's sled bumped and twisted, sometimes hardly moving. Almost two hours passed before we reached shore. We waited for Amos and the crew's third sled. Finally, we saw both teams through the snow curtain, curving toward us like moving pencil lines drawn against the whiteness.

Another sled approached—laden with pieces of whale flukes from a bowhead. It was Patrick Attungana, Amos's uncle. His crew had landed a forty-five-foot whale with the aid of four other teams. That was the scuffle we had seen north of us during the morning. The flukes, Patrick said, would be saved for the Nalukataq, Point Hope's annual whaling feast.

Patrick hurried to the village with the good news. When his sled reached Point Hope, the Episcopal Church bell would ring and happy Eskimos would dance to the captain's house for a traditional salute.

Amos was alongside our sled. His exhausted dogs flopped in the snow. Their coats were plated with ice and frost.

"They are plenty tired," he said. "They need a break."

We rested for a few minutes, then Amos shouted, "Let's go home!"

In the village, Amos swept snow off his boots and hurried into his house.

"This is about the hardest crossing I ever made," he told his wife, Eunice.

Disappointment showed in the whaling captain's tired eyes, but he did not regret the decision to leave the ice.

"My men are the important thing," he said. "They have families. It was just too risky out there.

"Now it is time to sleep. We will go out again to hunt the whales."

Amos went into the bedroom for a nap. I walked back to the mission house.

Perhaps, I thought to myself, the villagers will be dancing to Amos Lane's home one of these days.

✦ ✦ ✦

AMOS LANE WAS STANDING atop a tower of sea ice, silhouetted against the perfect blue sky, watching for whales. The storm had passed. We were back on the Chukchi Sea ice for another try at harpooning the mammoth bowhead whale.

Amos wore an urgent look. Soon the whaling season would end.

There was a new open-water lead near our camp. Sluggish chips of ice drifted past with a rustling sound. The hunters hacked a trench-like launching ramp at the edge of the ice for the umiak. The boat looked ready to leap to battle.

"We wait," Amos said.

Daisy, the cook, sliced muktuk from a slab of whale meat. Her hands glistened with oil. She placed the muktuk in a pan to boil for lunch.

"Maybe you won't like it," she said.

I cut into the blubber with a hunting knife. It had a warm, nutty flavor.

"Good," I said.

"You are becoming an Eskimo," joked Wilfred Lane, Amos's brother.

"I consider that a compliment."

Wilfred smiled and smeared his chunk of muktuk with mustard.

"I'll take mine plain."

"Mustard is good," he said.

Amos left the umiak for a few minutes and reached for a piece of muktuk.

"I can't get enough," he said.

Then the captain armed a harpoon gun and placed it across the bow of the umiak. He knelt in the snow to inflate a poke, a sealskin sewn into a ball-shaped float that would trail the harpoon as a marker.

"We should have sonar to help find a whale," he said with a laugh.

When all was ready, Amos scaled the ice spire again for lookout duty. His binoculars swept over the silent icescape. Hours passed. Amos remained at his lofty post.

Blue shadows of the spring evening were lengthening when Amos joined his crew.

"I heard a whale out there spouting," he whispered.

Amos prepared a second harpoon and coiled the lines meticulously in the umiak. He spent several minutes testing his timing in lifting and aiming the heavy weapon. It was ten o'clock. The sun was a red fireball, falling over the horizon. The hunters stayed with the umiak.

The long, cold night was upon us . . .

Dawn flooded the camp with light. Breakfast was ready—corn meal, fried whale meat, and muktuk.

Amos was restless.

The lead was narrowing. We used the umiak as a bulldozer to shove some of the floating ice away from the launching area so we would be able to move in a hurry if a whale were sighted.

A flock of eider ducks skimmed low over the water. Amos reached for his shotgun and dropped three of the ducks. We went out with the umiak to retrieve them.

"Oh, boy, duck soup, coming up," Daisy said, combining hunks of duck meat with rice, salt, and water for the soup.

Amos climbed again to the top of the ice column and searched down the lead.

"Come on, whales, do something," he muttered.

✦ ✦ ✦

DAYS WERE BLENDING, one into another, with only flaming sunsets to mark the dividing lines, as we waited on the ice. The cold was punishing. The diet was monotonous, and we were running low on food.

But there was powerful beauty in the arctic tableau around us. Cliffs of pressure-ridge ice were mirrored in the sea like marble statues. The luminous blue shadows of the arctic twilight provided a kind of stage lighting. Flights of murre birds rustled overhead with a sound like wind in trees.

Amos Lane, our whaling captain, was exhausted. He had slept only a few hours in the past three days—always on the alert for the first signs of a whale.

Harold Koonuk, a Point Hope teenager, warmed himself over the whale-oil stove and talked of his life as an Eskimo.

"I must finish school," he said. "But I don't think I will ever leave Point Hope. My mother and my father are getting old. They work too hard. They need me. I will never forget them."

We jumped at the sound of rifle cracks. It was three o'clock in the morning.

"Beluga!" Harold yelled as he sprinted toward the umiak. Amos and Kirk Oviuk, another crew member, had bagged a beluga. They struggled to haul the white whale onto the ice for butchering.

But there was no time to finish the job. A bowhead whale had been sighted down the lead.

We paddled, almost noiselessly, into open water, waiting for the whale to appear again. Boats from two neighboring camps converged in the misty lead. The chase was on!

The trio of umiaks glided north for more than a mile. Harpooners were ready to strike. But the bowhead did not surface again. We returned to camp.

"There will be more whales," Amos said.

The wind from the north was like an icy lash. Parka hoods were framed with frost. We waited. Daisy, the cook, served raw muktuk, crackers, and tea at the side of the umiak.

About noon another bowhead was spotted far to the south. The camp was hushed and tense. Jacob Lane, Amos's brother, climbed to the summit of a pressure-ridge boulder and waved a paddle toward a nearby whaling crew. It was a signal for quiet.

We could see two bowheads rolling in the distance. They were glossy and black, like twin submarines. We waited for them to come within harpooning distance. But they passed us under water.

Some of the hunters tried to nap, stretched out on caribou skins beside the boat. Henry Nashookpuk, exhausted, fell asleep in a sitting position. The lead was threatening to close again as the wind nudged big slabs of ice toward our camp.

Suddenly, there was a loud hiss not more than twenty feet away. We could see a small bowhead, just under the ice. Only its head was poking out for air. But Amos and his men were unable to break the ice that was choking the lead. They pounded futilely with their paddles.

Ice was forming all around, except for a puddle directly in front of the umiak. Icicles dangled like pendants from the boat.

"Wouldn't you know?" Amos asked. "When the whales are running, the ice moves in. Well, you can't win 'em all."

We could see Daisy walking from the cook tent with a pan of duck soup.

"Boy, that smells good," Amos said.

The hunters dipped into the soup like starving men. Spoons froze to the metal dishes in seconds.

"Kind of a cool picnic," Amos quipped.

It was almost midnight. The sky was a two-tone dome—pink where the midnight sun had dipped below the horizon; china blue to the east.

The hunters slept. All but Amos.

"I'm not giving up yet," he said.

The wind was bitter cold. The cook tent rocked with wind gusts. Again, Amos was a lone figure atop his icy lookout tower. Like a statue on an alabaster pedestal.

2:15 A.M. The sun was like a burning red ball as it burst out of its hiding place beyond the ice ridges.

"Boy, it must be 10 below out there," said Wilfred Lane, one of the whaling captain's brothers, as he ducked into the cook tent to get warm. "Amos, he's still up. Has been all night."

I could see Amos pivoting on his ice spire, searching for bowheads. The dog teams were huddled in the snow, their bushy tails tucked in for added warmth.

"Another helluva night," Amos said as he entered the tent. "Cold and nothing doing."

Henry Nashookpuk inspected the pan of leftover duck soup from last night's meal.

"Think I'll have some morning soup," he said. But the fire in the cook-stove was barely alive.

Henry punched holes in an empty milk can and pushed the can inside the stove for a makeshift grate. Oil from a piece of pinkish blubber atop the stove dripped through the milk-can perforations and burned brightly. Soon the stove top was glowing cherry red, and Henry was able to savor his soup.

Finally, Amos was asleep, but only a few feet away from the umiak.

And then we heard a bowhead cruising by the camp. We could hear it blowing. The sound was like the puff of a steam locomotive. *Whoosh.*

The Eskimos climbed into the umiak and lifted their paddles. Jacob Lane was in the bow with the harpoon. The whale's heavy breathing stopped. My heart pounded.

The bowhead surfaced several hundred yards to the north. But, again, the ice blocked us from moving. Umiaks from two other camps sped toward the whale.

Andrew Franklin's crew reached the whale first, drove the umiak onto the bowhead's back, and thrust a harpoon. The shaft quivered. The harpoon's "bomb" exploded inside the whale with a deep roar. Then a second harpoon found the mark. But its bomb misfired.

The bowhead tossed wildly. The Franklin umiak rocked on the waves and almost overturned in the icy water. Then the wounded animal sounded, vanishing under the ice with the hunters' gear.

"They lost it," Amos said.

Franklin's men searched a long time, hoping that their sealskin marker would bob to the surface. No luck. We watched as the weary crew paddled back to camp.

I asked Amos what Point Hope families would do for meat if they failed to harvest enough whales for the season.

"We will survive," he answered simply,

It was time for me to leave. There was a lump in my throat as I shook hands with my new friends after a memorable week on the ice.

Dazzling blue shadows were painting the snow and ice as I turned for a last look at the daring men who hunt whales by the light of the midnight sun.

Amos still was searching the horizons, a brave, determined figure against the cold sky. His men were ready in the umiak, like an arrow in a taut bow.

The dog team raced across the ice toward Point Hope. We turned a corner in a pressure-ridge canyon, and I could see the hunters no longer.

CHAPTER 9

LOVE LYRICS

TOK—A national TV crew was roaming the Alaska Highway in search of stories about the North Country.

"Tell me," said the New York producer, unfurling a hanky to wipe Alaska dust from her cherry-red high-heel shoes, "do you know of any interesting people around here?"

I was on hand for a few days as an unpaid consultant for the television team. My old friend Charles Kuralt had asked for help in mining human-interest features for his acclaimed CBS *Sunday Morning* show.

Stifling a giggle and wondering why anyone would wear fancy dress shoes for bush travel, I decided to introduce the producer to one of my favorite Alaskans.

"Maybe you would like to meet Donna Blasor-Bernhardt," I suggested. "She's called the poet laureate of the Alaska Highway."

The producer folded the handkerchief and stuffed it into a purse.

"Is it always dusty around here?" she asked.

"Sometimes it rains and then it's muddy."

"Well, where does this Donna live?"

"Close by, up the road, in Tok."

"Tok?"

"It's a little crossroads community, about two hundred miles southeast of Fairbanks. Milepost 1314 of the Alaska Highway. Population: 1,214. It's a junction point, where the Alaska Highway intersects a slice of road called the Tok Cutoff, which connects with the Glenn Highway into Anchorage. Altogether, it's a drive of about 325 miles from Tok to Anchorage. . . . "

The producer sighed. It was plain that she didn't want a geography lesson.

"Tok—that's a funny name," she said. "Indian? Eskimo?"

"Neither. I'll let Donna tell you how Tok got its name."

Donna Blasor-Bernhardt is a frontier woman who writes lyrics of love about Alaska. She lives alone in a cozy log cabin decked with blazes of summertime geraniums.

Of her life, she writes:

You don't need to buy me diamonds
And I don't need designer jeans,
Three hundred dollar an ounce perfume
Or riding in stretched limousines.

'Cause I've got diamonds in the stars at night
And Mister Levi made my jeans,
Wood smoke and spruce pitch are my perfumes
Howling huskies . . . my limousines."

Donna is a widow. Her husband, Dick, died in 1987. Donna found herself adrift with two small children, crushing debts, and no insurance. She turned to writing, mostly poetry, to make a living.

"Writing was the only thing I knew how to do," she recalls. "I never stopped to think how preposterous it might be to try to sell poetry."

Visitors marvel at Donna's courage, her determination to stick with a land that can be as cruel as it is beautiful.

"Courageous? No. I don't think so," she says, blushing. "I just believe that

Donna Blasor-Bernhardt composes a poem by her log cabin in Tok.

destiny has to do with where you are supposed to be. A real contentment comes with that. I wouldn't change a thing."

We drove into Tok and followed a gravel driveway to Donna's front yard.

The TV producer stepped out of the van and looked around, as if planning where the cameraman should plant his tripod.

"So this is Donna," she said, approaching my friend with the cranberry-red hair and a smile that could melt glaciers. They shook hands.

I winked at Donna. She caught the signal.

"Talk to her," the producer instructed me. "Talk to each other," she added, prodding us toward Donna's ready-for-winter woodpile. Maybe the producer saw the neatly stacked firewood as a rustic background.

Donna and I already were talking—about travels along the Alaska Highway, our pioneering parents, Donna's writings, our love for Alaska.

We hardly were aware of the camera. Our conversation went on after the TV crew had packed its gear.

"Cocktail hour!" announced the producer. "Is there a decent restaurant around here?"

"Try Fast Eddy's in downtown Tok?" I said.

Donna smiled.

"They'll never understand why we feel as we do about Alaska," she said, reaching out for a hug that never made the film.

It was a wrap. The TV team had its story. And so do I.

It goes like this . . .

✦ ✦ ✦

THE YEAR WAS 1977. Dick and Donna Bernhardt and their children, ten-year-old Ricky and eight-year-old Katherine, were snuggled in a 16-by-32-foot Army surplus tent on the edge of Tok. The outdoor temperature was 69 degrees below zero.

"We figured on the tent being our temporary home until we finished building a log cabin," Donna recalls. "But there was an early snow, followed by an early, bitter-cold winter that halted our cabin building. We ended up living in the tent for thirteen months."

There was only a woodstove for heat. And some days the greedy stove consumed almost a cord of wood.

"Dick and I took turns, in shifts, staying up to stoke the stove," Donna says.

Donna was on fire watch one frigid night. She pushed a log into the stove, and smiled as she watched her husband and children sleeping like bear cubs in a wintertime cave.

"I'm blessed," she whispered.

Then she stepped outdoors to check the thermometer.

"There was a full moon," Donna remembers. "The moonlight had turned the snow to diamonds. Stars flickered like swarms of fireflies. And the northern lights were in full motion, dancing to the music of a heavenly symphony.

"Even our tent was beautiful in the moonlight. It was covered in frost, like a house of jewels. Somewhere in the distance a wolf howled a song. I could feel the night enfolding me, wrapping its arms around me.

"I was standing there, having this love affair with Alaska.

"I thought of how our life had changed and all that we had left behind—the dishwasher, the washing machine, the clothes dryer, television, furnace. But it was here that we had found life, real life."

Donna remembers how the northern lights, beaming over the Alaska Highway, first welcomed her to Alaska.

That was in 1950, when her parents, Don and Bessie Blasor, were driving north from their home in Pittsburg, Kansas, in an old Dodge pickup that her dad had bought from a Kansas farmer.

Don Blasor, a barnstorming stunt pilot in early-day air shows, then a flight instructor during World War II, was unemployed. He hoped for a better life for his family in Alaska.

"That pickup that my father found in the middle of a cornfield had bald tires, a hole in the floor, and the heater didn't work," Donna says. "Daddy was driving. I sat next to him with my feet on top of our dog, Zipper, and my mom sat next to the other door. Most of the time my little sister sat on Mom's lap. We were all wrapped in blankets.

"Somehow, we made it to Alaska just eighteen days later. And that was counting a slight delay when a man robbed a bank in Edmonton [Alberta] and my dad inadvertently stopped the bank robber when the robber ran a red light and hit our truck. The Mounties arrested the robber and helped Daddy get the truck fixed—and we were on our way north again.

"I'll never forget when we were on the Alaska Highway and saw snow, tall mountains, and the northern lights for the first time. I was only six years old, but I was full of joy. I knew then that this would be my home forever. I still feel that way."

The Blasors settled in Anchorage, with a house trailer and an attached lean-to for a home. Don Blasor found a job as an aircraft mechanic.

"Our first years were very hard," Donna says. "I remember my mom doing a lot of crying. But she wanted us to be together, so this was it. Later my parents were able to build a comfortable home that evolved into a neighborhood.

"We pulled a salmon net in Cook Inlet. We smoked and canned salmon, put in a garden and canned the vegetables, picked berries, hauled lumber, drove nails—and we did it together. My parents were good examples of what parents should be."

Dick Bernhardt, born in San Antonio, Texas, came north with his parents, Arno and Agnes Bernhardt, in 1956. They also settled in Anchorage. Donna and Dick met in 1964 while working at the Anchorage International Airport

"Dick asked me out, then promptly stood me up," Donna says. "I was angry, but he said he was trying to find a new car and the time just went by. I gave him another chance. We went to a drive-in theater. *Isle of Love* was playing. Maybe it was an omen."

Donna was falling in love. But there was trouble at the post office.

"The boss thought he was a ladies' man," Donna says. "I had to go home and change shirts one day because he grabbed me and ripped my shirt. Another time, I had to slap him hard across the face just to get loose. He thought it was funny.

"Then I married Dick, and two weeks later Dick was laid off—and a month later I was fired. It was just in time for winter. We killed a caribou for meat and had a few veggies, and that was about it."

The couple found other jobs. Then along came the children, Ricky in 1966 and Katherine in 1970.

Anchorage was growing, especially with the discovery of the big oil field at Prudhoe Bay in Alaska's high Arctic.

"We wanted out," Donna says. "Our beloved frontier city was now a big city of 250,000."

One day as Donna was walking home from work at an Anchorage swimming pool, a man tried to pull her into his car. Donna was carrying a pistol for protection, and she shoved the weapon into the assailant's ribs. He fled. And so did the Bernhardt family.

A roadside sign and summertime flowers welcome visitors to Tok on the Alaska Highway.

"That did it," Donna says. "We wanted to find some place else to raise our kids."

They traveled much of Alaska in search of affordable property. It was early fall in 1977 when they were able to buy a few acres on the outskirts of Tok.

"We pitched our tent on our own land, and the four of us celebrated, toasting each other with Kool-Aid in paper cups," Donna says. "At last we were back in 'the real Alaska.'"

Tok (rhymes with "poke") began as a highway-construction camp during the desperate early days of World War II. Japanese troops occupied the islands of Attu and Kiska in Alaska's Aleutian Islands in June 1942. Alaskans braced for a possible invasion of the mainland. President Franklin D. Roosevelt ordered construction of an emergency military highway into Alaska's heartland.

Construction crews—mostly young, bewildered GIs far from their homes—swarmed into Tok and other key points in Alaska and western Canada to build what became the Alaska Highway. The job was done in less than nine months. And a year later American and Canadian forces drove the Japanese from the Aleutians.

"Here we were in Tok, with little more than our tent and our dreams," Donna recalls.

It was during one of those nights in the tent when Donna watched, spellbound, as the northern lights waltzed across the winter sky. She took a pencil in hand and began writing on a crumpled grocery sack. The poem began:

This is our "house" among the spruce,
The guy lines are taut and never loose.
It's all we have; it isn't much.
The walls are sewn from canvas duck.
Though life is hard, it's not so bad.
We've got more than we might have had. . . . "

And then she wrote a ballad titled "Midnight Moonlight."

An awesome night; full of mystery and romance,
The silent sky begins a slow blush of color. . . .
Fiery, rubied, northern lights
Spread by an artist's tranquil brush. . . . "

Dick read the scribbled lines during his fire-watch shift, and next morning he showed them to Beth Jacobs, editor of the weekly *Mukluk News* in Tok. They were published in the *News* a few days later—and ever since Donna has been writing lyrics about the land she loves.

"It's impossible to describe why I love Alaska so much," she says. "It's something in the heart."

And then with a laugh, Donna tells about a spring day when "the air was clear and full of cheer." She had decided to have an early-season barbecue. The coals were glowing and hot dogs were steaming on the grill. Then a surprise snowstorm turned the wieners to icicles.

Donna dismissed the cookout calamity with a rhyme:

Here's some advice concerning that ice;
When spring fever plays its tune,
Don't get caught with a "barbecue" thought
At least until it's June.

Donna still treasures memories of the family's first year in Tok. There were hardships, but there also were precious moments. One night she and Dick danced in the snow, under the northern lights, humming favorite melodies, kissing, and wishing on the bright North Star that life always could be that way.

But it was not to be.

The cabin was built. They christened it their Winter Cabin.

"Built with our own hands, with our own trees for logs," Donna says. "We couldn't have been happier."

A few years later, they added a log garage next door and went into business with a tire dealership.

"It was like a dream come true," Donna recalls.

But soon after, Dick and Donna were injured in a trucking accident. Dick checked into a Fairbanks hospital for knee surgery. The operation was a success.

Dick called home. "I've got a bionic knee now," he told Donna. "When I get better, I'll be able to chase you faster."

Hours later, Dick Bernhardt was dead. An accidental overdose of morphine was cited as the cause.

"Car lights in the driveway," Donna remembers. "A knock on the door. A state trooper standing there, telling me that Dick had died."

The dream had ended. There was no insurance. Creditors demanded payment of overdue bills. Donna lost the tire franchise.

"My heart ached," Donna says, "but I was determined to save Winter Cabin and keep a roof over our heads."

Donna booked a bush-plane flight on a blue-sky day to scatter Dick's ashes atop a mountain in sight of their Winter Cabin.

"Farewell my love," she whispered as the ashes drifted away.

Later, Donna wrote a poem about that last good-bye. She called it "One Last Flight."

It closes this way:

I sail in the wind without a mast,
Free to fly when the north wind blows;
Do not weep; I'm free at last.
Free to be where the wild rose grows. . . .

✦ ✦ ✦

MOST FOLK AROUND HERE expected Donna to leave Alaska after Dick's death.

"That never entered my thoughts," she says.

"This country can throw at me what it wants. It can keep testing me, and it will. I would never be happy somewhere else."

A few years ago Donna built a cluster of three little bed-and-breakfast cabins by her Winter Cabin. Guests have access to such amenities as running water and toilets in an adjacent bathhouse. Donna doesn't bother with either. She still hauls her water from a well, and she prefers an outhouse that she calls her private theater for northern lights shows.

Son Ricky works at a sawmill in Tok and lives just down the road with his companion, Brooke Baker. Ricky's eighteen-year-old son, Kenneth, is a basketball star at Tok High School. Daughter Katherine and her husband, Chris, live in Fairbanks. They have a daughter, Brianna, who was starting kindergarten, and infant twin sons, Michael and Erich.

"I still live alone, and I think I always will," Donna says. "It's not that I haven't had a chance to remarry, but I'm still in love with Dick. I believe one is fortunate to find true love in a lifetime. I'm content with my family, my writing, and life in general. Life is good."

I heard from Donna the other day. We're e-mail pen pals. She told me that she had shot a caribou for her winter meat supply. Ricky came by to help butcher the critter.

"All signs point to an early winter," Donna wrote.

"The ground is gold with fallen leaves. The fireweed has gone to cotton. The squirrels are busy stashing spruce cones. I hear them pitching cones and banging on the skylight above my bed. I think they know something, so I'm taking my cue from them and getting ready for winter."

Oh—about how Tok got its name.

Donna researched that with veterans of the U.S. Army's 97th Engineering Regiment, who helped build the Alaska Highway back in 1942-43. Tok was named for a dog, a Siberian husky puppy that used to tag along with the soldiers.

There's more. Tok, the dog, had a pal, a cub bear named Little Dynamite. Donna has written a book about Tok and Little Dynamite and the valiant men and women who built the Alaska Highway that passes by her front door.

She also has written a book about her happy years with Dick and her enduring love affair with Alaska.

"I leaked tears into the computer when writing that one," she says.

Someday, I told Donna, Hollywood is going to scoop up that manuscript and then my frontier friend will become a celebrity.

"I doubt that," Donna said with a laugh.

"I don't live in the past. I'm happy with what life has given me."

They say home is where the heart is
And mine is surely here.
My cabin and its woodsmoke
Fill my heart with cheer.

The sky is radiant (as my soul),
Its beauty told at night
With northern lights in full bloom
'Neath stars and bright moonlight. . . .

CHAPTER 10

MUDHOLE'S PARTY

CORDOVA—Jim Johnson, a friend from Alaska Airlines, was on the phone with an invitation.

"They're going to have a party for Mudhole, he said. "You don't want to miss this one—the whole gang will be there."

The gang consisted of most of the surviving bush pilots of early-day Alaska. They were bound for Cordova in April 1973 to toast (and roast) one of their own, Merle K. (Mudhole) Smith.

"There'll never be another evening like it," Jim Johnson said.

There never was.

They gathered in the Elks Club in Cordova and called the roll:

- Noel Wien, age seventy-three, the dean of Alaska's bush pilots. He came into the country in 1924. There was a period in 1924 and '25 when Noel was the only pilot in all of Alaska.
- Sigurd Wien, sixty-nine, Noel's brother, a pioneer arctic pilot. Rated by many of the pilots as the best of them all.

139

- Robert C. (Bob) Reeve, seventy-one, the daring glacier pilot who blazed the air trails through Alaska's Aleutian Islands.
- John Cross, still flying at age seventy-eight, with more than 21,000 hours in his logbook.
- Jack Jefford, sixty-two, a veteran of thirty-seven years of flying Alaska, from bush pilot to chief of flight operations in Alaska for the Federal Aviation Administration.
- Jack Peck, fifty-eight, longtime bush pilot, later chief of airport operations for the state of Alaska.
- Wyman (Lanky) Rice, sixty-three, once Peck's partner in a flying service, then executive vice president of Wien Consolidated Airlines.
- Ray Petersen, sixty-one, a pioneering bush pilot in the Kuskokwim region, later president of Wien Consolidated.
- John DeLeo, a United Air Lines Boeing 747 captain, who learned to fly in his native Cordova in 1935, with John Cross as his instructor.

And Governor William A. (Bill) Egan, a pilot himself during his younger days in neighboring Valdez. Egan told the crowd that it was a lucky thing for passengers that he gave up flying for politics after making a couple of botched landings in his 1939 Aeronca. Egan was elected Alaska's first governor when Alaska was granted statehood in 1959.

There were tears in Mudhole Smith's eyes when his fellow bush pilots led a standing ovation.

"I never thought I would see the day when these guys would be on their feet for me," he said.

It wasn't that many years ago that the old birdmen were hard-flying rivals, battling each other for business across this unforgiving frontier. Many of their comrades died in fiery crashes.

My elder brother, Ernest Patty Jr., was one of those bush pilots who wagered with the weather and lost. He flew into an ice

Merle K. (Mudhole) Smith, in 1973.

Pioneer bush pilots gather in Cordova in 1973 to honor Merle K. (Mudhole) Smith. They are (from left) Jack Jefford, Jack Peck, Bob Reeve, Smith, Ray Petersen, John Cross, Sigurd Wien, and Noel Wien.

storm northeast of Fairbanks in 1947—leaving behind a widow and a six-month-old son.

But mostly I remember how Ernie loved to fly. He soloed, secretly, at age sixteen. A few days later he buzzed our Fairbanks home with a dish-rattling, low-level pass. My mother, who suspected that Ernie was taking flying lessons from Bill Lavery, dashed out of the house, shook her fist at the Taylorcraft, and laughed.

"There goes that Ernest Patty!" she said. "I knew it!"

The testimonial dinner for Mudhole Smith—"Smitty" to home folk in Cordova—was arranged by the grateful citizens of the town on the occasion of Smith's retirement as a vice president and director of Alaska Airlines. Years before, he had built a little flying service called Cordova Airlines into a successful scheduled carrier that in 1968 was merged into Alaska Airlines.

What Cordovans remembered best were the times when their Smitty flew into remote bush strips on dangerous emergency runs—and opened his big heart to transport their school ball teams for little or no revenue when his income was as thin as the fabric on a Jenny's wings. They also remembered when Cordova was stranded by a shipping strike in 1946-47, and how Smith mounted a Cordova Airlines airlift that fed the entire Prince William Sound town with airborne groceries.

So the good people of Cordova decided it was time to tell Smith thank you and to invite his flying pals to the party.

I scanned the head table and thought about all the great stories these old-timers could tell. These were my heroes. I had known most of them since childhood. And, somehow, I knew they never would be together again.

✦ ✦ ✦

THERE WAS NOEL WIEN. He made aviation history July 15, 1924, when he and his mechanic, Bill Yunkers, flew an open-cockpit Hisso Standard J-1—a surplus World War I biplane—north from Anchorage to Fairbanks. It was the first flight ever between the two cities. Along the way, Wien almost was blinded by forest-fire smoke. He swooped down to about 150 feet and followed the Alaska Railroad tracks into Weeks Field in Fairbanks.

"The flight was made in the fast time of 3 hours and 45 minutes," the *Fairbanks Daily News-Miner* reported. Today jetliners cover the 260 miles in about forty minutes.

Other Noel Wien firsts:

The first flight and successful landing beyond the Arctic Circle, anywhere in the world, in 1925.

The first commercial flight from Fairbanks to then isolated Nome, on the Bering Sea coast, also in 1925.

The first round-trip flight between Alaska and Russia, to save a cargo of furs from a trading schooner that had been frozen in arctic ice off Siberia's North Cape. That was in 1929.

And the first commercial passenger flights between Fairbanks and Seattle—beginning with the race to rush news photographs to Seattle of the air crash near Barrow, Alaska, that killed Wiley Post and Will Rogers. That was in 1935. Post, first to fly solo around the world, and Rogers, America's beloved humorist, died instantly when Post's floatplane stalled on takeoff from a lagoon near the top of the world.

Noel's wife, Ada, said that when her husband saw his name in print, he reacted "as if he was reading about someone else."

"Sometimes it even sounds interesting," the famous flier quipped.

When I had my first airplane ride, Noel Wien was at the controls. I was twelve. The flight in a Ford Trimotor was first prize in a contest for creating a

Noel Wien, known as the dean of Alaska bush pilots, in 1974.

slogan based on the call letters of KFAR, the first radio station in Fairbanks. My winning entry: "Key For Alaska's Riches." The award also included a turtle, but it didn't survive the Fairbanks winter.

Noel died in 1977.

✦ ✦ ✦

THEN THERE WAS SIG WIEN. A quiet man. Short on words, long on performance. Not one to talk about his exploits. He was the first to provide air service to Barrow, Point Hope, Anaktuvuk Pass, and other arctic villages. He also may have been the first to fly the unmapped North Slope, where later the giant Prudhoe Bay oil field was discovered

"I always thought that country up there had a future because of the oil seepages I spotted from the air and what the geologists were saying," Sig said. "So the big strike [in 1967] didn't surprise me."

Sig still was jogging three miles a day in his seventies. He ran in 60-below weather, wearing a down parka and with a wool scarf over his mouth "to warm the air."

Sigurd Wien died in 1994. He was ninety-one.

✦ ✦ ✦

RAY PETERSEN began flying the bush in 1934. When he retired in 1978, he was president of Wien Consolidated, with a fleet of Boeing 737 jetliners.

"There were only fifty-five pilots in all of Alaska when I started," Petersen recalled. "Now there are thousands."

That's no exaggeration. The Federal Aviation Administration lists more than 10,000 licensed pilots among Alaska's 550,000-plus residents. Able pilots still fly Alaska's bush, but today's band of birdmen challenge the northern skies almost in anonymity.

"Flying is their job and they do it well," Petersen said. "Technically, the guys flying today are far ahead of where we were. We didn't even have radios in the beginning.

"But just as in the old days," he added, "there are good pilots and bad pilots. Those with good judgment stay alive. Those who do damn fool things get into trouble."

Ray Petersen was ninety-two as of 2003. Along with Ralph Savory, Bob Byers and a very few others, he is among the last of Alaska's pioneer pilots.

✦ ✦ ✦

JOHN CROSS RECALLED landing a Bellanca at night on Cordova's Eyak Lake.

"The lake was like an inkwell," he said. "I landed, turned on my light, and there was a rowboat right in front of me. My gosh!"

Cross came to Alaska in 1934, when he delivered a plane to M. D. Kirkpatrick, founder of Cordova Air. He flew awhile for Cordova Air, then joined Noel Wien for several years. It was Noel who taught him about arctic flying.

In 1939, Cross started his own outfit, Northern Cross Airways, flying mostly out of Kotzebue and Deering in the Arctic. Ocean beaches, gravel bars, lakes, and soggy tundra were his bush runways.

Cross also had the dubious distinction of being knocked out of the air by Jimmy Doolittle, later the much-honored Tokyo raider of World War II.

It happened in the early 1930s in Kansas City, Missouri. Cross was flying a biplane at an aviation show. He was shooting a landing when Doolittle made one of his trademark approaches by diving from 2,000 feet, then leveling off almost at ground level and snap-rolling before landing in front of the bleachers. But this time Doolittle's racing plane clipped Cross's undercarriage. Cross bailed out and landed in a cornfield, just missing railroad tracks where a freight train was rolling along at high speed.

Jimmy Doolittle lost his license for a while over this incident, but soon was flying again.

John Cross died in 1981 in Kotzebue. He was eighty-six. Someone figured out for Cross's obituary that he had flown almost 2 million air miles in the Arctic.

Retired General James H. Doolittle died in 1993. He was ninety-six.

✦ ✦ ✦

NEXT AT THE MICROPHONE was Jack Jefford. He pioneered instrument flying in Alaska when he flew for the Civil Aeronautics Authority, later the Federal Aviation Administration. Jefford was chief pilot for the FAA, flying dozens of mercy missions and creating vital air routes for supplying Alaska's military outposts in World War II.

But there was time for fun, too. Jefford confessed to a weekend of moonlighting for Mudhole Smith shortly after World War II, when there was a shortage of qualified DC-3 pilots in Alaska.

"I can't do it for you, Smitty," Jefford said when Smith asked him to deliver a surplus military C-47 (Douglas DC-3). "I just can't. I'm chief of the division for the CAA. What you are asking me is against regulations."

Smith countered: "I'll give you a hundred bucks."

"No, I can't," Jefford said.

Smith raised the ante—two hundred dollars, then three hundred, finally four hundred.

"OK, I'll do it," Jefford said. "So I flew down to Seattle that weekend and picked up the plane and a load of commercial fishermen for Smitty. By now, I hope the statute of limitations has run out."

Jefford, a master storyteller, also told about his pre-government bush-flying days. It was a time when the southwestern corner of the second floor of the old Nordale Hotel in Fairbanks more or less was reserved for pilots and hangar talk. Jefford had been dispatched to Fairbanks by a saloon keeper in Nome to hire a musician for the bar.

Jefford flew into Fairbanks and found a female pianist whom he rated "quite good, especially when she played 'Indian Love Call.'" He hired both the piano player and her partner, a drummer, also a woman, but was unable to load the bass drum through the Lockheed Vega's door.

"Hell," he told the musicians, "we can borrow a drum in Nome."

Nome residents thronged the airport to meet the plane. The *Nome Nugget* even published a special edition that day to announce the ladies' arrival. But it turned out that the two passengers had a genuine fear of flying—and a bottled remedy.

"We were airborne when I smelled gin, lots of gin," Jefford said. "The girls were drunk. But they sobered up after we reached Nome and played beautiful music, as promised. They played all that winter in Nome."

Jefford retired in 1972 with 26,600 hours of flying time. Then he and his wife, Ruth, moved to Wasilla, just north of Anchorage, and opened their own air-taxi outfit, Valley Air Transport.

Jack Jefford died in 1979. He was sixty-eight.

✦ ✦ ✦

BOB REEVE STEPPED to the microphone and looked over the crowd with a playful grin. There were many colorful pilots in early-times Alaska, but none more entertaining than Robert Campbell Reeve.

"We were at each others' throats in business years ago," Reeve told his buddies. "Now here we are, breaking bread together. I'm honored to be here with all of you."

With that surprisingly gentle opening out of the way, Reeve began teasing the guest of honor about his flying skills.

"There was a time in Anchorage when Smitty was taking off in a Boeing 80A. The plane got off track and flew into Art Woodley's hangar," Reeve said.

"And I want to take credit for giving Smitty his Mudhole nickname. It happened in 1939 at the Bremner Mine, south of the town of McCarthy, when Smitty's Stearman biplane hit a hole in the airstrip on takeoff and lurched off, into the mud, with the prop turning at about eighteen-hundred rpm. I was flying over at the time and saw him stuck in the mud."

Reeve arrived in Valdez in 1932 with twenty cents in his pocket. Or was it

Bob Reeve stands on the snow with his airplane after making a glacier landing on skis near Valdez in the 1930s. REEVE COLLECTION

fifty cents? I heard both versions from the glacier pilot. Anyway, Reeve reached Valdez by stowing away on a steamer from Seattle.

He rented an open-cockpit Eaglerock plane and began chartering for mining operations in the mountains around Valdez. In summer, he would take off—on skis—from the Valdez mudflats and make daring landings on crevasse-laced glaciers near the mining camps.

But his greatest adventures were in the Aleutian Islands during World War II, when Reeve was a civilian pilot hired to supply military bases in the Aleutians. Japanese forces were holding two of the islands, Attu and Kiska.

Legend has it that Reeve was on a flight to Adak Island in thick weather when the control tower advised him that the ceiling was too low for a safe landing.

"Just give me taxi instructions," he growled. "I'm already down."

And then there was the night that Reeve was grounded out at Umnak Island in the Aleutians. So he got into a poker game with a bunch of bomber pilots. Within an hour or so, the military fliers had cleaned him out of his ready cash.

"I'll pledge my airplane for five thousand dollars credit," he offered.

It took only an hour for Reeve to lose that, too.

He was granted a "second mortgage," and finally his luck began to turn.

**Robert C. (Bob)
Reeve, in 1966.**

Within a day, he had won back the propeller and wings. A few days later, the fuselage and landing gear, the ailerons, and the stabilizer.

But try as he would, there was no way Reeve could regain the rudder and elevators. The weather was clearing, and he needed the plane.

It was 3 A.M. on the tenth day when finally Reeve had title to the entire plane.

"Gimme that IOU—I gotta get going," he said.

Later, Reeve was inducted into the Aviation Hall of Fame and was named Alaskan of the Year. He also received an honorary Doctor of Science degree from the University of Alaska.

Reeve joked that what he called "my new cloak of respectability" almost led to disaster. In Anchorage, he gave up his old haunts such as the Cheechako Lounge and Mike's Place to join the posh Petroleum Club atop the Anchorage Westward Hotel.

March 27, 1964. Good Friday. It was Reeve's sixty-second birthday. It also was the day that one of the most powerful earthquakes in history hit Alaska. Reeve found himself in the Petroleum Club, swaying fifteen floors above Anchorage while, in his words, "the earth coughed and growled and crackled and cracked."

Finally, Reeve made his escape unharmed, but raged over "the foul and libelous slander that I was frightened."

"I was not scared," he said, "but on the way down I did pass four other guys who really were scared."

Occupants of the Cheechako Lounge and Mike's Place, down on street level on Fourth Avenue, came through unscathed.

"I wondered why I had ever forsaken my old friends," he lamented.

After World War II, Reeve made a down payment on a surplus C-47 transport and carved a new commercial-aviation route through the Aleutians. It was a territory that nobody else wanted. Reeve Aleutian Airways was the name of his new company.

"I knew the area could be developed with guts and hard work," he said.

Guts and hard work. That pretty well sums up the life of Bob Reeve. Reeve was a remarkable pilot. In 1937, Ernie Pyle (later a noted war correspondent) described Reeve as "the most amazing of all Alaska's amazing fliers."

Bob Reeve died in his sleep in 1980. He was seventy-eight.

✦ ✦ ✦

MISSING FROM MUDHOLE'S party were many of the old gang who had made their last flights:

Carl Ben Eielson, Frank Barr, Vern Bookwalter, Joe Crosson, Jim Dodson, Frank Dorbandt, Bob Ellis, Archie Ferguson, Harold Gillam, Dick Hawley, Alex Holden, Roy Holm, Herm Joslyn, Maurice King, Fred Moeller, Al Monsen, Russ Merrill, Hans Mirow, Frank Pollack, S. E. Robbins, Murrel Sasseen, Shell Simmons, Clyde Wann, Oscar Winchell, Art Woodley, Ed Young, and the others . . .

"I had fun tonight," said Mudhole Smith. "But I wonder if we'll ever get together again. Probably not. We're a bunch of old men."

Mudhole was right. It was the last gathering of Alaska's eagles.

Rest well, gentlemen.

CHAPTER 11

TWO SHEPHERDS FOR ALASKA

SITKA—It seems that I have been tagging along with Ivan Veniaminov for most of my life.

I found him here in Sitka, the nineteenth-century capital of Russian America. In Kodiak, site of the first Russian settlement in Alaska. In the wind-whipped Aleut village of Unalaska in the Aleutian Islands. In Irkutsk, in the heart of Siberia. At an ancient monastery near Moscow. And on a lonely coastal bluff in northern California.

It has been an unusual odyssey.

I'm not of the Orthodox faith, but since school days I've wanted to know more about the selfless missionary who gave Alaska's native peoples the gifts of language and self-respect. Nobody left a greater imprint on Alaska.

This shepherd for Alaska was born Ioann (Ivan) Popov in 1797, in a humble Siberian village. As a young widower, with the church surname of Veniaminov, he was named the first Russian Orthodox bishop of Alaska. Later he would be known as His Beautitude, Metropolitan Innocent, primate of the church in czarist Russia. Now he is Saint Innocent, one with the angels.

To tell his story, I will call him Veniaminov. That is how Alaskans remember him.

Saint Innocent (Innokenti, in Russian), first Russian Orthodox bishop of Alaska.
STANTON PATTY COLLECTION

Metropolitan Theodosius, courageous clergyman, in 1977.

"He was a truly great man, an all-around man," says His Beautitude, Metropolitan Theodosius, who retired recently as primate of the Orthodox Church in America. Early in his own career, American-born Theodosius followed Veniaminov as the Russian Orthodox bishop of Alaska.

Sometimes I almost feel Veniaminov's presence as I roam the Aleutian Islands and visit the native villages he loved. I figure he would be more than six feet tall, with a gentle voice, a merry sense of humor and, when needed, steely courage. In another time, he might have been a resolute clergyman in America's civil-rights movement, perhaps in the mold of Martin Luther King Jr.

Metropolitan Theodosius, another of Alaska's good shepherds, has guided my quest for more details of Veniaminov's life. There were clues in Orthodox publications circulated mostly among communicants. And there were shared conversations about Theodosius's sometimes harrowing experiences inside the Soviet Union when he helped sustain the beleaguered Russian church.

A golden sunrise silhouettes St. Michael's Russian Orthodox Cathedral in Sitka.

One day three Alaskans (all adrift Protestants) asked our mutual friend Theodosius why he was willing to give us so much of his precious time.

"Because you fellows need me," he responded with a laugh.

It's true.

Wonderful, I thought as I began this story, how the lives of Veniaminov and Theodosius have crossed over the years. It was Theodosius who helped lead the campaign to canonize Veniaminov as Saint Innocent. That was in 1994, when the church in Russia still was being harassed by government authorities.

"The agreement was that the canonization had to be done privately," Theodosius reported, with no public announcement in Russia. "That was part of the 'punishment.'"

Another penalty was that Theodosius was not permitted to be present for the ceremony. But word of Veniaminov's canonization leaked from Russia— and Alaskans exulted.

Veniaminov risked his life countless times to bring the word of God to

Alaska's native peoples—at a time when the natives feared and resisted intruders from Russia who tried to enslave them as fur hunters.

Veniaminov built lasting churches in the Alaskan wilderness. He compiled grammars of the Aleut and Tlingit languages for natives who had no written languages. He brought the blessings of inoculation against smallpox to the Tlingits. He found time to carry out important scientific studies in ethnology, meteorology, and other fields. He even built clocks and furniture as a hobby. For almost twenty-five years, he covered his vast diocese—stretching across parts of two continents, in Alaska and Siberia—by native skin boats, dog teams, and on foot. In the end he was blinded by years of travel across glaring snowfields.

Theodosius took bold chances as he traveled frequently to the Soviet Union to help keep the church alive during the grave days of Soviet persecution.

He met with Orthodox priests and parishioners in private homes, restaurants, and gardens—always trying to avoid eavesdropping bugs planted in churches and hotels. Some of the Russian priests undoubtedly were Communist agents. Others of the clergy had to walk the fine line that served as the church's accommodation with the heavy-handed government.

"There was danger. I knew it, but I wasn't afraid for myself," Theodosius told me later. "I was only afraid for the people who wanted to meet with me. I'm very proud of them.

"The church in Russia did not die, but it was suppressed for a very long time. Nikita Khrushchev [Soviet prime minister from 1958 to 1964] was especially hard on the church—even more so than Stalin."

So, it is little wonder that the Soviets despised the brave bishop from Alaska who a few years later would become metropolitan of the Orthodox Church in America. In 1970, Theodosius, while bishop of Alaska, returned to Russia to receive the document that recognized the American church as a self-governing entity, no longer responsible to the mother church in Russia. It was a historic event. The church in the United States, with more than 1 million members, officially became the Orthodox Church in America.

✦ ✦ ✦

THE AMERICAN CHURCH began in Alaska, in 1794, when eleven Russian Orthodox monks, all volunteers, sailed from Siberia to Kodiak. One of those trailblazing monks was known as Father Herman—now Saint Herman—the first Russian Orthodox priest to be canonized on American soil. Theodosius orchestrated that canonization, too, in 1970, with a memorable ceremony in Kodiak

In 1842, BishopVeniaminov was on his way from Siberia to Alaska when his ship was caught in a raging storm. He prayed to Father Herman, the monk of Spruce Island, near Kodiak: "If it is God's will, Father Herman, give us better weather." Immediately, a fair wind took over, and the ship reached Kodiak safely.

In gratitude, Veniaminov traveled to Spruce Island to say a prayer over the grave of Father Herman. Veniaminov said he looked up from the prayer book, and there before him stood Father Herman. The natives of Kodiak love to tell that story. It was Father Herman who first planted Christianity in their hearts.

During a trip to Kodiak in 1968, I heard rumors that plans were under way to canonize Father Herman. I wanted to see the little chapel in the spruce forest where the kindly monk spent his last years. Phil Anderson, Roy Madsen, and other Kodiak friends offered to take me there in a small fishing vessel.

It was a crossing of about eight miles north from Kodiak's small-boat harbor to reach Spruce Island. We landed at Monk's Lagoon, on the eastern end of the seven-mile-long island, then hiked a quarter-mile or so through the dark-green rain forest to a clearing with a tiny, white-frame building. Wild violets sprinkled the sun-dappled meadow like purple sequins.

There was the faint scent of incense as Madsen unlocked the door to the empty chapel. And then we saw Father Herman's bier, covered with a full-length likeness of the monk in repose.

Father Herman, who nursed the Kodiak natives through epidemics and defended them against brutal, hard-drinking Russian fur traders, lived simply. His garments included an old deerskin shirt and a tattered cloak. He wore a fifteen-pound chain of fetters with a crucifix as his personal penance. The heavy necklace was displayed in a glass-covered case near the coffin.

Father Herman died on Spruce Island December 26, 1837, at the age of eighty-one. Natives of neighboring Afognak Island saw a column of light beaming over Spruce Island that night. They fell to their knees, exclaiming, "Our holy man has gone from us!"

Our friend, Metropolitan Theodosius, started the process toward sainthood for Father Herman after a pilgrimage to Spruce Island when he was the newly appointed bishop of Sitka and Alaska.

"Father Herman will be the first saint of the church to be canonized on American soil," Theodosius told me. "He has done his work well. God has already made him a saint—we are simply acknowledging what God has done."

The canonization ceremony was scheduled for August 6-9, 1970, in Kodiak's historic Russian Orthodox Church of the Resurrection.

"Yes, you can be there and you can take pictures for your newspaper," Theodosius said. "But you must wait for my signal each time you wish to use the camera."

"Agreed."

And so there I was on a lovely day in Kodiak as church dignitaries from throughout the world gathered to honor the monk of Spruce Island. Metropolitan Ireney, primate of the Orthodox Church in America, led the delegation. It was an unforgettable tableau of color and pageantry. The little blue-domed church on a hill above Kodiak's harbor blazed with candles and holy icons. High-ranking clergy were attired in golden robes and the crown-like headdresses called miters.

Father Herman's casket rested on a crimson carpet in the center of the church, decorated with a wreath of red roses and white carnations. I found a camera position on a balcony above the church floor and watched for cues from Theodosius. Finally, he looked up, nodded his head, and I got my once-in-a-lifetime photographs.

✦ ✦ ✦

MY SEARCH FOR NEW information about Veniaminov, the Russian saint, put me on a collision course with the Soviet bureaucracy when I traveled to Moscow in 1968 for a meeting of the North Pacific Fur Seal Commission. Would it be possible, I wondered, to find Veniaminov's grave while in the Soviet Union? How much did today's Russians know of his good works?

Before flying to Moscow, I needed to identify Veniaminov's burial site. Records were sparse. Then I found an old, undated pamphlet in the Alaska State Historical Library in Juneau. The last page told of Veniaminov's death on March 31, 1879, and noted that he was laid to rest on the grounds of the Troitse-Sergiev Monastery. But where was the monastery?

Additional research pointed toward to the ancient city of Zagorsk, about thirty-three miles north of Moscow. Zagorsk, one journal said, might be likened to the Vatican for Roman Catholics. Now I had a target. I couldn't wait to play hooky from the Fur Seal Commission meetings.

The American delegation to the conference checked into the Leningradskaya Hotel on Moscow's noisy Komsomol Square. The hotel had a service bureau, an Intourist operation, that was supposed to assist visitors with reservations for sightseeing, ballet performances, and such. A Moscow guide-book promised that the service bureau would be "a big help." And so I hurried to the service bureau desk and announced a request to visit Zagorsk.

"Why?" asked a poker-faced attendant.

Enthusiastically, sensing that my goal was near, I explained that I hoped to find the tomb of a great Russian missionary who toiled in Alaska. With considerable restraint, I didn't point out how foolish Russia had been to sell Alaska to the United States.

"We will see what can be arranged," the service bureau woman said. "Please come again tomorrow."

Tomorrow came and several more days passed without an encouraging word from the service bureau. What could be difficult about a little trip to Zagorsk? Time was running out.

I took my request to the chairman of the Soviet delegation to the Fur Seal Commission meeting. He promised to investigate, and that broke the logjam. The service bureau notified me that I could visit Zagorsk the next day. The cost would be about forty dollars for the car, driver, and guide-interpreter. Fine. I would have agreed to almost any price.

It was a cool, early-spring morning when I left for Zagorsk with an attractive Intourist guide-interpreter named Lidya. Her first question to me, as if fired by a prosecuting attorney: "Why do you really want to go to Zagorsk?"

Accustomed to this query, I explained, patiently, about my interest in Veniaminov and my attachment to Alaska. Lidya nodded understandingly as I recited the many achievements of Veniaminov, who rose to be Metropolitan Innocent of Moscow, one of the Russian church's highest positions.

"Yes, but why do you really want to go to Zagorsk?" she asked again.

Lidya also wanted to know my preferences in American politics. She thought much of the late Robert Kennedy, but didn't care for Richard Nixon.

Once through Moscow traffic, we stopped to take photographs along the

A priest welcomes visitors to tiny St. Nicholas Russian Orthodox Church in downtown Juneau.

narrow Yaroslavl Highway. It was an area of weathered old homes with scroll-work trimmings. The Russians are proud of these antiques, but if you took away the scalloped edgings they could be cabins in rural Alaska.

Clusters of Russian Orthodox Church domes fill the skyline in the Russian holy city of Zagorsk.

The tomb and portrait of Saint Innocent (Innokenti) in a Zagorsk cathedral.

Holy Resurrection Russian Orthodox Church in Kodiak is crowded for the canonization of Alaska's Saint Herman, in 1970.

Lidya still was edgy about my desire to visit Zagorsk. Were there military installations or other forbidden sights along the route that I shouldn't see, I wondered to myself? We rode the rest of the way in silence.

Finally, I sighted the onion domes and turrets of Zagorsk and the Troitse-Sergiev Monastery. They soared against the gray sky, like a scene from a Russian fairy tale. Was this where Veniaminov, the apostle of Alaska, was buried? The name of the monastery matched the one in the old pamphlet in the Juneau library. This could be it!

The monastery, dating to about 1340, is studded with centuries-old churches adorned with priceless icons and frescoes. In 1920, after the Communist takeover of Russia, the godless Soviet regime designated the monastery as the Zagorsk Historical and Art Museum Reservation. Museum it was, but at the time of my visit, divine services still were held there in the hush of history.

We left the Intourist automobile at the front gate of the monastery and walked into a panorama of blue and gold domes, like bright Christmas ornaments. Reverent pilgrims moved silently along the stone-block streets, never making eye contact with the stranger from America.

Lidya asked a bearded clergyman where to find the grave of Veniaminov—or did he know him as Innocent (Innokenti, in Russian)?

"Nyet," he said with a shrug, and walked away.

Perhaps, I thought, this was not the correct monastery. We wandered through the grounds, reading inscriptions on tombstones, hoping to find, even by accident, one that was lettered Innokenti. Finally, a young priest being questioned by Lidya thought he knew the answer. He gestured toward a pale-white church topped with an array of bulbous globes. A golden stripe banded the highest of the sky-blue domes.

We double-timed up the steps of the church and tugged at the door handle. But the church was locked. A sign on the door said it would not be open for another hour. There was nothing to do but wait.

This was the Church of the Holy Spirit, built in 1554. An elderly priest, identified later as Feodorit, deputy head of the monastery, emerged from the church. Lidya outlined my request.

"First we will talk a bit," the priest said.

We walked to his study, where I explained again my interest in Veniaminov, or Innokenti. Father Feodorit, a gracious conversationalist, knew the name, but did not say more. Instead, he presented me with a book, in English, purporting to tell about the status of the Orthodox church in Russia. It was a masterpiece of propaganda, asserting that freedom of religion prevailed in the Soviet Union and condemning outsiders who criticized the government for its attitude toward religion. The book declared that the church was living "under new conditions," instead of being the instrument of the czars, as before.

I was tempted to ask Father Feodorit some penetrating questions about church-state relations, but thought better of it. My focus was on finding and photographing the Veniaminov tomb. Father Feodorit approved my request, saying that he would send word ahead that I would be permitted to take photographs inside the Church of the Holy Spirit.

An old priest was waiting for us in the church. He scowled and turned away so I could go about my monstrous business. It would have done no good to explain that I meant no disrespect. I stepped inside and looked to the right—and there it was, the tomb of Veniaminov!

The Russian letters on the sarcophagus spelled INNOKENTI, in a script I had memorized, although my knowledge of Russian is limited to phrases such as "Please" and "Thank you."

I scribbled notes quickly: "It is a richly colored double tomb. Buried to Innocent's left is Philter, Veniaminov's close friend and mentor, whom he succeeded as Metropolitan of Moscow in January, 1868. That was just a few months after the purchase of Alaska from Russia. The top of the tomb resembles a small altar, decorated with portraits of Innokenti and Philter, covered with brocade and fenced with a golden railing. . . . "

I stuffed my notebook into a shirt pocket and, with some trepidation, began photographing the tomb. Bright flashes of the camera's strobe light triggered alarms with the glowering priest. I half-expected him to shout an order to stop.

It turned out that I returned home with the first-known photographs of Veniaminov's burial site taken by an American journalist. But little did I know that the elaborate sarcophagus was only symbolic—that both Innokenti and Philter really were buried originally in a gallery just outside the church.

And I didn't know then that Communist thugs earlier had opened the tomb and tossed the remains of the two metropolitans into a pit beside the Church of the Holy Spirit and covered the hole with paving blocks. So much for the "new conditions" the church faced in the Soviet Union.

Theodosius later told me about the desecration of the tomb as he sketched the layout on a slip of memo paper.

"It was an awful thing," he said.

Archaeologists recovered the remains during planning for Veniaminov's canonization. It was quite easy, said Theodosius, to identify Veniaminov's skeleton. He was known to be a tall man in life, considerably taller than Philter and others whose relics had been discarded by the Soviets.

I had followed those giant steps around the world. To the old Russian Orthodox cathedral in Irkutsk, where Veniaminov began his missionary work. To Unalaska, Sitka, and Kodiak, where he ministered to Alaska's native peoples. To Spruce Island, where he held services over the grave of Father Herman. To Fort Ross, in California, where he visited lonely, far-from-home Russian colonists. To Moscow, where he served as metropolitan at the close of an adventurous life. And, finally, to Zagorsk, where I found him at the end of my quest.

I took one more look at the tomb as I packed my camera gear. Then I thanked the cranky priest and hurried outside to join Lidya.

"Did you find what you were looking for in there?" she asked.

CHAPTER 12

SHORT TAKES

EAGLE—E.A. (NIMROD) Robertson killed a bear, extracted the bear's teeth, made himself a set of false teeth—then sat down and ate the bear.

Ernie Pyle said it happened this way. Pyle (later to be a celebrated correspondent in World War II) stopped by the Alaska village of Eagle in 1935 to interview Nimrod.

Robertson told Pyle that he was working a gold-mining claim near Eagle when wolves destroyed his cache of meat and other groceries. Nimrod got scurvy and his teeth fell out. So, he decided to fashion a set of dentures. He used mountain sheep teeth for the front row. Back of the sheep teeth, he inserted a few caribou teeth. And for grinding molars he decided to use the departed bear's teeth.

"It took him a month," Pyle reported. "He made both uppers and lowers. And he wore them for nearly twenty-five years. . . . "

Fact or fiction?

"A bit far-fetched," said Barney Hansen, a family friend in Eagle. Maybe it was a case of Pyle being unable to resist a good story, Barney said. Or perhaps Nimrod couldn't resist embroidering the truth.

"Nimrod told me that most of the teeth in those dentures were sheep teeth," Barney said. "He never ate that bear.

"Years later, a couple of dentists from Seattle stopped by Eagle on a tour of Alaska. They examined Nimrod's homemade plates, went home, and made him a new set. They sent him the best they could do, but old Nimrod was never satisfied with them."

Nimrod, originally from Bangor, Maine, was a master craftsman, a jeweler by trade. It was said around here that he could make anything but a living.

The old sourdough met a tragic end in 1940. There are at least two versions of his death.

According to the late Elva Scott, an Eagle historian, Nimrod stayed too long on a prospecting trip to the Seventymile River and ran short of provisions. He was halfway home, starving and numb with cold, when he realized he could go no farther. "He stood his rifle against a tree . . . laid down in a creek bed and pulled his parka hood over his face, folded his arms and dropped off to sleep, never to awaken," Scott wrote in her book *Jewel of the Yukon.* The depression where he lay filled with water and Nimrod's body soon was encased in ice.

Another theory is that Nimrod suffered a crippling injury, perhaps a broken leg, on the trail. He was known to have what locals remember as "an intense fear of wolves," so chose his own death to cheat the wolves. He bedded down in a shallow creek overflow, knowing that he soon would freeze to death in the frigid water—and that his icy shroud would shield his body from wolves.

Searchers found Nimrod blanketed in ice, with his arms folded over his chest.

What became of Nimrod's false teeth?

Last I heard, a Seattle dentist took them home for his collection.

✦ ✦ ✦

EXCURSION INLET—This lovely fiord in Southeastern Alaska is the site of a strange tale from World War II.

Because of heavy censorship during the war, few Americans were aware of what was happening here. German prisoners-of-war were shipped to Excursion Inlet in June 1945 to demolish a huge U.S. military installation that probably shouldn't have been built in the first place.

German prisoners work in the repair shop of a World War II prisoner of war camp at Excursion Inlet in Southeastern Alaska. DEPARTMENT OF THE ARMY PHOTO

Military records show that seven hundred German POWs, guarded by about sixty U.S. soldiers, were transferred from a Colorado prison camp to Excursion Inlet. The POW outfit was identified as the No. 1933 Service Command.

The Excursion Inlet base—forty air miles west of Juneau—was designed to handle cargo for convoys headed for the Aleutian Islands. Japanese troops in 1942 had occupied the islands of Attu and Kiska in the Aleutians. But by the time Excursion Inlet's military port was in full operation, Allied forces had ousted the Japanese from the island chain.

Ernest Gruening, then Alaska's territorial governor, was among those who had questioned plans to construct the Excursion Inlet base. Gruening flew to San Francisco to tell Lieutenant General John L. DeWitt, head of the Western Defense Command, that the Excursion Inlet project would be a waste of money. Gruening suggested instead that the port in Juneau, Alaska's capital city, be expanded.

"No, I have signed the order [for Excursion Inlet]," DeWitt told the governor.

"Then why not unsign it?" Gruening asked. "Not a stick of lumber has been laid down at Excursion Inlet."

Visitors inspect a stone chimney, all that remains of the World War II American officers' club at Excursion Inlet.

"I never countermand my own orders," the general responded.

Bottom line: the Excursion Inlet boondoggle cost American taxpayers more than $20 million. And later, the German war prisoners arrived at Excursion Inlet to dismantle the useless base.

There was no problem with the POWs, locals reported.

"That was only one escape attempt," Robert Syre, superintendent of the Excursion Inlet Packing Company, told me. "Two or three prisoners took off, but they got hungry and soon came back."

Little is left of the military base. Last time I visited, I saw only crumbling foundations of shipping piers and the shell of a stone fireplace for the burned-out officers' club.

Glacier Bay National Park, one of Alaska's scenic jewels, begins just across the inlet. Far as I know, there were no wartime secrets there.

✦ ✦ ✦

NOME—Among the stampeders who joined the gold rush to Nome was an over-the-hill gunfighter by the name of Wyatt Earp. Yep—the same Wyatt Earp who was involved in the famous shootout at the OK Corral in Tombstone, Arizona, back in 1881.

And Earp brought with him to Nome a hair-trigger temper that would cause him to be arrested there for, of all things, interfering with a lawman.

Wyatt Earp in custody? It's true.

Wild West yarns cast Earp mostly as a steely-eyed marshal. For sure he did kill a few outlaws, and maybe some other fellows, too. But Earp also was a gambling man, a wanderer with dreams of hitting it big somewhere, some day.

His first trip to Alaska ended in Wrangell, a rough and tough gold-rush town in Southeastern Alaska. That was in 1897. "Hell on wheels," was how Earp described rowdy Wrangell.

Historical accounts vary, but it seems that Wrangell was "between marshals" when Earp and his wife, Josie, came ashore there. Earp, then about fifty years old, agreed to fill in for a week while the town recruited a full-time marshal. Nothing eventful happened on the streets of Wrangell during that week, perhaps because of Earp's ruthless reputation.

The Earps headed north again in 1898, hoping to reach Dawson City and the Klondike goldfields. But by the time they reached the Yukon River mining camp of Rampart, the river was choked with ice. The couple was stranded there for the winter. The following spring Earp took a job as manager of a small store in St. Michael, Alaska, the Norton Sound pivot point for river travel to Dawson City.

In the summer of 1899, the aging gunfighter moved on to Nome. There he and a partner opened a fancy establishment called the Dexter Saloon. Soon Earp was harvesting more treasure than most of the miners who swarmed the golden beaches of Nome.

June 29, 1900. There was an early-morning street brawl out front of the Dexter. Officers arrested two of the combatants. Then Earp and other spectators moved in to free one of the prisoners.

"Wyatt Earp was likewise taken into custody," reported the *Nome Daily News.* "He is charged with interfering with an officer while in the discharge of his duty." Earp said he really was just trying to help the local marshal. Charges were dropped.

There were other scrapes with lawmen in Nome, according to Terrence Cole, one of Alaska's best historians. In one incident, Cole says, Earp was showing the boys how things were done down Arizona way. U.S. Marshal Albert Lowe stepped in, relieved Earp of his revolver, slapped his face, and told him to "go home or he would run him in."

By the fall of 1901 the Earps were ready to move on again. Earp sold his interest in the Dexter Saloon and he and Josie retired to California. Earp was almost eighty-one when he died peacefully at home in Los Angeles on January 13, 1929.

History does not record whether he was wearing his boots at the time.

✦ ✦ ✦

FAIRBANKS—I played Ping-Pong with Howard Hughes—well, sort of.

It was July 13, 1938. Hughes landed that afternoon at Weeks Field here on the next-to-last lap of his record-breaking flight around the world. His twin-engine Lockheed transport crossed the Bering Sea from Siberia and paused in Fairbanks to refuel. Hughes stayed only seventy-eight minutes, then flew on to Minneapolis and finally New York to complete his journey.

Just about the whole town turned out to welcome the millionaire aviator.

"The airport had all the aspects of a country carnival except pink lemonade," the *Fairbanks Daily News-Miner* reported.

Pink lemonade in my hometown? Not on your life.

Fairbanks residents crowd around Howard Hughes' plane during a fuel stop for the aviator's around-the-world flight in 1938. The Lockheed Electra's wings were filled with Ping-Pong balls for flotation during over-ocean legs of the flight. STANTON PATTY COLLECTION

Hughes, then age thirty-three, emerged from the plane, smiled, and posed for photographs. He visited planeside with Joe Crosson, one of Alaska's legendary bush pilots, and Mae Post, the widow of Wiley Post, who in 1933 had set the previous world-circling record. Wiley Post and Will Rogers, the cowboy philosopher and actor, had been killed in an air crash near the Eskimo village of Barrow, Alaska, in 1935.

Also on hand to greet Hughes was Fairbanks Mayor Les Nerland, one of my favorite Fairbanks dads. His son, Jerry, and I were among the kids at the scene.

As Fairbanksans crowded around the silvery plane, it suddenly "snowed" Ping-Pong balls. Hughes had filled the Lockheed's wings with 36,000 table-tennis balls to help provide flotation in case he was forced to ditch at sea. But after reaching Fairbanks, Hughes decided he didn't them any longer —so he opened the wings' inspection plates and jettisoned the little white balls.

The *News-Miner* said there was a "mad scramble" to retrieve them as souvenirs. I grabbed some and took them home. So did Jerry and his father.

Neither Jerry nor I can now find those precious mementos. They probably got discarded with my Superman comic books when we moved to our new house on Cowles Street.

✦ ✦ ✦

CARCROSS, Yukon Territory—There's a mother lode of gold-rush history in this little town in Canada's Yukon Territory—and in its pioneer cemetery.

Here is the grave of Kate Carmack, the Tagish Indian common-law wife of George Washington Carmack. Kate said it was she who discovered the bonanza in 1896 that began the gold rush to the Klondike. But it was George Carmack who got most of the credit when Klondike histories were written.

Close by Kate's resting place are the graves of Tagish Charley and Skookum Jim, Kate's brothers, who were with Carmack the day he discovered the gold. They also claimed to have made the Klondike gold discovery. We'll never know.

Here, too, is the grave of Polly the parrot, another survivor of the Klondike stampede. Polly has one of the most impressive bronze markers in the graveyard. The inscription on the parrot's monument—in rhyme, maybe composed during a beery wake:

Under this sod lies a sourdough parrot
Its heart was gold, pure fourteen carat,
Polly now can spread her wings,
Leaving behind all earthly things
She ranks in fame as our dear departed,
A just reward for being good hearted.

When Polly died in 1972 at the age of 125 or so, he or she was described in an Associated Press obituary as "the oldest, meanest, dirtiest bird north of the 60th Parallel." Nobody knew for sure if Polly was a boy or girl. The Carcross parrot usually was referred to as "he" in this "he-man" country. But that was before the women's movement meandered north. Polly is a "she" on the grave marker.

According to local lore, Polly arrived in the Yukon in 1898. The bird's first owner of record was a miner remembered as a Captain Alexander. The captain and his wife left Polly in the care of the Caribou Hotel in Carcross in 1918 when they departed for a visit to Vancouver, British Columbia. Sadly, their ship sank on the way south, and it was believed the Alexanders perished.

Polly stayed on at the Caribou for the rest of his or her celebrated life.

The parrot had a nasty temper—and an appalling vocabulary.

"Polly want a cracker?" asked unsuspecting visitors.

"Go to hell!" was Polly's stock reply.

I was the target of Polly's wrath in the parrot's somewhat golden years.

"Go to hell!" Polly shrieked one afternoon as I aimed a camera toward his or her cage in the lobby of the old Caribou.

"I heard you had mellowed, Polly, but I guess I was wrong."

There was a time when Polly also had a reputation as a hard drinker. Friends would pour Polly a few belts, and after awhile the inebriated bird would fall from its perch and sprawl on the bottom of the cage. But later Polly swore off booze—even learned to sing a few lines of "Onward, Christian Soldiers."

They found Polly deceased—"drumsticks up," said the Associated Press—on November 13, 1972. Telegrams of sympathy from Polly fans poured in from afar.

He or she was laid to rest in a small, velvet-lined casket as Johnnie Johns, a noted Yukon guide, sang Polly's favorite song, "I Love You Truly."

CHAPTER 13

UNSTOPPABLE WOMEN

EVA McGOWN

FAIRBANKS—"Come in, Dearie! Come in!"

It was wartime in Alaska. Eva McGown was on duty.

The World War II years crowded my hometown with thousands of soldiers, airmen, and construction workers. Housing was so tight that the military command took over the city's two largest hotels and several buildings on the neighboring University of Alaska campus.

Government officials tried to discourage GI wives from following their menfolk to the North Country. Many came anyway—and found an angel named Eva McGown.

Eva, a widow with a meager income, had a part-time job as Fairbanks's official hostess. Her office was a cluttered desk just off the lobby of the Nordale Hotel on Second Avenue. There she presided like a queen, wearing a wide-brimmed fruit-salad hat, a fuzzy pink stole, teardrop earrings, and several loops of imitation pearls. On anyone else the ensemble might have been ridiculous. On Eva, it was positively regal.

"Come in, Dearie," she would call to all who ventured into her corner of the lobby.

Often the visitors were military wives, newly arrived in Fairbanks, with babies in arms and other tykes tugging at their skirts. They were tired and discouraged. They had no place to stay. Somewhere along their disheartening searches for lodging, sympathetic Fairbanksans had suggested that the women "go see Eva McGown at the Nordale."

"God love you," Eva greeted one tearful military wife. "Everything will be all right, ye poor darlin'."

Eva jotted down an address, handed it to the young mother, and sent her on her way. When the woman was out of hearing range, Eva placed a telephone call and calmly announced to a surprised homeowner: "I'm sending the loveliest lass to spend the night at your house."

Then, before the startled citizen could decline, Eva hung up the telephone.

"There," she said with a smile as bright as the midnight sun. "There's always a way."

It was said that Eva carried an inventory in her head of all the spare bedrooms in Fairbanks. She also arranged for beds to be set up in church basements and auditoriums—sometimes even at the city jail.

One day a young woman arrived from England to wed an Air Force sergeant stationed at Ladd Field, on the outskirts of Fairbanks. Eva arranged the ceremony, filled St. Matthew's Episcopal Church with her own friends—and paid for the couple's hotel room for the wedding night.

Then there was the time that a young man entered the hotel with a giant husky in tow. He approached Eva shyly.

"Come in," Eva called. "There's plenty of room. My, he's just a puppy. Now what can I do for you?"

The caller needed lodging for himself—and the husky.

"We'll find something, Dearie," Eva said.

During a visit to Juneau, Alaska's capital city, Eva was introduced to a stranger.

"Oh, I know who you are—you're the lady who puts everyone to bed in Fairbanks!" the man exclaimed.

Few who met Eva McGown during those hectic times knew that the cheerful, pixie-like woman with the golden heart had experienced aching loneliness here.

Eva McGown,
in 1969—the
"can do" hostess
of Fairbanks.
STANTON PATTY
COLLECTION

In 1914, at the age of thirty-one, Eva Montgomery departed her native Belfast, Ireland, for the love of Arthur McGown, a part owner of the Model Cafe in Fairbanks. Yes, truth be known, Eva was a mail-order bride. She crossed the stormy Atlantic in what she described as "a filthy boat," then traveled by train to Seattle. There she boarded a steamer bound for Valdez, then spent more than a month on the trail in winter to reach Fairbanks. She traveled by horse-drawn sleigh and dogsled in bitter cold, staying nights in roadhouses that were little more than shacks.

"There were rough and tough men on the trail," Eva recalled. "But never a cursing word did they say in my hearing. They gave me hot bricks for my feet and wrapped furs around me."

Eva Montgomery and Arthur Louis McGown were married the night that Eva arrived in Fairbanks, February 26, 1914.

Fairbanks back then was a raw mining town—wooden sidewalks, muddy streets, rickety store buildings, riverboats, saloons, and brothels.

"At first, I asked myself, 'What am I doing here?'" Eva recalled. "Then I was taken by the beauty of Alaska, with its tall sentinel trees, pure white snow, and a glorious sky like a sea of glass on fire. I love Alaska with every bit of me—and I always will."

Arthur McGown died in 1930, the victim of a bone tumor. Eva was left a bewildered widow with almost no money.

"That's when I learned about loneliness," she said. "It's a heavier load than any woman should have to carry. In our little log cabin I heard no sound but the clock ticking and my own footsteps.

"Then came a day when I knew I must get busy. I went to the wee church, and I knelt down and said, 'Lord, I am ready.'"

Eva left the cabin and moved into the Nordale Hotel—Room 207—for the rest of her life. She supported herself by selling magazines and taking odd jobs until the topsy-turvy years of World War II, when Fairbanks put Eva on the payroll as the city's helpful hostess.

In 1953, Alaska's territorial governor, B. Frank Heintzleman, issued a proclamation naming Eva McGown Alaska's honorary hostess. It happened as Eva was being honored during a broadcast of the television program *This Is Your Life*.

A few years later, Eva became the first woman ever to win the Fairbanks Chamber of Commerce distinguished-service award. She stood on tiptoes to see over the lectern and told a cheering audience: "I never thought I would qualify for this. Now the only thing left is Heaven."

I've known Eva McGown all of my life—literally.

Other than my mother's voice, Eva's Irish trill probably was the first sound I heard the morning I was born. Mom said Eva brushed past the nurses at St. Joseph's Hospital and rushed to her bedside moments after I was placed in my mother's arms.

"God love you, Kay," Eva fairly shouted. "And who do we have here?"

Later in my young life, while I was learning to play trumpet in the school band, Eva drafted me for a duet in church. She would play the organ, and I was to follow along with the trumpet. The chosen hymn was "Onward, Christian Soldiers." I muffed a few notes, but Eva said we were a success. However, I don't remember anyone, not even my parents, requesting an encore.

Who says you can't go home again? I did, many times, while covering Alaska news for the *Seattle Times*. And the old Nordale Hotel was my base. Arne Lee, the longtime desk clerk, knew I was traveling on a skimpy expense account and always provided a bargain rate. He also told Eva when I'd be in town.

One July evening in 1970 I flew into Fairbanks from Prudhoe Bay, where I had been touring the fast-developing arctic oil field. I checked into my room at the Nordale, reviewed the Prudhoe Bay notes, and turned in early.

Next morning I found a message that Eva had slipped under my door:

Dear,

It's almost midnight—no light in your room. You were probably asleep.
Open your door first thing in the morning. I am leaving a plate of cookies
for you. I can't find the wee scotch that I know you like. Good night.

Love, Eva

Goodness. Eva even knew my brand of scotch. There were no secrets in
small-town Fairbanks.

Eva's Room 207 was a gathering place for friends. There she would serve
tea in fine-china cups, along with cookies—and sometimes a glass of sherry or
Irish Mist. The tiny hotel room was strewn with keepsakes and clothing; Eva's
spectacular hats, scarves, gloves, costume jewelry, fancy pillows, books, letters,
postcards, newspaper clippings, and faded photographs. And there was a little
hot plate that Eva used to cook her morning porridge.

Even Eva's bed was covered with garments and mementos. There seemed
to be no place for her to sleep. We figured that maybe she just pushed things
aside at night and slipped under a blanket.

The clutter may have cost Eva her life. On the night of February 22,
1972, the Nordale Hotel caught fire. Eva McGown, age eighty-eight, was
trapped in her room and died in the flames that destroyed the hotel.
Investigators said she probably couldn't find her door key in time to escape.

In the rubble, they discovered the hotel safe. It contained a small box
belonging to Eva. Inside were a clump of soil and several pieces of dried Irish
moss—wee bits of Ireland that Eva kept with her all those years in Fairbanks.

✦ ✦ ✦

SUSAN BUTCHER

FAIRBANKS—The first time I met Susan Butcher she was kissing a newborn
husky.

"I always do this with a new litter of pups," she said. "I make sure mine is
the first voice they hear and then I blow my breath into their mouths. That's
how we bond."

The bonding technique must be working. Susan Butcher, her dogs' best friend, has won the tough Iditarod Trail Sled Dog Race four times—and mushed a dog team to the top of Mount McKinley, the highest peak in North America.

"I love all of my dogs," she said. "They're my pets, not just sled dogs."

During an interview with a national magazine writer a few years ago, the Massachusetts-born musher recalled being teased by schoolmates because she suffered from a learning disorder called dyslexia. She was unable to recognize most written words.

"I spelled god 'd-o-g,'" she said. "Dogs didn't care whether I was dyslectic or not."

Susan grew accustomed to having to prove herself, especially when she began competing in Alaska sled-dog races—once considered a sport for he-men only. The male mushers used to snigger about the way Susan pampered her dogs. Now the guys cringe when someone reminds them of a popular bumper sticker seen around Alaska:

"Alaska—where men are men and women win the Iditarod."

Susan wasn't the first woman to win the Anchorage-to-Nome Iditarod race. That was Libby Riddles, who conquered the trail in 1985. Libby never won again.

It was six minutes after midnight on March 13, 1986, when thirty-year-old Susan Butcher won her first Iditarod. She reached the finish line on Nome's Front Street in a record time of eleven days, eighteen hours, and six minutes for the 1,049-mile distance. First prize was fifty thousand dollars. She won the next two years, then again in 1990.

Susan might have been first in 1991, too, but surrendered the lead that year to protect her dogs from a savage blizzard. Her archrival, Rick Swenson, winner of five Iditarod races, pushed on through the storm and won the race. Swenson told reporters that Susan, who placed third, was "too soft."

"It hurt to lose, but taking care of the dogs was the most important thing to me," Susan told me.

In 1979, Joe Redington Sr.—known as the father of the Iditarod—asked Susan if she wanted to join him in climbing Mount McKinley with a team of sled dogs.

"Sounds good to me," Susan said.

And so they set off on a forty-one-day journey to the summit of 20,320-foot-high Mount McKinley. Along the way, they were pinned down by a

Susan Butcher,
Iditarod
champion,
cuddles a
newborn husky
at her Fairbanks
kennel.

storm with winds estimated at one hundred miles an hour. Susan huddled with the dogs as the wind howled. With the two mushers were Ray Genet, a veteran mountain guide, and Rob Stapleton, an Anchorage photographer.

It was Memorial Day—May 28, 1979—when they mushed four of the dogs to the rooftop of the continent.

"I've always been a great believer in dogs," Redington said.

Then Genet, who had a fiery temper, asked Joe how he planned to steer the dogs down to sea level.

"I don't know," Redington said. "I've been so busy trying to get 'em up here I haven't figured out how we're going to get 'em down."

Lew Freedman, author of the Redington biography *Father of the Iditarod,* said Genet reacted by flailing his ice ax "in a fit." Freedman also quoted Stapleton as saying: "Joe had trained the dogs to go. They hadn't been trained to stop."

It was tricky going, but somehow all descended the mountain safely.

In 1994, Susan announced her retirement from the Iditarod. The next year she and her mushing husband, Dave Monson, welcomed their first child, a daughter, Tekla—named for Susan's lead dog that toiled to the top of Mount McKinley. Two of Susan's faithful lead dogs—Tekla and Granite—were ring bearers when Susan and Dave were married.

"Both of the dogs are gone now," Susan said. "But we have lots of their descendants."

One recent summer day I saw Susan waiting on the bank of the Chena River in Fairbanks to greet passengers cruising aboard the sternwheeler *Discovery III*. The paddleboat paused alongside Susan and David's Trailbreaker Kennel. Then, with a wireless microphone beamed to the vessel's loudspeaker system, Susan told the travelers about her adventures on the Iditarod Trail.

Like the time she and her dog team crashed through a patch of ice on the Yukon River and almost drowned. They went on and finished the race.

As she talked, huskies of all ages dashed around the kennel like kids at play. Susan caught one of the high-energy puppies and gave it a hug and a kiss.

"I guess I've done OK," said Susan Butcher, one of Alaska's all-time great athletes.

✦ ✦ ✦

SADIE NEAKOK

BARROW—Sadie Neakok was on the roof of her little frame house in Barrow, digging through a stack of frozen fish and caribou for her family's supper, when the president of the United States called. The rooftop pantry was the Eskimo woman's outdoor freezer for arctic winters.

She descended a ladder and went to the telephone.

"Where is this call from?" Sadie asked the operator.

"The White House."

"I thought somebody might be pulling my leg," Sadie recalled, "but then a man's voice asked if I was Mrs. Sadie Neakok. He asked some more questions and then said: 'I think you would be the right person to come to my conference.'"

There was a pause.

Sadie Neakok stands on the roof of her home in Barrow in 1971 to gather frozen arctic char for her family's dinner.

"Who am I talking to?" Sadie asked.

"The president."

It was.

President Richard M. Nixon was telephoning District Judge Sadie Neakok of Barrow to invite her to attend a White House conference on children's nutrition. "I can come," Sadie told the president.

Later, in Washington, D.C., she apologized to Nixon for "seeming kind of impatient."

"I had been in court all day," she said. "I thought it might be the FBI calling about a post office break-in we had in July."

Sadie Brower Neakok, one of Alaska's most distinguished women, was born into two cultures near the top of the world. Her father, Charles D. Brower, a native of New York City, was the first white settler in Barrow.

Brower, who was known widely as the King of the Arctic, established a trading post in Barrow village in 1884 to serve whaling fleets that were roaming the Far North.

Barrow (sometimes mistakenly called Point Barrow) is America's farthest-north community. The Eskimo town huddles on the shore of the Arctic Ocean at 71 degrees north, only about eleven hundred miles from the North Pole.

Brower made sure that his daughter had a proper western education in California. Sadie also was reared in the ways of her Eskimo mother, Asianggataq, who taught her to hunt and sew.

I met Sadie in 1971. She was a small woman of fifty-five then, with dark eyes that seemed to burn from an inner fire. She already had a reputation as a fierce advocate for Alaska's native peoples. She won the right for the Inupiaq (Eskimo) language to be the language of the court in cases where the defendants were unable to understand English. She also refused to handle cases against Eskimos who exercised their aboriginal rights to hunt caribou and other wildlife for their families. Such subsistence hunting, she said, was necessary for good nutrition.

Once, when a storm washed a villager's body out of its grave, a call went out for Sadie. State and federal agencies refused to help pay for reburial. Sadie fashioned a new coffin out of some leftover lumber and lined it with tent cloth. She was digging the grave herself when her husband and a local police officer arrived to help finish the task.

In 1960, when Alaska was a brand new state, Sadie was appointed magistrate for Barrow. Later she was advanced to the position of district court judge. Her district stretched from Barter Island, near Alaska's eastern border with Canada, down to Point Lay, on the west coast of Alaska. Sometimes her caseload was so heavy and her court facilities so meager that Sadie threatened to quit—and one day she did.

Tundra Times, the statewide native newspaper, told the story in 1978:

"I didn't have a [court] reporter," Sadie complained. "They gave me a clerk for 15 hours a week and I used her up the first day.

"My kitchen was my courthouse. And I was sweeping out the jail because there was no one else to do it.

"I just walked out until somebody woke up to the fact that I meant business."

George Boney, then chief justice of the Alaska Supreme Court, called and asked Sadie to return to the bench. Boney began his attempt at friendly persuasion by calling Sadie "Honey."

"Don't you 'Honey' me unless you have some kind of solution," Sadie replied.

Relief was granted, and Judge Sadie went back to work.

Sadie Neakok agonized over the difficulties her fellow Eskimos faced in making the transition from nomadic ways to the white man's cash economy. Before she donned a judge's robes, she spent several years as a teacher and social worker in Barrow.

"I got involved in the welfare of my people when I began visiting their homes," she told me as we walked a beach by the village, where icy waves crashed ashore with a gloomy cadence.

"The people here were so poor," she said. "They lived on what they could scrounge. Some homes were never really warm. Some of the people didn't have enough fuel, not even driftwood, to melt snow or ice for water."

Later, when Sadie became Barrow's magistrate, she decided the position would give her an opportunity "to get a fair deal for my people."

"They needed somebody who would understand their problems," she said. "Someone coming in from the Lower 48 and not knowing the people and our ways that have been handed on for generations couldn't do it."

Sadie stopped walking, looked back toward her village, and sighed.

"If I have to, I can be very severe in court," she said. "The people understand that I have to be that way sometimes. I try to explain fully why I am sentencing a person—that sometimes it's for their own good."

Sadie could be creative in court, too.

Case in point: the 1960 Barrow Duck-in.

It involved a confrontation between the Eskimos, who depended on migrating waterfowl for food, and zealous state game wardens.

"I want to know about it when someone gets arrested," Sadie told Eben Hopson, a state legislator from Barrow. "That will be the day when everyone here is going to get a duck from his neighbor and stand in front of the game warden. The only way to solve this is to have everybody arrested and see how it comes out."

It happened, just as Sadie hoped it would: one hundred and fifty Barrow Eskimos were arrested in one day and charged with illegal possession of migratory birds. The case was to be heard in a rented theater, with all defendants present.

Governor William A. Egan intervened. All charges were dropped. End of case.

Sadie Brower married Nate Neakok, a Bureau of Indian Affairs mechanic. They had twelve children. In 1968 she was named Alaska's mother of the year. In 1968 she received an honorary doctor of laws degree from the University of Alaska.

And about that telephone call from the president . . .

Sadie did go to Washington as requested and met with President Nixon.

"It was a great honor," she said.

And then she returned home and climbed the ladder to the rooftop to rummage through the cache of frozen fish and caribou for her family's supper.

◆ ◆ ◆

ETTA JONES

ALEUTIAN ISLANDS—It was a sunshine morning in August 1941—four months before the Japanese attack on Pearl Harbor—when Etta Jones first saw the island of Attu from the deck of a Coast Guard cutter.

"The American flag flew from the village flagpole," she recalled. "The village looked neat and serene, with well-painted houses and a beautiful, little white church."

Ten months later, Etta Jones would see the Japanese flag flying over the tiny village, also called Attu, at the tip of the Aleutian Islands. Her husband, Charles Foster Jones, would be murdered by Japanese soldiers. She and the fifty-seven Aleuts of Attu would be on their way to prisoner-of-war camps in Japan.

What happened at Attu, to the Joneses and to the Aleut people they loved, is a story that never has been told in full. Over a period of several years I searched government records and interviewed veterans of the Aleutian campaign to collect clues. But there was little solid information.

Then one day, paydirt! Lulu Fairbanks, a family friend and longtime Alaska journalist, called me at the *Seattle Times*

"I heard that you want to know about Etta Jones," Lulu said. "Well, I think I can help. Etta is gone now. I spent some time with her here in Seattle right after the war ended."

Lulu guided me to Emma Lambert, then residing in Seattle, who had met

Etta Jones while serving as a government nurse in Alaska. Lambert suggested I get in touch with Eleanor Meyers, Jones's niece, in Michigan.

I wrote to Meyers. Yes, she replied, she had her late aunt's scrapbook and was willing to lend me some of the letters and keepsakes that Jones had saved from the tragic wartime years. Lulu Fairbanks added more details.

Finally, I was able to piece together Etta Jones's story.

Etta Jones was captured by Japanese forces in the Aleutian Islands in World War II. STANTON PATTY COLLECTION

Etta Jones and her husband were nearing retirement when the Coast Guard delivered them to Attu. She was to be Attu's new schoolteacher. Her husband— she called him Foster—was assigned as the village weather observer. The couple already had spent twenty years serving other Alaska communities with the Indian Service of the U.S. Department of Interior.

December 7, 1941: Japanese warplanes bombed Pearl Harbor. Alaska tensed for an attack.

"But life goes on very peacefully here," Etta Jones wrote relatives.

"'Don't go to Attu,' our friends warned us as we left Seattle. We laughed at them. What would Japan want with Attu?"

Attu was unarmed, except for a couple of shotguns that villagers used for bird hunting. Mike Hodikoff, the Attu chief, a bright, brawny man, much admired by the Joneses, assured the couple that no Japanese scouts had been spotted on the island.

"We would know," Hodikoff said. "This is our home."

Nevertheless, the Joneses were advised that an American military vessel would arrive in a few weeks to evacuate all Attu residents.

Sunday, June 7, 1942.

About eleven o'clock that morning an Attu woman named Martha hurried to Etta Jones, spun the teacher around, and pointed excitedly to the hills above the village.

"Japs coming!" Martha shouted.

"They were swarming down like an army of ants!" Etta Jones recalled. They must have surrounded the island in their landing barges, closing in from all sides at once. Such a waste of effort. One rowboat could have come in through the open harbor and encountered no resistance.

"Bullets began raining through the windows. . . . At almost the moment of their [the Japanese] arrival, Foster had been trying to send the weather report through to Dutch Harbor on his regular eleven o'clock schedule.

"Now he added something else. Four words. 'The Japs are here.'"

Quickly, Etta Jones thrust all letters and reports she could find into the fireplace. Her husband smashed his radio. Japanese bullets still were hammering Attu village when Charles Foster Jones prepared to leave their village house and surrender to the invaders. Just then, a Japanese soldier smashed through the door and thrust a bayonet toward Etta Jones's stomach.

"The soldier kept saying, over and over, 'Do not cry. Do not cry,'" she said. "I had no intention of crying.

"The whole world seemed to whirl and totter. I knew in my heart that I would never see Foster again."

Several days later, Etta Jones was told she would be transported to Japan as a prisoner. It was while saying good-bye to her beloved Aleuts that she learned of her husband's death.

"We buried Mr. Jones near the church," one of the villagers whispered.

Etta Jones was confused and angry. Each day on Attu a Japanese guard had told her, "Your husband is well. He sends his love." But the truth was that he had been executed shortly after being taken prisoner.

"I was put into a launch and taken to a big ship outside the harbor," she said. "On the floor of the launch was something I tried not to see, but it kept burning itself into my eyes, into the very core of me. It was the American flag, torn to ribbons and rubbed in the bilge and dirt of the launch."

In Japan she was placed with eighteen Australian nurses who had been captured in New Guinea. The women were moved through a series of prison camps for the next three years. Food was skimpy, but Etta Jones said she was treated kindly by her guards.

"Perhaps because of my white hair," she said.

With a teacher's foresight, she had packed crayons, drawing paper, and other school supplies among her belongings from Attu. The Aussie nurses joined with their American friend each holiday to make table decorations. Wax-crayon drawings of turkeys, cranberry sauce, and other treats of the season decorated the table for their first Christmas dinner. No matter that rice was all they had to eat.

In my files is a little note on school paper that an Australian nurse handed Etta Jones in 1944. It must have been the Fourth of July.

"Mrs. Jones," the nurse had written, "my message to you today is, 'By next Independence Day you will be back home in America.'"

The prophecy almost was correct. It was August 11, 1945, when Etta Jones was freed by American troops in a village near Yokohama. Soon after, she arrived in Seattle for a visit with her friend Lulu Fairbanks.

"She was such a wonderful lady," Lulu told me. "I took Etta to a restaurant on Pike Street in Seattle. . . . I asked her what food she missed most in the prison camps. 'Mince pie,' she said, 'but I haven't had rich food in so long and I fear I couldn't hold it down.' So we settled for a waffle."

Etta Jones worried about her Aleut friends. She heard that they had been interned on Japan's northern island of Hokkaido and that many had died there. Official records show that of the fifty-seven Attu natives taken prisoner by the Japanese, twenty-two died in the Hokkaido prison camps. The dead included Chief Mike Hodikoff.

Lulu Fairbanks asked Frank Lakinoff, one of the surviving Aleuts, where Charles Foster Jones had been buried at Attu after being executed by the Japanese invaders. Lakinoff, who had helped dig Jones's grave, sketched a map showing the grave ten feet to the left from Attu's Russian Orthodox church.

That was exactly where a U.S. military graves-registration team found Jones's remains in 1948. He rests now in the post cemetery at Fort Richardson, on the outskirts of Anchorage.

On Pearl Harbor Day in 1945, Interior Secretary Harold L. Ickes handed Etta Jones a check for $7,374.21. It was her back pay as an Indian Office teacher at Attu, and included a bonus for valor. The Interior Department news release noted that she was the only white woman to be taken prisoner on American soil in World War II.

Etta Jones died December 12, 1965, in Bradenton, Florida, at the age of eighty-six.

The village of Attu no longer exists.

✦ ✦ ✦

AND SOME MORE of the many unstoppable women of Alaska:

✦ ✦ ✦

RUTH ALLMAN, *keeper of history.*

FOR MORE THAN twenty-five years, Ruth Allman served travelers generous helpings of history—and sourdough waffles—at the House of Wickersham in Juneau. The gracious Victorian home once belonged to Judge James Wickersham, Alaska's colorful delegate to Congress in territorial times. Wickersham in 1916 introduced the first Alaska statehood bill in Congress, but it would be 1959 before Alaska would win statehood. Ruth Allman, Wickersham's devoted niece, maintained the historic hilltop home on a meager budget, and made certain that visitors knew about her uncle's remarkable life. Ruth Allman died in 1989.

✦ ✦ ✦

EDITH BULLOCK, *frontier businesswoman.*

EDITH BULLOCK ARRIVED in Alaska in 1939 and found a job as a bookkeeper for a gold-mining camp near Nome. By the 1950s, as president of B&R Tug and Barge, she was the world's only female tugboat operator in arctic waters. The company was based in the Eskimo community of Kotzebue, just north of the Arctic Circle. Bullock also served two terms in Alaska's territorial House of Representatives and was a University of Alaska regent. She died in 1994.

✦ ✦ ✦

LILLIAN CROSSON, *bush pilot's wife.*

ONE DAY IN 1930 Lillian Osborne stepped into the cockpit of an open-cock-pit plane for a flight from Fairbanks to Nenana. At the controls was Joe Crosson, one of Alaska's best-known bush pilots. They were flying secretly to

Nenana to be married—to avoid a noisy shivaree by Joe's fellow pilots back in Fairbanks. It was Crosson who flew to Barrow in 1935 to retrieve the bodies of two of his friends, pioneer aviator Wiley Post and humorist Will Rogers, who died when Post's plane stalled and crashed in a lagoon near the arctic village. Joe Crosson died in 1949 of a heart attack at the age of forty-six. Lillian went on from this tragedy to raise the couple's four children and to open a Seattle travel agency that she ran for more than thirty years. Lillian Crosson, now in her nineties, represents dozens of courageous wives of early-day Alaska aviators—women who endured lonely days and nights in frontier towns while their husbands flew dangerous missions. I also should report that Lillian was one of my baby-sitters in Fairbanks. I hope I was on my best behavior. She won't say.

✦ ✦ ✦

JOSEPHINE CRUMRINE, artist.

PROBABLY THE PROUDEST footnote an Alaskan dog owner could add to the pedigree of a husky or malamute would read: "Painted by Josephine Crumrine."

Josephine Crumrine paints an Alaskan sled dog.

Jo Crumrine has painted a gallery of handsome sled dogs for dozens of clients. However, some of her best-known paintings of these dogs adorned menu covers that were featured aboard Alaska Steamship Company passenger vessels in the days before mega-liners. The menus are treasures for collectors. Josephine Crumrine Liddell is the shy artist's full name; her late husband was Robert Liddell, an Alaska businessman. A personal note: Jo painted three of our beloved huskies, teasing them into poses with bits of hamburger while she sketched and painted. Those huskies are gone now, but the paintings are reminders of wonderful times.

✦ ✦ ✦

DALE DeARMOND, artist.

MANY OF ALASKA'S master painters have portrayed Alaska on a grand scale, with dramatic landscapes and seascapes. Dale DeArmond does it with exquisite woodcuts that capture ticks of time in Alaska's long history. It might be a print of a little Russian Orthodox church that seems to leaning into a southeaster. Or of a single-minded raven that appears to be busy building a mountain—as in a favorite Tlingit Indian legend of how Raven created the world. Many of Dale's subjects are based on long-treasured legends of Southeastern Alaska's Tlingit and Haida Indians. She treats their stories with deep respect, and as the native peoples often do, also with gentle whimsy. There is another distinguished DeArmond, Dale's husband, Robert. Bob DeArmond is one of Alaska's most-honored historians, a man who has generously redirected my writings from errant places over the years.

✦ ✦ ✦

NEVA EGAN, Alaska's first first lady.

NEVA EGAN CAME to Valdez from Kansas in 1937 to teach school. She intended to stay only one year "to see what Alaska was like." But romance changed her plans. In 1940 she married William A. (Bill) Egan, a Valdez lad—who years later would be elected the new state of Alaska's first governor. Bill Egan died in 1984. "I love Alaska so much that I can't find words to

**Alaska Governor
William Egan
and Neva Egan
in 1963.** JAPAN
AIR LINES PHOTO

describe my feelings," Neva Egan told me one day as we cruised the fiords of Southeastern Alaska aboard one of the state ferries that her husband had commissioned when he was governor. Alaskans feel the same way about their gracious first first lady.

✦ ✦ ✦

ADA BLACKJACK JOHNSON, *arctic heroine.*

IN 1972, I MET a tiny Eskimo woman from Alaska who was the only survivor of an ill-fated expedition to the Soviet Arctic in 1921. Not until our interview had she been willing to tell about that tragedy. She was close to tears as we talked. The story: Vilhjalmur Stefansson, the noted arctic explorer, had hired Ada Blackjack (later Johnson) as a seamstress for a four-man party that was instructed to colonize Wrangel Island, eighty-five miles off the northeastern coast of Siberia. Wrangel Island was disputed territory. Czarist Russia had claimed the island in 1916 and the Soviet Union continued the claim. Expeditions representing both the United States and Great Britain had made feeble claims to Wrangel Island many years before. Stefansson hoped his 1921 plan for colonization—defying the Soviet Union—would cause England (or maybe Canada) to exercise a definitive claim. But Stefansson's scheme failed. A supply vessel for the little expedition was unable to smash through the pack ice and reach Wrangel Island in 1922. Ada and the four men were stranded and low on food. Three of the men set off on foot in a desperate attempt to reach Alaska. They never were seen again. "Maybe they fell through the ice, or maybe they were killed by the Russians—I don't know," Ada said. Ada nursed the last man until he died of scurvy in June 1923. Only Ada Blackjack was alive when a rescue vessel arrived two months later. Ada Blackjack Johnson died in 1983 at age eighty-five. Her son, Billy Johnson, placed a plaque on her grave in Anchorage: "The heroine of Wrangel Island." Wrangel Island remains Russian territory today.

✦ ✦ ✦

MARGARET (MARDY) MURIE, *conservationist.*

MARDY MURIE LIVED more than one hundred years, and spent most of those years fighting to preserve the wild lands of Alaska. Admirers have described her as the spiritual grandmother of America's conservation movement. She was reared in Alaska, and with her late husband, Olaus Murie, a noted biologist, was instrumental in establishing national parks and national refuges across Alaska. Mardy Murie also had the distinction of being the first female graduate of the University of Alaska. That was in 1924. The university followed in 1976 with an honorary Doctor of Humane Letters degree for the indomitable Mardy Murie. She died in October, 2003 at age 101.

CHAPTER 14

DAN McGREW, SAM McGEE, AND THE LADY KNOWN AS LOU

DAWSON CITY, Yukon Territory—It is quiet now in the Klondike. Weeds and willows hide the scars where miners tore at frozen gravels during the great gold rush more than a hundred years ago. Bonanza Creek, the little stream that surrendered the first precious nuggets, still wanders through the valley of the Klondike River.

Some say ghosts of the goldfields still roam the dusty streets of Dawson City:

- George Washington Carmack, the ornery prospector who said he was first to find the gold, then after striking it rich abandoned his Indian wife.
- Robert Henderson, the loner whose bigotry cost him a fortune.
- Klondike Kate, Diamond Tooth Gertie, the Oregon Mare, Gussie Lamore, and other dance-hall queens who parted the miners from

their hard-won gold. Gertie sported a flashy diamond between two of her front teeth.

■ And Robert Service, the shy stranger who told the stories of the stampede with rousing rhymes. With lyrics such as these, from "The Shooting of Dan McGrew":

A bunch of the boys were whooping it up
   in the Malamute Saloon;
The kid that handles the music-box
   was hitting a jag-time tune;
Back of the bar, in a solo game,
   sat Dangerous Dan McGrew,
And watching his luck was his light o' love,
   the lady that's known as Lou.

Up on Eighth Avenue, on a hillside above the boardwalks and saloons of old Dawson, there is a little log cabin framed with birches and alders and flaming fireweed. That is my destination on a fine summer afternoon. I hike up Church Street, pausing along the way to catch my breath. I look back and see the Yukon River surging by the city of gold toward the faraway Bering Sea. The river here is the color of coffee au lait, laden with particles of ground-up rock and mud chiseled by distant glaciers. I continue toward the cabin, and hear a cheerful medley of bird songs.

I also hear the bothersome buzz of Yukon mosquitoes.

Slap! One down. Slap! Slap!

Visitors are gathered by the little cabin. They have come to hear Robert Service's ballads about such gold-rush characters as Sam McGee from Tennessee, Dangerous Dan McGrew, and the Lady that's known as Lou. It's all make-believe, of course.

Well, maybe not.

A slender, slope-shouldered man wearing a black bow tie, a frock coat, and matching trousers walks from the cabin and settles into a rocking chair made of braided willow twigs.

The ghost of Robert Service?

Not today.

This is Tom Byrne, an actor from British Columbia, maybe the best

Tom Byrne recites rousing Robert Service verses by Service's cabin in Dawson City

interpreter ever of Service's ballads. He leans forward in the rocker, and in a voice trembling with excitement, begins telling about the bard of the Yukon who used to live in the little log cabin.

"Robert Service found his gold in the beauty of the north, and put that beauty into words for us to enjoy," Byrne says, reciting from "The Spell of the Yukon":

> It's the great, big broad land 'way up yonder,
> It's the forests where silence has lease;
> It's the beauty that thrills me with wonder,
> It's the stillness that fills me with peace. . . .

**Robert Service,
bard of the
Klondike.**
STANTON PATTY
COLLECTION

"Robert Service could be a man of mirth, too," says Tom Byrne. "This is one of my favorites, and it may be yours, too."

There are strange things done in the midnight sun
by the men who moil for gold;
The Arctic trails have their secret tales
That would make your blood run cold;
The Northern Lights have seen queer sights,
But the queerest they ever did see
Was the night on the marge of Lake Lebarge
I cremated Sam McGee. . . .

Many in the hushed audience know the lines that begin "The Cremation of Sam McGee." Some even lip-synch the familiar verses as Byrne describes

194

how Sam McGee from Tennessee finally found warmth in the frozen north "in the heart of a furnace roar."

The crowd laughs and applauds. Byrne smiles. "Wonderful fun," he says.

"Now I want to tell you more about Robert Service," he says. "The first thing you should know is that Mr. Service was not here to witness the momentous gold rush to the Klondike. He wrote most of his famous poems before arriving in Dawson City."

Well, there goes the legend.

But wait, the real story of Robert Service may be better.

✦ ✦ ✦

ROBERT WILLIAM SERVICE, the man who immortalized the Klondike gold rush, was born in England, reared mostly in Scotland. He was a bashful boy, given to daydreaming and reading. He was trained in banking, but found that occupation unexciting. In 1896, Service traveled to Canada, then drifted along the American West Coast, working at various jobs: spreading manure on a cattle ranch, picking oranges, milking cows, clerking in a store, washing dishes for a cafe, and working as a gardener at a San Diego bordello.

Flat broke and jobless, Service landed in Vancouver, British Columbia, in 1903 and decided he might as well give banking a try. He applied rather diffidently to the Canadian Imperial Bank of Commerce and, to his surprise, was hired.

As Service was rambling through the West, doing his best to prove a failure at anything that didn't hold his interest, big things were happening up in the Klondike.

August 16, 1896: George Carmack, a drifter from California, and his Tagish Indian companions were at their fish camp at the mouth of the Klondike River. With Carmack were Kate Carmack, his common-law Indian wife, and Kate's brothers, Skookum Jim and Tagish Charley. Along came Robert Henderson, a veteran prospector far from his native Nova Scotia.

"I'm going up the Klondike," Henderson told Carmack. Then he described a possible show of gold on a creek that empties into the Klondike—known then as Rabbit Creek, later renamed Discovery Creek.

Dawson-born Pierre Berton, the Klondike historian, says their conversation went something like this:

A croupier spins a roulette wheel at Diamond Tooth Gertie's in Dawson City.

"What are the chances to locate up there?" Carmack asked. "Everything staked?"

Henderson glanced at Skookum Jim and Tagish Charley and uttered the remark that probably cost him a fortune.

"There's a chance for you, George," Henderson said, "but I don't want any damn siwashes [Indians] staking on that creek." Henderson soon would regret that insult.

Next day, the Carmack party made the amazing gold discovery near what now is Dawson City—and triggered the Klondike stampede. It isn't clear who found the gold. Carmack insisted he did. Tagish elders say it was Skookum Jim.

"At any rate," writes Pierre Berton, "the gold was there, lying thick between the flaky slabs of rock like cheese in a sandwich."

Carmack hurried downriver to register rich claims for himself and Jim and Charley. He told other prospectors about the great discovery, but didn't send word to Robert Henderson.

"Gold!"

At first it was a whisper—then a shout heard 'round the world.

A city of gold—Dawson City—sprouted where the Klondike River joins the fabled Yukon River in Canada about 260 miles south of the Arctic Circle. In less than two years, it grew to be the largest city north of San Francisco and west of Winnipeg.

More than a hundred thousand gold-crazed argonauts set out for the Klondike—scrambling over mountain passes thundering with avalanches, crowding aboard leaky steamships and riverboats, rafting raging rivers, trudging across crevasse-pocked glaciers.

"There has been nothing like it since, and there can never be anything like it again," Pierre Berton says of the gold-rush madness.

The National Park Service estimates that fifty thousand stampeders reached the promised land by way of Alaskan and Canadian routes. But by the time they arrived, most of the best claims already had been staked. Still, desperate miners drove shafts into the Klondike muck, battling clouds of mosquitoes in summer and killing cold in winter.

In the end, only about three hundred found enough gold to be considered wealthy—and only

Gold nuggets from the Klondike.

thirty managed to hang on to the riches for the rest of their years. Many emptied their pokes here for Diamond Tooth Gertie and her co-workers.

"The poor ginks have just gotta spend it, they just can't help themselves," Gertie said of the lonely miners.

Dawson City ran wild until most of the easy gold was gone. Then the prospectors moved on, to new goldfields—to Nome in 1899 and 1900, to Fairbanks in 1902 and 1903. Dawson City faded like a tattered dream.

Robert Service missed it all.

In 1904 the Canadian bank transferred Service to Whitehorse, in the Yukon, where gold-rush tales, tall and true, still were being heard on the north wind. Fortune was about to open a golden door for the reluctant bank teller.

In Whitehorse one day a friend asked Service to write a ditty for a church social. Seeking a quiet place to compose the words, Service returned after banking hours to his teller's station and began writing. It was a Saturday night, and he could hear in the background the sounds of honky-tonk pianos and merry voices from saloons down the street. The first line came quickly: "A bunch of the boys were whooping it up in the Malamute Saloon. . . ."

But Service forgot to tell a nervous night watchman that he would be working that night at the bank. The guard heard noises back by the teller cage, drew his revolver, and fired.

"Fortunately, he was a poor shot," Service said later, "or 'The Shooting of Dan McGrew' might never have been written."

"Anyhow," Service added, "with the sensation of a bullet whizzing past my head, and a detonation ringing in my ears, the ballad was achieved."

"Dan McGrew" proved too racy for the church program. But soon after, with publication of several of his poems, Service was on his way to fame and fortune—and Dawson City.

In 1908 the Canadian Imperial Bank of Commerce transferred Service to Dawson, about three hundred miles north of Whitehorse. Fellow employees welcomed him as a celebrity but were surprised to find the shy poet not at all like the characters in his bawdy ballads. Service never was "one of the boys." He kept mostly to himself, preferring solitary hikes in the hills back of town to evenings of whiskey and poker, then returning to his cabin to write the lively gold-rush ballads.

Service quit the bank the next year to write full time. And the little log cabin where Tom Byrne recites the rhymes of Robert Service on a sunny summer afternoon became Service's home until 1912, when the bard departed the Yukon forever.

He loved the cabin. "Everything was snug and shipshape," he wrote later. "I would not have exchanged my cabin for the palace of a king." In "Rhymes of a Rolling Stone," he wrote:

O, dear little cabin, I've loved you so long,
And now I must bid you good-bye!
Yet well do I know, as I quit you to-night,
It's Youth that I'm leaving behind. . . .

These days a visitor isn't likely to travel far in Canada's Yukon Territory without hearing a Robert Service ballad. Motorcoach drivers spin Service's tales of the northern trails while rolling along Yukon highways with flocks of summer tourists. Tour guides bow their heads and invoke "The Spell of the Yukon" as they stop by the Bonanza Creek discovery site on the outskirts of Dawson City. Misty-eyed entertainers recite Robert Service poems during variety shows in Whitehorse, in Dawson City, and across the border in neighboring Alaska.

Alaskans claim the Yukon bard as a favorite son, one of their own. Truth is, Alaska never was on Service's itinerary. Far as I know, he never set foot in Alaska.

It doesn't matter. Nobody captured the spirit of the north better than Robert Service. And nobody recaptures it better than Tom Byrne at the little log cabin on Eighth Avenue as he breathes new life into such classics as "The Spell of the Yukon":

It's the cussedest land that I know,
From the big, dizzy mountains that screen it
    To the deep, deathlike valleys below.
Some say God was tired when He made it;
    Some say it's a fine land to shun;
Maybe; but there's some as would trade it
    For no land on earth—and I'm one.

What is it about the Yukon that calls men such as Robert Service and Tom Byrne?

"I can't really explain it," Byrne says. "But I know that it's something that gets a grip on you. You just feel closer to nature, closer to God."

How did Service find this magic?

"Robert Service was a good listener, but he did tend to twist stories around a bit," Byrne says.

Case in point: "The Cremation of Sam McGee."

The ballad tells of a luckless miner, Sam McGee, from Tennessee, who froze to death on the shore of Lake Lebarge, not far from Dawson City. A companion sighted the wreck of a steamer, the *Alice May,* and decided then and there to cremate poor Sam in the vessel's boiler.

The real Sam McGee—a name that Service plucked from a Whitehorse bank ledger—was anything but pleased when the poem was published. It seems that Service needed a name to rhyme with Tennessee. Sam's was handy.

There really was a Yukon steamboat named *Olive May* (Service called it the *Alice May*) that had been beached for the winter by Lake Lebarge (also spelled Leberge). It's also true that a North West Mounted Police physician came across a prospector who had died of scurvy. The doctor decided to utilize the Olive May's firebox as a crematorium.

I heard the story in 1976 from Earl Sugden, of Seattle, grandson of the Mountie who did the deed on the marge of Lake Lebarge. His grandfather was Leonard Sugden, surgeon-general of the North West Mounted Police. It was the middle of winter, and the Mountie was faced with a problem. The ground was frozen, so he couldn't dig a grave. Cremation seemed to be the only choice. So the doctor went aboard the steamer, asked the crew to fire up the boiler, and performed his grisly task.

"Later," Earl Sugden told me, "Robert Service spent a winter with my grandfather in Whitehorse and heard the story of the cremation from him. And that is how 'The Cremation of Sam McGee' came to be written. That's the truth."

As I write this, I am listening to a rare recording of Robert Service, late in life, reciting some of his rhymes. His pace is slow and measured, as in a soliloquy. He apologizes for sounding like an "old chap." But his voice is strong and filled with emotion. Often, he ascends a crescendo and ends on a high note, a vocal exclamation point—as when delivering a punch line in "The Cremation of Sam McGee." And then the listener almost expects to hear a chuckle from

Robert Service relaxes on the steps of his log cabin in Dawson City, about 1912. A.J. Gillis photo, from the Stanton Patty collection

the author. It is clear that the old vagabond was enjoying himself to the fullest as he relived those adventurous years in the Yukon. And why not?

My parents spent several summers in Dawson City in the 1950s, living across the street from what became listed in the Parks Canada inventory as the Robert Service Cabin. Dad was managing gold-dredging operations in the creeks around Dawson City. My mother was writing occasional feature stories about life in old Dawson City for the Seattle-based *Alaska Weekly*. Her byline was Kathryn S. Patty.

One of Mom's articles was headlined "Mr. Service Doesn't Live Here Any More." This is what she wrote:

"I can look out my window to the Service cabin directly across the street. Visitors from all parts of Canada and the United States stand before the cabin, its front door inviting all to enter.

"This is what they see: The porch railing and floor made of birch saplings, a rocking chair at one end fashioned entirely of twisted saplings and roots. Up one step to the front room, 12 feet by 16 feet in length, and a pair of well-worn snowshoes hanging precariously near a framed copy of "The Cremation of Sam McGee." Autograph leavers have cheerfully written their signatures here and there on the yellowed walls. A mounted ptarmigan and hawk perch morosely on their pedestals under a set of caribou horns. Nearby there are an old seven-legged couch, several chairs and a low desk—we wonder if this is the desk where Service worked. There is a balloon ceiling of flimsy cheesecloth and a low-slung Yukon stove.

"In the back room of the cabin, same width and half as long, there is a narrow packing box table, some cupboards and a single iron bed with a feather-stitched blue denim coverlet.

"Mr. Service doesn't live here any more. He is now living in France and keeping nice and warm."

Later, Mom visited Service in sunny France and invited him to return to the North Country for a lecture program. She said that he declined, graciously, joking that he had "done his time" in the frigid north.

"To him, the Yukon seems very far away and long ago," she said. "He has little desire to remember it. But he is remembered in all of our hearts."

Service died in the sleepy seaside town of Lancieux, France, far from the Yukon, in 1958, at age eighty-four.

His widow, Germaine, told Tom Byrne: "Late in life, my husband was afraid that he would be forgotten."

"Never," Byrne responded.

✦ ✦ ✦

Later, much later . . .

It was August 17, 1973—Discovery Day in the Klondike—and a bunch of the boys were sitting around in the Sluice Box Lounge at the Eldorado Hotel in Dawson City. Captain Dick Stevenson was telling his pals about a pickled human toe he'd found in a cabin he had purchased from a trapper.

One thing led to another, and Stevenson decided the toe would make a unique ingredient for a drink he named the Sourtoe Cocktail. He would charge five dollars for anyone willing to down the fearsome drink.

The original rules called for the toe to be immersed in a beer glass filled with champagne—with the customer guzzling the brew until the toe touched his or her lips.

"Disgusting," said a woman at an adjoining table in the bar.

Dick Stevenson
displays one of his
infamous "sour toes"
for visitors to
Dawson City.

Stevenson flashed a blinding smile: like Diamond Tooth Gertie, he has diamond chips fixed to one of his front teeth.

"Not really," he said. "I call it a challenge drink. Think of the toe as you might an olive when it garnishes a martini."

"Outrageous. Fiendish. Disgusting," the woman said. "I'm outa here."

Captain Dick just beamed another grin.

"This is the home of the brave," he said.

Later, Stevenson said it would be OK for customers to choose any beverage, maybe beer or wine, to accompany the marinated toe.

"But Diet Pepsi is for sissies," he added.

One night, by the light of the midnight sun, the terrible toe was swallowed by a visitor who was downing his unlucky thirteenth glass of champagne and, as Stevenson remembers, "sort of fell over backward and swallowed the toe."

"The guy wasn't feeling so good the next morning," Captain Dick recalls. "He just sat there in the restaurant, stirring his scrambled eggs."

Stevenson had other toes in reserve. One had been severed by a power lawn mower and mailed by its owner to the creator of the Sourtoe Cocktail. Stevenson hints that he also has connections with certain physicians and morticians.

Toe No. 3 also was swallowed, this time on purpose, by a macho baseball player.

"His girl friend told him he had to swallow the toe to prove his manhood, and he did," Stevenson reported. "The chap wasn't too bright."

One night Stevenson said it was time for me to try a Sourtoe Cocktail. The prize would be a genuine Sourtoe Certificate signed by Captain Dick, certifying that I would be considered a person capable of almost anything.

And so, with cold sweat upon my brow,
I leaned way back and took a sip;
The hellish toe ascended through the bubbly
Until it clipped my lip—and that's a fact.

"Now you're one of us," said Captain Dick.

About then, I was remembering that it was the same Dick Stevenson who staged a Miss Nude Yukon beauty contest here—until the Royal Canadian Mounted Police halted the show.

Well, what's a guy to do?

At last count, more than ten thousand candidates had joined the Sourtoe Cocktail club.

"I've decided that I am going to will all of my little piggies to good old Dawson City," Stevenson said. "Can you think of a better way to maintain a toehold in history?"

Oh, for the return of Robert Service to write "The Ballad of the Sourtoe Cocktail."

"There are strange things done in the midnight sun. . . . "

"Aye, Lad," says Tom Byrne, "that much hasn't changed in the dear old Yukon and maybe never will."

CHAPTER 15

ICEBOUND

PRUDHOE BAY—It was the summer of 1975. The largest flotilla of tugs and barges in peacetime history gathered near Seattle for a 3,300-mile dash to the Prudhoe Bay oil field near the top of the world.

The fleet: twenty-three tugboats, with forty-seven barges in tow.

The mission: deliver more than 160,000 tons of equipment to bring the great Alaska oil field into production.

It was a high-stakes gamble.

Would the arctic ice pack open in time for the tugs and barges to reach Prudhoe Bay, unload, and retreat before the ice closed in again for another year? Unless the sealift reached Prudhoe Bay on schedule, there would be a delay of a year or more in moving oil through the trans-Alaska pipeline to the tanker port of Valdez.

Most of the cargo consisted of components for prefabricated buildings to be assembled like a city of Lego bricks at Prudhoe. Those oil field modules ranged from living quarters and a gymnasium for workers to the flow stations that would pump crude oil into the 800-mile-long pipeline.

Everything depended on finding a path through the ice.

The tug *Warrior* tows a barge into Prudhoe Bay.

In a normal summer, wind, weather, and tide combine to nudge the ice pack far enough offshore to allow shallow-draft vessels to maneuver around the frozen rooftop of Alaska. But this was not a normal summer. The 1975 sealift would face the worst polar-ice conditions of the century.

Maybe the oil companies should have consulted the Eskimo whalers of Barrow, America's northernmost community, before rolling the dice. Something strange was happening in the high Arctic, springtime whaling crews reported. The ice wasn't moving as it usually did. Stubborn winds were holding the ice on shore.

I didn't know any of this when I begged Arctic Marine Freighters, the joint-venture company directing the tug-and-barge operation, for a reporter's berth aboard one of the tugs. The company granted my request, but with a chilly lack of enthusiasm. Maybe they figured a nosy reporter could complicate things on a crowded tugboat.

My supervisor, Bob Twiss, the *Seattle Times* travel editor, also was cool to the idea.

"How long will you be gone?" Twiss snapped, taking a bite out of the soggy cigar that wobbled from the right corner of his mouth.

"I should be back in ten days or so, no longer than two weeks."

"Make sure you do, Twiss said.

Well, things didn't go as planned. The flotilla was icebound in the Arctic for more than two months. And so was I. As things turned out, I was the only reporter in the fleet. I was delighted, of course. The story was ours, all the way.

So, there I was in Barrow in mid-July, waiting for the signal to board the tug *Warrior* for the run to Prudhoe Bay.

Bulging into the Arctic Ocean ten miles northeast of the Eskimo community of Barrow is Point Barrow, a spear point of land at 71 degrees north. From the air, on my first ice-reconnaissance flight with sealift officials, it was easy to see how pack ice pressing against Point Barrow works as an icy gate between the Chukchi Sea to the west and the Beaufort Sea to the east.

Would that gate swing open in time for the tugs and barges to reach the Beaufort Sea and Prudhoe Bay?

The fleet was mustering off the village of Wainwright, about eighty-five miles west of Point Barrow. Captain Neil (Sparky) Borgert, the sealift director, was flying daily ice-recon missions.

"I don't know what's going to happen," Borgert shouted over the roar of the twin-engine plane. "Things can change fast up here. Give us just twenty-four hours of a good southwesterly wind and we'll be on the way."

It was summertime in the Arctic, the season of the midnight sun. But the brief summers here can torment planners with snow, below-freezing temperatures, and dangerous whiteout conditions for aircraft pilots.

Thick fog closed around the Beechcraft Baron as we probed the pack ice. We were skimming over the ice, flying blind, at an altitude of less than one hundred feet. The pilots, Jack Johnson, from Kodiak, and Ed Hansen, from Anchorage, were navigating by instruments. The sensation was like flying inside a bottle of milk.

"I see nothing but solid ice at Point Barrow," Sparky said in disgust as we broke out of the fog. "We'll just have to sit tight."

We turned easterly, toward Prudhoe Bay. The scene there was surreal. We could see the tops of oil-drilling rigs poking like church steeples through the fog. Cranes and small tugs were clustered by the beach, ready to unload the high-priority cargo. Arctic Marine Freighters planned to sink two 400-foot-long barges to create a docking area. But those barges were in the delayed tug-and-barge fleet, too.

Day after day, Sparky Borgert continued his aerial searches to find a passage through the ice.

"Solid ice," he said on July 19, gulping a cup of lukewarm coffee from the flight thermos. It was the same verdict July 20, July 21, July 22, July 23 . . .

The stubborn ice barrier was holding the fleet off Wainwright village, more than 250 miles short of Prudhoe Bay. Each lost day was robbing Arctic Marine Freighters and the pipeline builders of precious time.

Some would-be experts said the sealift wouldn't get through. And even if it did, they said, there would be corpses of ice-gored tugs and barges on the ocean floor.

"They're wrong," said Sparky Borgert. "I'm an optimist—we're going to make it."

✦ ✦ ✦

JULY 24. IT WAS TIME for me to board the tug *Warrior*.

"Good luck," Sparky said as we parted on the gravel airstrip at Wainwright. "Hope to meet you at Prudhoe in a few days."

Warrior and the other tugs were milling like lost lambs off the little Eskimo village as I rode a skiff to the vessel. The ice formations near shore were so dense that Sparky—now back in the air—had to guide the skiff operator through the maze from one patch of open water to the next.

Imagine a ten-mile-long stretch of the Chukchi Sea, between Alaska and Siberia, dotted with tugs and barges—bracketed by drifting icebergs and facing an over-the-horizon expanse of impenetrable ice. And aboard these tugs, were 184 tired and frustrated crew members.

Tension was building. The tug crews had been away from home since departing Puget Sound on the Fourth of July. Now, three weeks into the voyage, lettuce, milk, and other fresh groceries already were in short supply. Also lacking was mail from home

Duke DeLaHunt, skipper of the tug *Warrior*.

But there was surprisingly little griping. These towboat mariners were solid professionals. In the weeks ahead I would witness inspiring acts of heroism and sacrifice.

"Welcome," said Captain Thomas R. (Duke) DeLaHunt, *Warrior*'s skipper. "I can't tell you what's going to happen. But, damn, this ice has to move some time and let us by. All we can do now is wait."

I handed Duke a peace offering, a fifth of Cutty Sark.

"I don't allow any liquor aboard my boat," he growled. "I'll have to confiscate that."

"Meet me in my cabin at five o'clock," he added with a grin.

Duke said there was an upper bunk for me in the fo'c'sle.

But he didn't brief me about what happens when the engineer "air starts" the powerful, 9,000-horsepower diesels. The ignition triggers an ear-splitting, high-frequency screech like a scream in a horror movie. The first time I heard it I heaved from the bunk and banged my head against the steel bulkhead. Shipmates laughed.

And then, while trying to sleep, there was the unnerving sound of ice hammering against the tug's thin-skinned hull—like crashing kettle drums in a symphony finale.

"We're not an icebreaker, but sometimes we have to be," Duke said.

DeLaHunt, from Seattle, was a tugboat officer in the Aleutian Islands campaign of World War II. A cultured man, he listened to Beethoven recordings in his cabin during quiet hours. He could discuss subjects ranging from literature to anthropology with scholarly precision. But the sea was his life.

Duke DeLaHunt headed a crew of seven men, packed together for the duration on a 137-foot-long tugboat, managing to get along under difficult circumstances. I was proud to be with them.

Warrior had two giant barges in tow—the *Barge Ketchikan* (400 feet long and 78 feet wide) and *Barge 415* (400 feet long and 100 feet wide). They were tethered to the tug by thick cables. Duke worried that the cables, now slack and rubbing on the abrasive sea bottom only thirty feet below, would fray and part before the *Warrior* could get under way for Prudhoe Bay.

Each time a big chunk of ice bore down on the tug, the helmsman on watch tried to dodge by swiveling the *Warrior* from side to side in the shallow water. And each time the towboat moved there was slack to be taken up or let out on the cables. It was a constant battle against wind and current as the ice boulders threatened the tug.

Sometimes there wasn't sufficient warning to steer away from the tumbling slabs. Then the glacier-blue ice battered the *Warrior* and its barges, until rolling away with noisy splashes. The long towing cables danced violently through the water with the strain—now taut, now slack.

Finally, when we were able to turn into open water, the barges followed like well-behaved dogs on a double leash.

It was a bizarre caravan wandering in a white desert. The tugs and barges, with their weary crews, moved restlessly through the arctic twilight. Dodging. Stopping. Moving again. Dropping the anchor. Lifting the anchor. More ice. Moving again. Tense, tiring, frustrating.

Sparky Borgert was on the radio.

"I don't know what to say." he told the sealift crews. "There's just no way I can move you yet."

Nothing had changed. The fleet was icebound about where it was more than a week ago.

✦ ✦ ✦

TWO DAYS LATER we were forced to fall back—first to Icy Cape, then farther south, to Point Lay. Now we were more than 350 miles from Prudhoe Bay. Wave after wave of polar ice had clogged the first rendezvous area off Wainwright, then Point Lay. The ice could put holes in the tugs or run them aground. There was no place to hide.

Up anchor and run . . . rest . . . run again . . . circle . . . rest . . . run again. A crazy carousel of ice and fog.

Morale, sky-high a week ago, was falling. Some of the tugs were short of water and fuel. Showers and laundering were out of the question.

"You'd better not stand downwind of me," joked Jack Barker, an impish-featured deckhand from Snohomish, Washington.

Time blurred. Only X marks on the girlie calendar in the galley showed the current dates as days dragged by like the monotonous beats of a musician's metronome. All we could do was to keep running, away from the ice. Gray, gloomy fog settled around the flotilla.

Neighboring tugs and barges vanished in the fog, visible only as slow-moving

Barges loaded with construction modules for the Prudhoe Bay oil field in Alaska's High Arctic tag along behind tugboats in the icy Chukchi Sea, in the summer of 1975.

blips on *Warrior's* radar screen. Occasionally the fog lifted for a few moments and the barges, with their towering oil field modules, were ghostly shapes swinging though a gauzy haze.

Warrior threaded through the ice, as if on a toilsome slalom course. Cold rain dripped from the faces of the men as they worked on deck to adjust the tow lines. Icebergs slammed into the *Warrior*, one after the other. The tug lurched, straightened, and waited for the next impacts.

"I should have listened to my dear old mother," Duke DeLaHunt said with a weak smile. "She wanted me to be a man of the cloth."

One day we happened on a herd of walrus traveling across the Chukchi Sea on scattered cakes of ice. The big mammals lifted their ivory tusks and stared at the passing tug.

"Maybe we should follow them—they seem to know where to go," said Jack Kem, the *Warrior's* chief mate, from Medford, Oregon.

And then it began snowing, the white flakes whizzing past almost horizontally.

"Snow on the fifth of August!" Kem said. "Can you believe it?"

✦ ✦ ✦

TOM GEORGE, the cook, said it would be OK for me to use a galley table to write my reports for the *Times*. I missed a few keys on the portable typewriter as *Warrior* twisted and rocked to elude the ice. No matter. I would dictate the stories via a marine-radio hookup to the *Times* newsroom. My typos would remain visible only to me.

DeLaHunt and the other skippers needed their radios full time. But every other day or so, Duke would grant me a few minutes on the radiophone in the wheelhouse.

The procedure was for me to dictate a story, word for word, line by line, to a staffer at the *Times* who would write the text on his typewriter as we talked. Between paragraphs, we would say "Over" each time we were ready to resume dictation.

It was slow going through a clatter of pesky static. A scowl on Duke's face told me when it was time to end the calls.

Bob Twiss broke in on several of the calls.

"When are you coming home?" the boss asked.

"I have no idea. How are things in Seattle?"

"Don't change the subject. When are you coming home?"

Tom George, the cook on the *Warrior*, posts a menu in the tug's galley.

These truly were long-distance conversations. Each call traveled from the Arctic through a marine-radio operator in Oakland, California, then north from Oakland to Seattle.

I never dared to ask about the telephone bills when I returned home.

Meanwhile, I was writing a batch of background stories to provide more details about the arctic drama. But there was no way, either off Wainwright or Point Lay, to travel to shore and find a post office. And so the stack of features was growing—and quickly becoming outdated.

Then one lucky afternoon, near Wainwright, I sighted two Eskimo seal hunters in an aluminum skiff. I waved and shouted to catch their attention. The skiff skittered through the ice and came alongside *Warrior.*

"Could I give you an important package to mail?" I asked Homer Bodfish, one of the hunters. "Maybe you could take it to Wainwright and get it aboard the next mail plane."

Bodfish said he would be happy to help, but first he had more hunting to do. He took the envelope with my stories and a five-dollar bill for postage, waved, and sped away.

The envelope reached the *Times* a few days later by what I called Eskimo Post. But my seal-hunting mailman never returned for another dispatch. I was back to pleading for time on the marine radio.

✦ ✦ ✦

THE BATTLE WITH the ice was taking a toll. Several of the barges deployed around Point Lay had suffered ice damage. We also heard urgent messages on the radio network as the ice-recon plane circled overhead.

A message from Seattle to a crewman on one of the tugs: "His father has cancer. He will receive a letter shortly."

A conversation with another tug: "One of our crew is suffering from internal bleeding and somehow must be evacuated as soon as possible."

Another radio report : "Our cook quit. He says he's had enough."

"Don't let our cook off the boat," DeLaHunt quipped.

Tom George, the gregarious Greek from Seattle who was our cook, was worth guarding. The day before, despite a dwindling pantry, he managed to come up with hearty servings of chicken cacciatore. This day the main course was teriyaki steak.

Tempers throughout the fleet were nearing the boiling point.

"Come on, damn it, one crew member muttered. "Let's get going!"

Duke DeLaHunt tried to keep his voice low and calm.

"We're all getting jumpy," he said.

The eight men on the *Warrior* were alone with their thoughts as the days wore on. Some wrote letters or read worn pocketbooks or played cards in the galley. Others sat by themselves for long periods, staring into space as if thinking in long distance.

Finally, some good news.

"We are bringing in some stores—perishables, meats, and other things," Arctic Marine Freighters told the tug crews by radio.

"I wonder if they'll bring us a Christmas tree, too," said Jack Kem. "Sometimes it seems like we're be here 'til then."

Three days later, with the first rosy streaks of dawn lighting the sky, a craft named the *Skilak* was alongside and swinging a pallet of food onto *Warrior's* deck. The temperature was near freezing and the wind was raw.

All aboard pitched in to unload the flour, sugar, eggs, bread, butter, scallops, shrimp, steaks, bacon, coffee, lettuce, tomatoes, potatoes, cantaloupes, green onions, cabbage, celery, apples, and oranges. Tom George negotiated with the *Skilak's* crew for a two-pound sack of rice from the *Skilak's* own pantry.

There was mail, too.

The biggest share, a stack of letters from his girl friend, was addressed to Ed Irish, the second mate, from Hood River, Oregon.

"It should take me all night to read these," he said with a grin.

❖ ❖ ❖

NEW TROUBLE WAS brewing with a howling wind and a falling barometer.

"A storm is headed this way," the skipper said.

The tug was pitching and rolling on heavy swells and the barges were tossing great clouds of spray as they bucked into the waves. The wind ripped foamy crests off the waves, pitching spray over the wheelhouse windows twenty feet above the churning sea.

"It's going to be a long grind," DeLaHunt said. "We have to keep just pulling hard enough to keep the gear [the towing cables] tight. It's touchy." A sudden jerk on the deteriorating cables and they could break like fragile threads.

The blow had come up as suddenly as a sneak punch. Mountainous seas rose around the tug. *Warrior* rocked and slammed into the waves.

Behind the tug, our two barges on their cable tethers rammed against giant waves. *Warrior* fell into deep, dark canyons of green sea water, rose, plunged again . . . and again . . .

"Damn!" DeLaHunt yelled.

The blow was lifting the chain bridles on the snouts of both barges out of the water—putting a terrible strain on the lines. The skipper raced to the winch controls near the stern to let out more line.

In mariner's terms, we were "hove to," almost into the teeth of the gale—steering a few points off the wind to cushion the shock to the cables with each surge of the sea.

Then it happened. *Barge 415's* main towing gear broke!

Quickly, crewmen fastened a slender emergency line to hold the barge from drifting onto the beach. Three of the sealift's barges already had been driven ashore in the storm.

"We have to get a stronger line on the *415*—we can't wait any longer or we'll lose her," Duke said.

Then the skipper grew silent. He was rehearsing each step in his mind.

"OK," he announced. "We're gonna give it a whirl."

It was 7:30 P.M. Rain, wind, and danger.

First, the *415* was pulled close to the tug with *Warrior's* towing winch. Then DeLaHunt placed the tug along the port side of the barge. There were only seconds to get heavy lines aboard the barge before *Warrior* and the barge pitched apart.

Seaman Ralph Kasdorf, a hawser in hand, was poised on the *Warrior's* tossing bow, ready to vault onto the slippery deck of the barge.

"Jump!" DeLaHunt shouted. "Now—jump like hell!"

Kasdorf covered the space with a daring broad jump that might have qualified for the Olympics, fell, picked himself up, and raced up the barge's deck to fasten the line from the tug to a cleat. The taut hawser strained, almost to the breaking point.

Ed Irish, the second mate, crash-dived onto the barge. He and Kasdorf, somehow, made fast a stern line and then a spring line.

With its big diesels roaring, *Warrior* managed to stay close to the barge all during the process. And now, with the new lines in place, *Warrior's* crew had fair

Crew members aboard the tug *Warrior* haul in a damaged towing cable during the sealift to Prudhoe Bay.

control of the *415*, but still struggled to hold the enormous barge into the wind.

It was a fight. The barge wanted to kite away, toward the beach. We were drifting perilously close to the Icy Cape spit.

The tug and barge, now lashed together, slammed violently together with each swell, a nightmare of crashing metal. Kasdorf and Irish were tiny figures in the dim light as they mounted a catwalk on the bow of the barge to retrieve and repair what was left of the mangled towing gear that had snapped during the storm.

It was after 1 A.M. before DeLaHunt was ready to let out lines and put a proper working distance between *Warrior* and the endangered barge.

"We'll know in a minute if this is going to work," he said.

A few seconds later *Barge 415* was following obediently behind the *Warrior* on its new towing gear.

DeLaHunt grinned, reached for a pen, and made an entry in the tug's log: "Gear up and hooked on."

It was a happy crew that gathered for coffee in the mess room.

"By golly, we've really got hold of that barge now," said Jack Barker.

Ed Irish flashed a bright smile. "Time flies when you're having fun," he said.

Duke DeLaHunt, the *Warrior* skipper, repairs a frayed towing cable.

"You guys did a helluva job out there," the skipper told them.

Ralph Kasdorf was playing solitaire, as if nothing much had happened. Tom George slapped Kasdorf on the back and kidded him about the long, risky leap to the deck of *Barge 415*.

"At least Superman goes into a phone booth to change his clothes before he makes a flight," the cook said.

Kasdorf smiled and turned a card.

September 1. Labor Day. A day to remember.

✦ ✦ ✦

ARCTIC MARINE FREIGHTERS began calling the tug captains, one by one, by radio with this message:

"We want you to pick up your gear and head for Point Barrow."

Duke DeLaHunt was not certain that he had heard correctly. He asked for the message to be repeated.

"I can't believe it," he said after the confirmation. "We're on the way!"

Arctic Marine Freighters had decided that it was a now-or-never situation: try to get through to Prudhoe Bay or lose the entire season. It was the boldest kind of crapshoot. The tempo changed suddenly throughout the fleet. Engines thundered and the barges stretched out on towing cables behind the tugs.

"Under way," DeLaHunt wrote in *Warrior*'s log.

There was light snow, then fog. The end-of-summer temperature was 34 degrees. The polar ice in the distance looked like a long, low, whitewashed wall.

We passed Wainwright, then Point Belcher, and Point Franklin. Still ahead, Point Barrow—then, maybe, Prudhoe Bay.

But in midafternoon there was a change of signals. Sealift officials began rearranging several of the tug-and-barge combinations so that the tugs with the least draft—the ones that could maneuver in the shallowest water—could haul the priority cargo to Prudhoe. DeLaHunt was ordered to stop, wait for the tug *Sioux*, and hand off *Barge 415* to the *Sioux*.

The men of the *Warrior*, who had saved the *415* from certain disaster a few days before, were disappointed. Now *Warrior* was told to stand by in the Wainwright area.

"The decision is understandable," DeLaHunt told me. "The *415* must get through to Prudhoe. But I wish we were going, too."

Sioux was alongside the *Warrior* by eight o'clock that night, and fifteen minutes later was headed for Point Barrow with *Barge 415*. Less than an hour later, *Sioux* was plowing through scattered slabs of ice on the hoped-for path to Point Barrow and beyond.

Arctic Marine Freighters suggested that I transfer from the *Warrior* to the *Sioux*, and I agreed. It was difficult to say farewell to the men of the *Warrior* after more than a month aboard their valiant tug. There were many fine crews in this fleet, and *Warrior*'s was one of the best. Not a quitter in the lot.

Captain Byrd Perry, from Montesano, Washington, was the *Sioux*'s skipper. He had the kind of quiet confidence that comes with years of dueling with danger.

In the inky darkness of the arctic night, Perry steered cautiously through thickets of ice. Sometimes he had to slow the tug almost to a dead stop and nudge aside the craggy bergs. *Sioux*'s searchlight swung in the blackness, helping to pick a course.

And then it began to snow again, big, fluffy flakes. The temperature was 34 degrees and falling. Behind the *Sioux*, I could see that three other tugs with barges were bunched up, slugging cautiously through the ice, trying not to rip holes in the vessels.

"Stay in as close as the Good Lord will let you," Sparky Borgert radioed from the ice-recon plane circling overhead. "You're going to find more ice, but it is beginning to look really good ahead."

We were almost out of the ice, then it closed in again around the *Sioux*. Thunderclaps of ice banged against the tug's hull. Wind-driven snow flashed by the searchlights. Winds: 20 to 25 knots. Temperature: 27 degrees.

Past Point Barrow—then Cape Halkett, Harrison Bay, the Colville River delta. Now fifty miles to Prudhoe Bay.

"It looks like the homestretch," Borgert called.

Cheerful, bright sunshine tinseled the arctic panorama. It was Thursday, September 4, and the lofty drilling rigs of Prudhoe Bay were in sight.

"We're almost there," Skipper Perry said.

Workers at Prudhoe set up a betting pool for guessing the arrival time, with a prize of six thousand dollars. The winning time was 8:24 P.M. That's when *Sioux* dropped anchor at Prudhoe Bay. Close behind were the tugs *Sea Monarch, Spartan,* and *Jeffrey Foss.* Within a few minutes, stevedores were at work aboard the snow-slick barges, stripping them of the oil field modules.

There were no fanfares or shouts of congratulations. The towboaters didn't expect any. They were just doing their jobs.

✦ ✦ ✦

SEVERAL WEEKS LATER, back in Seattle, I was at Pier 17 to meet the *Warrior* and her crew.

Warrior looked like a warship returning from combat, scraped and bruised, ready for the repair yard. And her men had that look of exhaustion that follows a terrible battle.

"That's it," Duke DeLaHunt said, signing off the ship's log with a flourish and a big grin.

The skipper hugged his wife, Peggy, and turned to look at the *Warrior.*

"Really," he said, "there's no way to describe what happened up there in the Arctic. It was a bloody nightmare. It was the stuff of miracles, too."

In all, twenty-five of the forty-seven barges reached Prudhoe Bay. *Warrior* reached Prudhoe, too, with a couple of those barges.

"So long," Duke said. "I'm going home."

CHAPTER 16

SHORT TAKES II

DIOMEDE—I got my face slapped on Little Diomede Island. And it saved me from a painful case of frostbite.

I was flying from Nome to Diomede village in 1971 to write a story about the seventeen Eskimo families who lived there—in Alaska, but only two and a half miles across Bering Strait from Russia.

There were no navigational aids on Little Diomede then, not even a radio beacon. Drift slightly to the west, across the invisible International Dateline, and we would be in Soviet airspace.

Peter Donaghue, the Munz Northern Airlines pilot, set a careful compass course for the island, a blue-white lump of rock rising from the arctic ice pack. Then we sighted the village, a bleak huddle of buildings hanging from a sheer mountainside above Bering Strait.

Donaghue flew between Little Diomede Island and Russia's Big Diomede Island, so close to the Soviet military base on Big Diomede that we could see its wooden observation tower. The pilot looked down and grinned.

"I like to keep them guessing," said the former Royal Australian Air Force fighter pilot.

Then Donaghue landed the bush plane—on wheels—on a patch of sea ice in front of Diomede village. The two-mile-long island had no airstrip. The only time that aircraft—other than helicopters—could land or take off was when Bering Strait was frozen.

Diomeders with bright, friendly faces crowded around the plane to collect their mail and groceries. Other villagers were hurrying toward us, making a path through the jumbled heaps of ice known as pressure ridges.

The temperature was about 40 degrees below zero. A stinging wind made it colder.

I was standing near the plane, taking photographs, when a brown hand sped toward my face and covered my nose.

"Frostbite," said John Iyapana, one of Diomede's best hunters. "I saw your nose turning white and decided to give you the warmth of my hand to stop the frostbite from getting worse."

I was in the prop wash of the plane, with its idling propeller, adding to the already dangerous wind chill.

"You will be fine now," Iyapana said with a smile.

A few moments later, his warm hand lifted and we walked together toward the village a quarter-mile away.

That night, with Dennis Corrington, a trader from Nome, I crawled into one of the village huts through a doorway that was too small for us to enter standing, to meet with some of the Diomede men. They were seated in a circle, taking turns to drink from a bottle of Everclear—190-proof grain alcohol. Dennis and I were invited to join the group.

"You better not have a tape recorder with you," one of the Eskimos told me. "They tell lies about us in books and articles. We resent being regarded by the press as people in a freak show."

I showed the men my little spiral notebook and assured them that I don't carry a tape recorder.

Jacob Ahkinga, Diomede Island elder, in 1971.

221

A Diomede villager hikes across a stretch of Bering Strait pack ice.

"Is it OK if I take some pictures?"

"First," said one of the still-suspicious villagers, "you must give us your social security number."

"Sure, but why?"

"Because if we don't like what you print, we will come get you."

"You know my name. Why do you want my social security number, too?"

"Because when the government people come here, they always ask us for our social security numbers. They act like we don't have names. We are just numbers to them."

One of the Eskimos recorded my social security number on a scrap of paper and stuffed it in his pants pocket.

I was embarrassed by the "government people," the bureaucrats.

I gave all of the men names in my notes that night—Robert and Michael Soolook, John and James Iyapana, Albert Iyahuk, Aloysius Ahkvaluk, Jacob Ahkinga . . .

And then I reached for the bottle of Everclear, instead of a camera.

✦ ✦ ✦

JUNEAU—It's likely that I had one of the last interviews with Charles Lindbergh.

It happened in March 1968 when Lindbergh slipped into Juneau for a surprise address to a joint session of the Alaska Legislature. I had been tipped in advance by a secretary in Governor Walter J. Hickel's office and was present for the Lone Eagle's first public appearance in more than ten years. His visit was cloak-and-dagger stuff all the way.

Lindbergh, accompanied by his close friend Sam Pryor, a retired executive of Pan American World Airways, flew here secretly from Hawaii. They went directly to the governor's mansion, where they were welcomed by Ermalee Hickel, the governor's wife, and escorted to an upstairs apartment.

About the only Alaskans who knew of the visit were the Hickels and leaders of the Legislature. Instrumental in bringing about the visit were State Senator Lowell Thomas Jr. and his wife, Tay, a daughter of Sam Pryor. They

Charles A. Lindbergh addresses a joint session of the Alaska Legislature in 1968. In the background are State Senate President John Butrovich (left) and Bill Boardman, speaker of the State House of Representatives. STANTON PATTY COLLECTION

encouraged Lindbergh to talk to Alaskan leaders about one of his favorite subjects: the need for resource conservation.

On March 19, legislators were called into joint session in the House chamber. Then the surprise announcement from the rostrum:

"Ladies and gentlemen—General Charles A. Lindbergh."

It was if a ghost from the past had appeared.

Lindbergh walked briskly down the aisle and beamed a shy smile as legislators and spectators in the jammed gallery gave him a warm standing ovation. He seemed embarrassed, even ill at ease, as the applause exploded.

Speaking without notes, Lindbergh began by apologizing for being "rusty." He said he had given up making public appearances.

There was no need for the apology. The listeners—all but one—were charmed from the outset by the man with the piercing blue eyes and the soft, resonant voice. He was as humble as a beginner in a speech class. But his words penetrated.

"Alaska," he said, "is one of the key areas of the world as regards conservation, so what you do here is going to be watched closely by the rest of the world. It is absolutely necessary that we take steps now to protect what to us at this time seems commonplace."

But when he suggested eliminating bounties on predators, Bob Blodgett, a maverick state senator from Teller, stalked out of the chamber. It was too much for the legislator whom journalists had nicknamed "the Heller from Teller."

If Lindbergh noticed Blodgett's stormy departure, he didn't let on.

"It is too easy to kill," Lindbergh said of the since-discarded bounty system.

Later, upstairs in the governor's office, I had a few moments with the great aviator.

We talked about his trailblazing flight across the top of the world in 1931 when Lindbergh and his wife, Anne Morrow Lindbergh, piloted a little floatplane they called *Sirius* from New York to China. They made short stops in Barrow and Nome as they hopped around Alaska. Then I asked about his little-known combat flights in the South Pacific during World War II.

"I'd rather not go into that," he said.

I told Lindbergh how much my father admired him.

"Yes," he said, "I remember your father. We talked once, I think it was in New York, and I was interested in his view that some day the Arctic Ocean would become a sort of northern Mediterranean for the nations banked around its shores."

Then he asked: "What is it you do?"

I explained that I was representing the *Seattle Times* and would write a news story about his speech.

"Alaska is a very special place, but then since you are from here, you must know that," he said.

Would he autograph my copy of *The Spirit of St. Louis,* I asked him. The book is Lindbergh's account of his solo flight across the Atlantic, from New York to Paris, in 1927.

"Of course," he said, reaching for a pen.

To Stanton Patty
With Best Wishes
Charles A. Lindbergh
Juneau, Alaska 1968

✦ ✦ ✦

KETCHIKAN—Most visitors go sightseeing around this salmon and timber town aboard crowded motorcoaches. A fortunate few book tours with Lois Ellen Munch.

You can't miss her.

Lois, garbed in a '50s-style outfit that includes poodle skirt, saddle shoes, and jingling charm bracelet, is the owner of Ketchikan's only red-and white 1955 Chevy. The snazzy sedan is her tour chariot.

Why the 1950s theme?

"It was a cool time, the last nice time for America," Lois says.

How did she come by the classic car?

"It belonged to my ex-husband's dead aunt, and he didn't want it in the divorce."

Munch, who describes herself as "sort of a free spirit," taught school here for twenty years before starting her tour company, Classic Tours, in 1989.

"I still do some substitute teaching," she says. "And when I'm out driving visitors around, the schoolkids all wave at me. Sometimes I feel like I'm in a scene from *Happy Days.* It's neat."

Lois Munch, in poodle skirt and saddle shoes, shows off her 1955 Chevrolet in Ketchikan. PHOTO PROVIDED BY LOIS MUNCH

Lois shows her guests Indian totems, bald eagle nests—and Creek Street, Ketchikan's red-light district in earlier times.

Visitors have left her with mixed memories. A few seasons ago, Lois was touring a young couple that wasn't much interested in sightseeing.

"It was a romance on one of the cruise ships that call here," she remembers. "They were hugging and kissing in the back seat, really steaming up the windows. They were a married couple—but not married to each other.

"After the tour, I asked the guy, 'Are you two going to go on seeing each other after the cruise?'

"He replied: 'Of course not. I'm a married man.'

"Oh, well. He gave me a forty-seven-dollar tip. I can't explain that, either."

Ketchikan's unconventional tour guide also has been a part of true romance.

Among her favorite customers was a couple from Houston, Texas, who had been married for fifteen years and told Lois they wanted to renew their vows while in Ketchikan.

"They left all the details to me," Lois said.

And so she arranged for a local clergyman to meet the wedding party at a pretty waterfall just outside Ketchikan. Lois was filming the ceremony with a camcorder when a rain shower drenched the scene.

"No problem," she says. "I had an umbrella for two."

They had a picnic by the waterfall, with smoked salmon and cider.

"It was beautiful," Lois says. "I cried."

✦ ✦ ✦

VALDEZ—The tanker *ARCO Juneau* sailed south from Valdez on August 1, 1977, with the first shipment of crude oil from the Prudhoe Bay oil field on Alaska's North Slope. The oil had been delivered to the Valdez tanker terminal by the just-completed trans-Alaska pipeline.

It was cause for a celebration in the Prince William Sound community that had been virtually destroyed by the Good Friday Earthquake of 1964.

"Now we are the center of the universe, at least for a day," said Susy Collins, a Valdez city councilwoman.

They called the Valdez festival an "Oil-in." Among the events was a contest featuring young women in oil-soaked T-shirts.

"Crude and unrefined," spectators said.

Captain Emery A. McGowen, master of the *ARCO Juneau*, readied the huge tanker for the 1,230-mile journey down to Cherry Point, in Washington state. I was aboard to cover the story for the *Seattle Times*. Also in the press pool was the late Ward Sims, a crack reporter for the Associated Press.

We assured the safety-conscious skipper that we would do our best to stay out of his way so the vessel's routine would not be disturbed.

"If you don't, I'll shine my shoes on somebody's rear end," McGowen said during a briefing. But there was a twinkle in his eyes.

No McGowen shoe shines were necessary during the trip.

"How much oil are we carrying, Captain?" we asked.

"Eight hundred and forty thousand barrels," McGowen replied.

"What is the dollar value of the cargo?"

"Seven-point-two million dollars—exactly the amount the United States paid in 1867 to buy Alaska from Russia."

"Coincidence, Captain?"

"No comment."

ARCO—the Atlantic Richfield Company—had a savvy public-relations team on the job back when Prudhoe Bay was big news.

We found out later that the actual value of the shipload of crude was $11.5 million.

Alaska was worth more than its initial price, too, as things turned out.

Maybe we should have made an offer on Siberia while we were at it.

✦ ✦ ✦

WAINWRIGHT—Our little bush plane lifted off from Wainwright village on a blackening arctic night.

"I think we had a good meeting," said Wally Craig, superintendent of the Fairbanks agency of the federal Bureau of Indian Affairs, as he settled back for the return flight to Fairbanks.

Craig had traveled to Wainwright, a tiny Eskimo community on the Chukchi Sea, to talk with residents about the transition of village schools from federal to state jurisdiction.

There was an orange streak of sunset to the west as we flew into the October night. And then—as suddenly as if a curtain had fallen on a theater stage—we were enveloped in a blinding whiteout.

The plane droned on. Wally caught a nap.

"I think I'm lost," the pilot said.

Wally was awake instantly.

"Lost?"

"Yes, sir, I'm kind of new up here in Alaska. I came up hoping to make some money on the oil pipeline, but there were no flying jobs open on the pipeline, so I'm doing this for now."

"OK," Wally said calmly. "We'll work things out."

A few minutes later, the whiteout thinned. But it still was like looking through sheets of gloomy, drifting gauze.

There, just ahead, to the left, maybe five hundred feet below, was a flashing beacon atop a metal tower.

"What do you think?" Craig asked me.

"I'm not sure, but it could be the beacon at Umiat."

Wally thought for a moment, then made a decision.

"Yes, let's call that Umiat—that's where it should be."

"OK," he told the pilot. "Turn right—let's get some altitude to get over the Brooks Range and fly us home."

And that's how we made it safely back to Fairbanks.

I would have flown anywhere with the unflappable Wally Craig.

✦ ✦ ✦

KETCHIKAN—We went flying one day with Dale Clark. Destination: Anan Creek, a bear sanctuary sixty miles north of Ketchikan. And that put the veteran bush pilot in mind of a story.

Clark said he had landed a floatplane on a lake near the village of Klawock on nearby Prince of Wales Island. He was taxiing the plane to shore when a bear swam alongside and ripped one of the pontoons with its teeth.

"That bear took a big chunk out of the float, but luckily the hole was above the water line," Clark recalled. "I got out of there in a hurry and flew back to town."

All in a day's work, Alaska-style.

✦ ✦ ✦

NOME—It was winter in the Arctic. Tommy Johnson and his crew were out on the tundra clipping antlers from reindeer. The antlers were to be sold to a dealer in South Korea who would turn them into a powder that promised men vigor and virility.

This "essence of reindeer," swallowed straight or added to food as a seasoning, was worth big money in Asia.

"Don't worry about the reindeer—the antlers grow back again," Tommy said as we joined the reindeer roundup.

Back in Nome that afternoon, I asked Tommy's wife, Myrtle, if the Eskimos ever used the stuff.

"Our guys never needed it," Myrtle said.

CHAPTER 17

CLEAR FOREVER

DELTA JUNCTION—It was a moment to treasure.

Our twelve-year-old granddaughter, Christine, planted her feet smack in the middle of the Richardson Highway near Delta Junction.

"Mush!" she said with a giggle and a north-south swing of her blonde pony tail.

"Better move to the shoulder, Honey—a car could come along any moment," I called.

"No cars in sight," she said. "You're clear forever, Papa."

Clear forever. . .

"Papa, there are tears in your eyes."

"Maybe a few, Honey. I was here a long time ago, when I was about your age, and it's still as beautiful as I remembered."

"So, why are you crying?"

"I'm not, really. Got some Alaska dust in my eyes, that's all. Now, get off the highway, please."

The years fell away as I looked across the Tanana River toward the ice castles of the Alaska Range. Mount Hayes (13,832 feet high). Mount Deborah

A solo traveler rolls along a scenic section of the Alaska Highway near Haines Junction, Yukon Territory.

(12,339 feet). Hess Mountain (11,940 feet). And far away to the southwest, out of sight from here, the monarch, Mount McKinley (20,320 feet).

Fairbanks, my hometown, was only ninety-eight miles up the Richardson from Delta Junction.

Christine, Mabs, and I were driving the Alaska Highway, the Richardson, and other North Country highways during a 2,300-mile journey from Seattle to Fairbanks. It was a plum assignment from the *Seattle Times*. The concept:

Drive north to Alaska's Interior, then return to the Seattle area aboard an Alaska ferry.

"We'll call it 'Wet and Dry,'" said John Macdonald, the new travel editor at the *Times*.

Christine came along on the trip to, as she expressed it, "find some of my Alaskan roots."

✦ ✦ ✦

A LITTLE GEOGRAPHY: The Alaska Highway begins in Dawson Creek, in northeastern British Columbia—not to be confused with old Dawson City in the Klondike region of Canada's Yukon Territory. From Dawson Creek (designated in guidebooks as milepost 0 of the Alaska Highway), it is a journey of 1,390 miles to the end of the Alaska Highway at Delta Junction, Alaska.

The Alaska Highway meanders for hundreds of miles through British Columbia and Canada's Yukon Territory before reaching Alaska. In fact, almost two-thirds of the highway is in Canada. So why not call it the Alcan (for Alaska and Canada) Highway? I still think that Alcan—the highway's long-discarded World War II nickname—was the right name for this adventure route. But the official name, through the magic of bureaucracy, is the Alaska Highway.

From Delta Junction, Fairbanks-bound motorists continue north on the Richardson Highway. The 366-mile-long Richardson—which began as a gold-rush wagon trail more than a century ago—connects Fairbanks, in Alaska's heartland, with Valdez, on Prince William Sound. Drive straight ahead from Delta Junction to reach Fairbanks; turn left for Valdez, 266 miles to the south.

Here in Delta Junction with Christine and her doting grandmother, I was remembering a boyhood afternoon when my family was headed to Valdez to board an Alaska Steamship Company liner for Seattle. Three boisterous brothers were scrapping in the backseat of the 1935 Plymouth.

"Stop that, boys!" my father shouted, blowing a nauseous blue cloud of cigar smoke over his right shoulder.

"I'm getting carsick," I complained.

"If you don't quit fighting, we'll stop right here and cut a switch from one of those willows," Dad said. "I mean it."

He meant it.

But just then, the Plymouth began swaying.

"Flat tire, damn it," Dad muttered.

"Watch your language, please," Mom said.

Back in those days, the Richardson was a gravel road through the wilderness. Alaska Road Commission grader operators bladed excess gravel to a center berm. Sometimes the grader missed rocks as sharp as spears.

We had a flat tire *and* a leaking gasoline tank. A stray rock had punctured the tank.

My mother reached into her purse and produced two packages of chewing gum.

"Quickly, boys—chew!" she said.

We chewed big wads of rubbery gum until our cheeks puffed like busy chipmunks.

"I'm running out of spit," said my big brother, Ernie.

"Never mind, just chew!" Mom said.

A few minutes later she collected the masticated goo, patted it into a sort of flapjack, and handed it to my dad.

"Get under the car and patch the gas tank with the gum," she instructed.

Dad did, and we managed to reach Rika Wallen's roadhouse on the Tanana River before running out of fuel.

The chewing-gum incident happened just about here, where our granddaughter with the happy giggle was prodding us to "Mush!" on north to Fairbanks.

My parents and Ernie are gone now. So is Rika Wallen. But Rika's old roadhouse still is here. It's a state historical park now, and with some of the best food in the northland. And that "clear forever" view of the Alaska Range across the Tanana still is glorious.

"Christine, did I ever tell you about the time we used chewing gum to patch a gasoline tank?"

"Yes, Papa, you did."

✦ ✦ ✦

I AM PERSUADED that Alaska is viewed best through the eyes of the young.

How many times have I traveled the Alaska Highway and its tributary roads? Maybe a dozen. In all seasons. In family cars, RVs, and aboard highballing freight trucks while gathering stories for the *Times* and other publications. But with Christine for company, her grandparents were getting a fresh view of Alaska and western Canada.

One day, on a lonely stretch of the Alaska Highway, Christine said she had counted more than forty shades of green in forests that seemed to be rolling toward infinity. She wrote in her journal about "air so fresh that it blew me over." She talked about early-day gold stampedes—and during one stop hammered two chunks of quartz, like brass gongs, in hopes that a shower of gold would fall from the fractured rocks.

In the Canadian Yukon, she panned for gold with Dean Elston, a prospector who called himself Old Griz. The kindly Yukoner made certain that Christine would find some glitter in the bottom of her pan. She squealed with delight.

"Now I understand why they call it gold fever!" she said.

Old Griz said he helped build the Alaska Highway as a bulldozer operator in 1942. That was an epic effort. Construction crews completed the lifeline to Alaska in just eight months and eleven days.

Christine learns how to pan for gold in the Canadian Yukon with Dean Elston, known as Old Griz.

"We didn't have enough sense to know that it couldn't be done," said Old Griz.

For sure, the new highway in '42 was only a muddy, single-lane military road punched through mountains and forests. But for the first time in history, Alaska was joined to the forty-eight conterminous United States by an overland route.

Down at Muncho Lake, British Columbia (mile 436 of the Alaska Highway, measured from Dawson Creek), we were filling our gasoline tank when a grouchy tourist pulled to a stop. Christine listened as the visitor complained about "all this empty space, with not that much to see."

"How can you stand to live around here?" the traveler asked Jack Gunnesss, the service-station owner.

"Just look around you," Gunness suggested.

"Well," said the unhappy traveler, "the guidebook says we are supposed to see wildlife around here—where is it?"

"Keep looking," Gunness said. "It's here."

Christine was quiet as we drove north from jade-green Muncho Lake.

A few miles later, she sighed and said, "I don't get it. Why was that man so upset? This must be about the most wonderful place in the world."

On cue for Christine, a mountain sheep with curled horns pranced onto a ledge twenty feet or so above the highway.

"Wow!" said Christine.

By the time I attached a telephoto lens to my camera, the sheep had vanished. Christine snapped a great shot with her no-frills camera.

"Mr. Gunness was right," she said. "There is wildlife around here. Now— let's find a moose!"

A few days later we stopped for a midday picnic on the shore of Kluane Lake (mile 1039 of the Alaska Highway). We walked awhile to get some exercise, then began picking through leftovers in our ice chest. The July day was unseasonably chilly. Thick clouds draped the mountains beyond the lake. I wished that hot soup were on the menu.

Presto!

"Hi, there," called the driver of an RV parked in the Yukon campground. "Why don't you folks have lunch with us?"

Christine beamed. No mushy-bread turkey sandwiches and broken potato chips this day.

Our fellow travelers, Raul and Yvonne Miller, from Escondido, California, were on a two-month loop around Alaska.

"We're having the time of our lives," Yvonne said.

"That's more like it," Christine whispered. "That guy back at Muncho Lake was a real sourpuss."

Raul weighted a tablecloth with rocks and pieces of firewood. Yvonne served toasted-cheese sandwiches and lentil soup.

"Dig in," she said.

As happens often on northern highways, strangers get acquainted easily. They tell stories about their travels and swap addresses for Christmas cards. They attach Alaska Highway bumper stickers, like combat medals, to their vehicles.

My favorite is a cartoon showing a thirsty mosquito attacking a highway traveler. It reads: "I gave blood on the Alaska Highway."

We thanked the Californians for their hospitality and drove on, toward the Alaska border, still more than 150 miles to the north. Suddenly the gloomy clouds parted. Shafts of sunshine poured down on a chain of snow-crowned mountains just ahead. The peaks seemed to be hanging in the sky like castles. A blue-white glacier high in a mountain notch flashed like a gaudy diamond.

It was a North Country overture—big, bold, and beautiful. I almost expected to hear trumpet fanfares.

"Gosh, I never knew there were mountains like that anywhere," Christine said.

Her grandparents wondered if they had marveled at this dazzling view last time they drove through the Yukon. Or were they in too much of a hurry?

"I wish you could stay twelve years old forever, Honey."

"No way," Christine said. "I want to be sixteen—and soon."

✦ ✦ ✦

"CHRISTINE, DID I EVER tell you about the time your great-grandfather and I had to change a tire in a snowstorm near Whitehorse?"

"Isn't Whitehorse where we had dinner last night in that neat motel?"

"Right."

The year was 1953. My father, Ernest N. Patty, just had been named

My twelve-year-old granddaughter Christine Danielson writes in her daily journal during the Alaska Highway journey she took in 1986 with me and my wife, Mabs.

president of the University of Alaska. He asked me to share the driving from Seattle to the headquarters campus in Fairbanks.

The Alaska Highway back then was a grueling series of narrow, twisting stretches with sheer dropoffs, soggy swamps, and little maintenance. Even getting to mile 0 at Dawson Creek was a challenge. There were curves in British Columbia's Fraser River Canyon, north of Vancouver, where the road was so skinny that a vehicle's tires rode for a few frightening seconds on little wooden platforms built over the roiling river.

"Why are we doing this?" my mother asked. "It would have been better to take a plane."

"Because we'll need the car when we get to Fairbanks," my father explained as he steered around one of the killer curves.

In 1953, Alaska was still a territory. Statehood was six years in the future. There was no Alaska ferry system. The Alaska Highway, such as it was, provided the only surface route to Alaska.

We survived the Fraser River Canyon and made good progress until nearing Whitehorse on a black, icy night. Blizzard conditions. The highway surface was like a skating rink. The temperature was almost 30 degrees below zero.

"Oh, oh, I think we have a flat tire," Dad said, braking the Oldsmobile with a gentle skid. A sliver of steel sheared from the blade of a snow-clearing rig had shredded the right-rear tire. There was no choice but to unpack the trunk until we could free the spare tire.

Can you imagine resting a precious painting on a snowbank in the middle of the Yukon wilderness? The treasure was a painting by Sydney Laurence, greatest of the "old masters" who portrayed early-day Alaska. But it was blocking our access to the tire jack. Mom had purchased the canvas from the artist in the 1930s for $220. Today his masterpieces sell for thousands of dollars.

Dad and I draped a blanket over Laurence's scene of an Athabascan Indian's campfire, then took turns with the tire wrench. Our bare fingers were so cold that we were sure we had suffered frostbite. Mom helped by holding a flashlight on the work zone.

Finally, the job was done. We drove on, to Whitehorse.

Christine shivered as I told the story.

"Hope you never have to change a tire in freezing weather, Honey," I said.

"Me, too.

"When do we eat?"

North of Whitehorse, the Yukon capital, there are ghostly sections of the Alaska Highway—abandoned pieces of the original World War II road. They veer off the main highway for a few hundred yards, then dead-end in thickets of bushes and trees that have reclaimed the land.

No longer is the Alaska Highway a wilderness highway. Most of it is paved, although seasonal blisters in the pavement, known in the north as "frost heaves," can mangle axles of fast-moving vehicles. Christine called them "whoopee bumps"—for cries of "Whoopee!" when we were airborne.

We stopped the car and walked into one of the ghost roads until its wartime ruts vanished in the greenery.

"Spooky," said Christine.

"History," said her grandfather.

✦ ✦ ✦

THE YEAR WAS 1942 and America was at war. Japan had bombed Pearl Harbor in Hawaii. There were fears that enemy forces would invade Alaska.

President Franklin D. Roosevelt ordered construction of an emergency highway to Alaska. Less than a month later, thousands of shivering, bewildered American soldiers found themselves in tent camps fanning out through fifteen hundred miles of savage, unmapped wilderness. Their assignment: build the Alaska Highway.

"Make it fast and make it crooked."

Legend has it that those were the instructions from Brigadier General William M. Hoge of the Army Corps of Engineers.

Crooked, to make it difficult for enemy planes to strafe highway convoys? That's also part of the legend. But it's not true. The hurried-to-completion Alaska Highway was built with more curves than a Hollywood starlet, but not because of the threat of aerial strafing.

Jerome F. Sheldon, who served with the 18th Engineer Regiment during the 1942 construction season, told me that the real reason for the crooked highway was that terrain problems caused the fast-moving highway builders to loop around problem zones. Swamps, cliffs, and other nasty obstacles were described in official journals as "terrain peculiarities that would impede the rapidity of progress."

And then there was the story about a soldier who was driving a trailblazing bulldozer during the construction. He asked his sergeant what markings he should follow. The sergeant looked toward a slope about a half-mile ahead.

"See that dark thing at the foot of the hill? Let that be your guide."

The "dark thing" turned out to be a wandering moose.

I do hope that one is true.

African-American soldiers, most from poor towns in the South, made up about a third of the workforce. Residents of the long-isolated Athabascan community of Mantasta Lake, deep in Alaska's Interior, were startled when black troopers of the 97th Engineers marched through their village.

"The Athabascans said the African-Americans were the first white men they had ever seen," said Walter Mason, a young officer with the 97th.

I know that story is true.

More than ten thousand Army troops worked on the road in '42. Later, sixteen thousand civilian workers for the federal Public Roads Administration labored to upgrade the highway. The Corps of Engineers called the project "one of the greatest undertakings in U.S. history." But there was little mention of casualties in the congratulatory press releases.

Conditions were brutal for the highway builders.

A convoy of trucks heads north on the muddy Alaska Highway early in World War II. ARMY CORPS OF ENGINEERS PHOTO

Bottomless swamps swallowed trucks and bulldozers. Flash floods ripped away dozens of newly built bridges. Clouds of mosquitoes tormented workers. Steel snapped in temperatures that fell to 70 degrees below zero. Trucks overturned on sharp curves around rivers and lakes, taking their passengers to frigid graves. Tired rookie truckers, unaware of the hazards of hypothermia, pulled off the road to nap—and never wakened.

It was at Soldiers Summit, fifteen hundred feet above the Yukon's frozen Kluane Lake, on November 20, 1942, that American and Canadian officials cut a red, white, and blue ribbon to open the Alaska Highway.

The temperature was 15 below. The 18th Engineers Band played "The Star Spangled Banner" and "God Save the King." And the first U.S. Army truck bound for Fairbanks rolled northward on the brand new Alaska Highway.

After the ceremony, the dignitaries retired to a barracks building where a military band played Strauss waltzes as guests dined on moose meat.

"It was like a scene from some improbable opera," wrote Lieutenant

Richard Neuberger, an aide to one of the Army generals. (Neuberger later would be elected a U.S. senator for Oregon.)

In June 1943, Japanese troops occupied the islands of Attu and Kiska in the Aleutians. The war had come to Alaska. The Alaska Highway was ready.

✦ ✦ ✦

CHRISTINE WAS NAPPING in the backseat, her pretty head resting on my camera case, as we reached Northway Junction, milepost 1264. Mabs was reading ahead in *The Milepost,* the essential guide to highway travel in the North Country.

I was daydreaming, recalling a solo trip in 1991, when I turned off the highway at the junction and drove into nearby Northway village to meet Walter Northway, traditional chief of the tiny Athabascan village. Walter was an estimated 111 years old then. Nobody, not even Walter, knew his exact age.

The first military truck travels the brand-new Alaska Highway in 1942, from milepost 0 in Dawson Creek, British Columbia, to Whitehorse, Yukon Territory.
ARMY CORPS OF ENGINEERS PHOTO

Maybe Walter could tell me more about the war years, when he and other Alaska natives helped build a string of airfields along the Alaska Highway for ferrying thousands of American-built warplanes to the Soviet Union. Russia was fighting for its life against Nazi forces.

The United States offered to fly Bell P-39 Airacobras, Curtiss P-40 Warhawks, and other planes all the way to Siberia. But the wary Soviets didn't want us learning about their Siberian airfields.

Chief Walter Northway, at age 111, in 1991. The Athabascan Indian elder died in 1993

So it was agreed that American pilots would deliver the planes to Fairbanks, where they would be turned over to Soviet crews. The Soviet pilots then would whisk the aircraft from Fairbanks to Nome, then across Bering Strait to Siberia and on to the Eastern Front in Europe.

Soon a string of landing strips was sown across more than two thousand miles of Canada and Alaska. The network of airfields was known as the Northwest Staging Route. But most who were there remember it as the Alaska-Siberia Route, ALSIB for short.

Chief Walter Northway was hired as a dollar-an-hour laborer to clear brush for the airstrip at Northway. He watched in sorrow as other workers spread asphalt for the runway, the tar slopping across an ancient village cemetery.

There were tears in his eyes as Walter told me about that hard-hearted act carried out in the name of wartime expediency.

"It didn't have to be done that way," he said. "We told them so, but nobody cared."

Walter's Athabascan name was Haa Chi'jinii'aa. It means "Looking Back"—back to a time when time, as we know it, did not exist.

Northway was the name given to Walter's father by Captain James A. Northway, a gold-rush trader. The captain couldn't pronounced the father's Indian name—T'aaiy Ta ("Strong Man")—so gave him his own.

Walter told me about meeting white men for the first time when he and his father happened across two starving gold prospectors on the Chisana River. They helped the strangers to their camp and fed and nursed them for several days.

"After that, white men came like ants," he said.

As we parted, I looked long at the old chief, as if photographing him in my mind. Tousled hair crowned his head like fresh snow. His golden-brown face was etched with the map lines of a strenuous life. His smile was as warm as the summer sun.

We will meet again," he said

I went home to write about Walter Northway and other memorable characters along the Alaska Highway. One morning a Midwestern editor called and asked: "I have your story about an old Indian chief up in Alaska. Is he still alive?"

"You mean Walter Northway? I'll check."

I telephoned Northway village. Lee Northway, the chief's son, answered.

"How's your dad?"

"Doing OK. He's outdoors, chopping wood."

It was sure fun to call back to that editor and tell him that 111-year-old Walter Northway was out whacking firewood.

But two years later, on November 21, 1993, Walter died in his sleep.

Village men toiled all day with picks and shovels to open a grave in the frozen earth of Northway's modern cemetery. His casket rested across the tops of folding chairs in the gymnasium of the Walter Northway School. Mourners reached out to touch his leathery face.

"He was Alaska's oldest person, the elder of elders," Cheryl Silas, Walter's granddaughter, told the crowd. Walter was Northway's last traditional chief. The community decided that's how it should be.

I returned to Northway some years later to find Chief Northway's grave. It is atop a hill above the little village, hidden from outsiders by a thicket of willows. I parked my car and hiked alone up a dusty path too steep for a Jeep.

Just as I reached the chief's resting place, two ravens sounded an alarm, cawing nonstop with earsplitting shrieks.

Sentinel ravens? Perhaps.

Ravens are powerful symbols for many Alaska natives. One native legend tells of how Raven created the world, and launched the sun, the moon, and the stars into the sky.

The raucous raven cries continued as I raised a camera to photograph the village cemetery. Most of the graves are sheltered with traditional Athabascan spirit houses, like wooden dollhouses, memorials to the deceased.

"I mean no disrespect," I told the noisy birds. "I am here to pay my respects to an old friend."

Still, the relentless cawing continued.

A few minutes later, I closed the camera and headed down the trail. The moment I was out of sight, there was silence again.

Christine was busy making notes as we drove north from Northway Junction, watching a jet trail streak across a blueberry sky. Alaska's pioneer past is mostly memories now. Good memories.

"Never try to write a journal while riding on the Alaska Highway," Christine wrote. "You must understand that the highway has a lot of potholes."

The *Seattle Times* had asked Christine to keep a journal and write a feature story for readers her age. There was ample incentive: a promise of one hundred dollars if her story passed muster with the editors.

She wrote about finding her roots in Fairbanks—especially when she stood by a metal pole on the University of Alaska campus where her mother, Kay, as a ten-year-old, managed to freeze her tongue to the post on a frigid winter day. It took a pan of warm water to free her tongue.

"I love that story," Christine said, with a merry laugh.

She also wrote about me.

"My grandfather snores a lot, so I was glad that I brought ear plugs," she wrote.

But what about the Alaska Highway, Honey?

"We did many fun things," she wrote. "This was the trip of a lifetime."

It still is.

CHAPTER 18

HERE LIES SOAPY

SKAGWAY—It was in the misty fiordlands of Southeastern Alaska that I mined some of my best travel memories.

Southeast, as Alaskans call the emerald archipelago that sweeps north from Ketchikan to Haines and Skagway, is a wondrous realm of lofty totems and bald eagles; shimmering glaciers and high-jumping whales.

And history . . .

Alaska's first gold rush happened in Juneau, now Alaska's capital, in 1880. That was sixteen years before the discovery of gold in the Yukon's fabled Klondike.

Later, thousands of stampeders raced through Skagway and neighboring Dyea toward the goldfields of the Klondike in Canada's Yukon—and through Southeast's rowdy Wrangell town and up the Stikine River to reach the gold of British Columbia's Cassiar country.

Wrangell. It boomed under three flags—Russian, British, and American.

It was in Southeast, in the waters of the Tongass, America's largest national forest, that salmon barons from the Lower 48 built their giant canneries—and bold fish-pirates rafted by to help themselves to more than a few salmon from company fish traps. I knew at least two of those salmon purloiners who themselves became wealthy cannery owners. There were plenty of fish back then for everyone. But I tell no tales about dead men.

It was in Southeast—in Sitka—that czarist Russia planted its capital when Alaska was Russian America. It was in old Sitka that the Stars and Stripes were raised when we bought Alaska from Russia in 1867, for two cents an acre. What a deal!

And it was in rip-roaring, gold-rush Skagway, here at the head of glacier-rimmed Lynn Canal, that Bobby Sheldon witnessed Alaska's most famous gunfight. That was on July 8, 1898, when Jefferson Randolph (Soapy) Smith and Frank Reid faced off in a feud that cost both men their lives.

"I guess I am the last living eyewitness to that event—at least I claim to be," Bobby told me in 1980. He was ninety-seven then.

I'll take his word for it.

Robert E. (Bobby) Sheldon was postmaster in Fairbanks when I was a youngster. He was a peppery adversary for noisy Fairbanks kids who crowded his post office to warm up on winter days. We managed to outrun him every time he tried to clear the lobby.

"You've mellowed," I told Bobby when we met in 1980.

"You used to be a real pest," he said.

"Peace, Bobby."

"Sure, what the hell?"

Sheldon didn't have to tell tall tales. This pioneer Alaskan's true adventures would fill a better-than-fiction book.

For openers, he built what probably was the first automobile ever assembled in Alaska—without ever having seen one. That was in 1905. Five years later he made the first auto trip—this one in a Model T—down the wintertime trail from Fairbanks to Valdez, a wilderness route that later became the Richardson Highway. The journey, 375 miles in those days, was regarded as impossible; Bobby did it in three and a half days.

Sheldon also found time to serve four terms in the Alaska Legislature, including the first state legislature after Alaska pinned its north star to the flag in 1959. He also provided the first visitor transportation in Mount McKinley National Park until, he said, "greedy politicians decided that the government should take over the concession."

Now it's Denali National Park, with Mount McKinley as the centerpiece.

When Sheldon built that first horseless carriage in Skagway, it truly was a labor of love. It seems that Bobby was competing with a well-to-do physician's son for the affections of the town belle. He decided to best his rival's fancy horse and buggy with a real automobile.

All he had to go by were some photographs in a magazine. He used a 3½- horsepower, two-cycle engine from a boat, some cut-down buggy wheels, and assorted other parts built from scratch—and soon he was putt-putting by startled Skagway citizens at ten miles an hour.

The doctor's son won the girl. But Bobby thought he came out a winner, too.

"I heard she married four times and caused four guys a lot of misery," he said.

❖ ❖ ❖

BOBBY SHELDON ARRIVED in Skagway from Washington state in 1897 with his widowed father—at the crest of the Klondike gold stampede. A heart attack felled his dad while the two were trying to scale Chilkoot Pass on the way to the Yukon. The father returned to Washington, where he died soon after. Bobby decided to stay in Skagway, alone.

"When my father died he left me the biggest estate any orphan boy ever inherited," Bobby said. "He left me the entire Territory of Alaska in which to try to make a living.

"I've been trying to collect on the estate ever since. Sometimes the collecting wasn't so bad, and sometimes it wasn't so good. But Alaska was always a wonderful place."

Bobby was a fifteen-year-old newspaper boy in Skagway that fateful night in '98 when Soapy Smith, Skagway's notorious badman, marched down to the Skagway waterfront to break up a secret meeting of vigilantes who were planning to run Soapy's gang out of town.

Robert E. (Bobby) Sheldon, in 1969. He witnessed the gunfight between Soapy Smith and Frank Reid.

The secret didn't keep. Soapy, back at his saloon, heard about the meeting. So did several excited townspeople who set out for the wharf. Enterprising Bobby Sheldon, with a bundle of for-sale Seattle newspapers under one arm, followed the crowd.

Along the way, he saw Harriet Pullen, proprietor of Pullen House, Skagway's landmark hotel, hurrying toward the Juneau Wharf, where the vigilantes were gathered. She was searching for her young son, Royal, fearing he might wander into trouble.

Soapy, fortified with a few belts of whiskey, passed Pullen without a greeting.

"I'll fix 'em," Soapy muttered to himself, hefting his Winchester rifle.

Four days earlier, on the Fourth of July, Pullen had been persuaded by Soapy to participate in Skagway's patriotic parade with her fancy horse-and-wagon outfit for hotel guests. Soapy was the grand marshal, spurring a white horse up and down Broadway, the gold town's main street.

Depending on who is telling yarns about Skagway's crime boss, Soapy comes across either as a charming swindler or a ruthless gangster. Historical accounts describe him as shrewd and fearless.

One of Soapy's scams was his "telegraph office." There he would charge newcomers five dollars to send a telegram anywhere in the world. Never mind that Skagway was not yet connected by telegraph to "anywhere." Soapy's telegraph wires ended just outside his office window. Hapless customers usually received a message back asking them to send money home.

Soapy and his bullies held Skagway in a grip of terror. Killings and robberies carried out by Soapy's thugs discouraged many prospectors from taking the White Pass Trail through Skagway to the Klondike. Instead, newcomers detoured to neighboring Dyea and Chilkoot Pass.

Skagway merchants worried about losing business. They decided Soapy had to be stopped, and formed what became known as the Vigilance Committee. One of those posted as guards for the vigilante meeting was Frank Reid, the town surveyor.

Soapy was in what Sheldon remembered as a "black rage" when he reached the Juneau Wharf about 9 P.M. Quickly, Reid stepped forward to block Smith from crashing the meeting.

Bobby Sheldon was standing about 150 feet away from the two men.

"Halt!" Reid shouted.

Jefferson Randolph (Soapy) Smith's saloon in 1898, in gold-rush Skagway.
STANTON PATTY COLLECTION

"Then they started talking real tough to each other," Sheldon recalled.

"All of a sudden, Soapy brought his rifle down from his shoulder. Reid reached out and grabbed the muzzle to get it away from his middle. Soapy pulled the trigger and the slug went through Reid's left groin.

"Reid went to his knees, still hanging onto the barrel of Soapy's rifle with his left hand. Soapy was jerking, trying to get the rifle free to fire another shot. Reid got his revolver out of his pocket and fired three shots.

"One of Reid's bullets left a red streak on Soapy's arm. Another creased his side. The third went through Soapy's heart—and down went Soapy."

Word spread quickly through Skagway that Soapy Smith was dead.

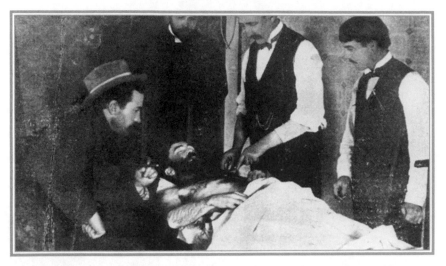

The body of Soapy Smith lies in the Skagway morgue after a shootout with Frank Reid. STANTON PATTY COLLECTION

Harriet Pullen said members of Soapy's gang "took to the hills like a flock of goats."

"Before I could realize what had happened, my son Royal and I were practically alone with the dead outlaw," Pullen said.

"Then it was that my small son, not half as scared as I was, pulled me by the hand up to where the dead bandit lay and looking him in the face exclaimed, 'Why Mama, that is the man that brought all of us kids candy, and now he's dead.'"

Bobby Sheldon said he "just kept staring" at Soapy's corpse.

"They carried Frank Reid to the hospital in a piece of canvas—he was moaning and groaning something awful," Sheldon said.

"But Soapy lay there for some time before they took him to the morgue. Nobody would touch him. Sentiment was so strong that anybody looking like he wanted to help might have been shot as a sympathizer."

Soapy Smith was buried July 11 in Skagway's Gold Rush Cemetery—six feet outside the cemetery boundary "so as not to desecrate the cemetery," Sheldon said.

The Reverend J. A. Sinclair, who preached the funeral sermon, chose for his text a verse from the Bible's book of Proverbs: "The way of transgressors is hard."

"He has paid the penalty of his mistaken and misguided judgment," Sinclair told the few persons who had gathered at the cemetery. "His remains lie here today cold and still in solitary death, no worthy mourner near his bier, no tears of sorrow shed by his fellow citizens. . . . "

Soapy's wood-slab grave marker (the original was stolen long ago) was lettered as follows:

> JEFFERSON R. SMITH
> DIED
> JULY 8, 1898
> AGED 38 YEARS

Frank Reid's grave marker has a place of honor in Skagway's Gold Rush Cemetery. STANTON PATTY COLLECTION

Frank Reid, mortally wounded, lingered for twelve days in Skagway's Bishop Rowe Hospital. There, with Reverend Sinclair's assistance, Reid "renewed his Christian faith and prepared for the end," said Glenda Choate, a Skagway historian.

"To lift the spirits of the lonely man," Choate added, "Sinclair had his church choir visit and sing hymns. . . . music filled his final days."

Reid died July 20. He was fifty-four.

Never had there been such a funeral in Alaska. So many mourners turned out for the funeral that Reverend Sinclair conducted part of the services out front of his little Episcopal church.

"Nearly all the population followed the dead hero to his last resting place," witnesses reported. "The procession marched out of town to a dirge played by the band of the leading variety show. Many tears were shed over the dead hero's bier as his remains were lowered into the grave."

Reid's grave, just a few yards from Soapy's, is marked with a tall granite shaft inscribed:

He gave his life for the
Honor of Skagway

Harriet Pullen, the grand dame of Skagway's gold-rush years, enjoyed dramatizing the story of Soapy's demise for her guests at Pullen House. Old-timers said she would tell how she "held Soapy's head in my lap," then show the enthralled audience her bloodstained kitchen apron. One Skagway detractor swore that it was chicken blood—from the chickens that Pullen had killed for that evening's hotel supper.

Who knows? It made a colorful story for the tourists.

Harriet Pullen's death in 1941, at the age of eighty-six, left Bobby Sheldon as the last witness to the shooting of Soapy Smith.

"It was quite a time for Skagway," Sheldon said. "And I was there to see it."

Sheldon died at age ninety-nine on January 4, 1983, in the Fairbanks Pioneer Home.

"I've had a great life, kid," he told me shortly before he died. "No complaints."

✦ ✦ ✦

IT IS A BLUE-SKY DAY in Skagway.

The golden dome of the old Golden North Hotel on Broadway glitters like a newfound nugget. Engine No. 73, the antique steam locomotive of the White Pass & Yukon narrow-gauge railroad, howls by Skagway's waterfront.

Giant cruise ships are tethered to the piers where Soapy Smith met his inglorious end. Helicopters lift into the mountains where passengers are invited to stroll on glaciers as bright as diamonds.

Hikers strap on backpacks at the National Park Service visitor center and head out of town for the Chilkoot Pass gold trail. A piano man is playing a ragtime tune at the Red Onion Saloon, where ladies of the evening parted lonely miners from their pokes back in the days of '98.

And out front of the Arctic Brotherhood Hall, Steve Hites is gathering customers for a tour of Skagway's yesteryears. I decide to tag along for a new travel story about Skagway.

Wearing a derby, a mortician's frock coat, and a chain of gold nuggets

Steve Hites rides a White Pass & Yukon Route train into the "high iron" country above Skagway.

across his bright-red vest, Hites looks every inch a gold-rush dandy. Steve and his ever-patient wife, Gayla, operate the Skagway Streetcar Company, with a fleet of vintage touring cars for excursions around Skagway.

"Here lies Soapy Smith," Hites tells visitors as we reach Gold Rush Cemetery.

(Well, maybe. More about that later.)

Then, darting back and forth like a nervous raven, playing both roles, Hites reenacts the showdown between Soapy Smith, the villain, and Frank Reid, the hero. The tour guide supplies the dialogue with his inimitable version of the brawl:

"Soapy, rifle in hand, walks up to Frank. 'Get out of my way!' he says.

"'Never!' says Frank in an ice-cold voice.

"There's a scuffle. Shots ring out . . .

A White Pass & Yukon Route train emerges from a rock tunnel high above Skagway. The narrow-gauge railroad was built during the epic gold rush to the Klondike.

"Smith dies instantly, a bullet through his heart. Reid perishes several days later of his own wounds."

Hites pivots and gestures toward the grave of Jefferson Randolph (Soapy) Smith, just outside the cemetery's boundary line.

"The good people of Skagway were not about to plant his remains in hallowed ground," he tells his spellbound audience. "And so, the rascal Soapy was cast adrift for all eternity."

The visitors applaud.

"Mr. Hites," one woman says, "you should be on the stage."

"Madame," Hites responds, with a great sweep of his arms by the mountain backdrop, "this is my stage."

And here in Gold Rush Cemetery lies Martin Itjen, Skagway's first tour conductor—a high-voltage character (not unlike Steve Hites). In 1935, Itjen traveled to Hollywood to have dinner with Mae West, the brassy movie star.

"Why don't you come up and see *me* some time?" Martin asked the actress, borrowing one of Mae's famous film lines.

Steve Hites, Skagway historian and gold-rush guide, dresses the part of a gold-rush dandy as he guides tours for summer visitors.

Itjen's last joke was a huge granite boulder by his grave—painted gold and proclaimed (by him) to be "the largest nugget in the world." He chained it to a tree before his death in 1942, "to make darned sure that nobody steals it."

Martin Itjen founded the first Skagway Streetcar Company, in 1923. The operation consisted of a combination taxi and coal-hauling rig and the owner's nonstop banter.

President Warren G. Harding—the first U.S. president to visit Alaska—rode in Martin's car when he made a three-hour stop here in 1923. Itjen swept out the coal dust, installed a couple of seats, and took Harding on a sightseeing tour. There was a reception over at the Pullen House, then Skagway's finest hotel. Legend has it that a dog named Buck joined the presidential reception line at Pullen House and Harding leaned down to shake hands with the pooch.

Only in Skagway . . .

Steve and Gayla Hites decided in 1985 to revive the Skagway Streetcar Company and follow Itjen's original touring route. It was easy to map the drive; Itjen left behind a 78-rpm recording of his narration.

There are folks around here who wonder if Martin Itjen lives on somehow as Steve Hites. Itjen, like Hites, was a born promoter. One of his touring cars carried a life-size mannequin of Soapy Smith, with the words "Soapy lives!"

Remember, this was before Elvis.

Itjen worked awhile for the White Pass & Yukon Route railroad before going into the tourist business. So did Hites. The White Pass & Yukon, completed in 1900, is a genuine nugget of the Klondike gold rush. Today the old railroad offers some of Alaska's most popular excursions, with trips into the snowy mountains above Skagway.

When first we met, Hites was a singing conductor on those White Pass & Yukon trains. He's still a rail buff. Ask for a song, and Hites reaches for his guitar and croons a rousing railroad ballad.

The saga of Soapy Smith, as told by Hites, ends with a tip of Steve's derby to Frank Reid, who gunned down the outlaw, and a steely glance toward Soapy's tombstone.

But is Soapy Smith still here?

Maybe not.

Some folks around here say that Soapy was washed out to sea many years ago when the Skagway River flooded the graveyard. But that's not what the tourists want to hear. And it's not in Steve Hites's script.

Whatever, Soapy still haunts dear old Skagway.

We depart Gold Rush Cemetery and motor across the Skagway River to a hillside vista point that happens to include Skagway's "new" cemetery. The cemetery borders the city's garbage dump.

"Just think," Hites quips, "some day I will be buried near my old refrigerator."

The tour ends at the Arctic Brotherhood Hall. Well, not the original A.B. Hall, but a theater in Steve and Gayla's handsome Skagway Streetcar Company office, across the street from the White Pass & Yukon depot.

The first Arctic Brotherhood Hall, dating to 1899, still is one of Skagway's showpieces. Its facade is a collage of more than twenty thousand sticks of driftwood gathered from nearby tide flats.

The Arctic Brotherhood was formed by eleven miners—"as true of heart and as hardy of brawn as ever came together for fun, fight, or foot race"— aboard the steamship *City of Seattle* en route to Skagway in 1899. President Harding was made an honorary member here in 1923, at what turned out to be the brotherhood's last official meeting.

Steve Hites decided he would resuscitate the long-dormant organization.

"I have reorganized the Arctic Brotherhood, and I have recommended each of you for membership," he tells visitors during the tour finale.

The initiation ceremony includes a rendition of "Home on the Range," with special lyrics.

"Home, home in the snow," Hites sings, "where the moose and the caribou play . . . "

"More!" the audience shouts. "Encore!"

Hites wears a grin as big as the northern sky.

"Welcome to the Arctic Brotherhood, brothers and sisters," he says.

I tuck my Arctic Brotherhood membership card into my wallet, shake hands with Steve, and go on my way.

"Be sure to give my regards to Mollie Walsh," he calls.

✦ ✦ ✦

MOLLIE WALSH.

Now, there was a true heroine of the gold rush.

There's a bronze bust of Mollie by a children's playground in downtown Skagway. "The Angel of the White Pass Trail," is how old-timers remembered her.

The story begins in 1897, when twenty-four-year-old Mollie arrived in Skagway from Seattle aboard the S.S. *Quadra,* with hopes of joining the stampede to the Klondike. She soon found Skagway a wicked and dangerous place for single women.

Back then, the women of Skagway were divided into two categories: the "Respectables" and the "Unfortunates"—the latter referring to prostitutes. Mollie was one of the "Respectables," but risked censure for befriending a "soiled dove" who lay dying in a Skagway brothel. She found a preacher to read a prayer as the young woman breathed her last, then helped arrange the funeral.

The Reverend R. M. Dickey, who conducted the service, made this entry in his diary:

"The funeral service . . . was held in the (Presbyterian) church, which scandalized some people. Nearly 50 unfortunates were there, their painted faces and gaudy ornaments marking them from the respectables, some of whom sat aloof and disapproving."

Soon after, Mollie left Skagway and hiked thirty-three miles up the White Pass Trail to a camp called Log Cabin. There she pitched a tent and began serving hot meals to tired and hungry stampeders. She fed, nursed, and comforted lonely men far from home, asking nothing but fair pay for the groceries.

"She's an angel, a real lady, pure as the driven snow," said a grateful prospector.

Two men wooed Miss Mollie: Jack Newman, one of the best-liked packers on the trail, and Mike Bartlett, the hot-tempered owner of another pack train. Mollie chose Bartlett. They married and moved to Seattle.

An article published in 1973 by the White Pass & Yukon Route railroad tells the rest of the story:

Claude G. Bannick, a Seattle mounted policeman, was covering his Pike Street beat on the night of October 27, 1902, when he heard a woman's scream. Then there was a pistol shot.

Mike Bartlett had killed his wife.

Bartlett was tried for murder, but was acquitted as being temporarily insane. Later, he took his own life,

Jack Newman was beside himself with grief when he learned of Mollie's death.

Newman also had left Alaska for Seattle, and there he married a widow by the name of Hannah Berry. In 1930—twenty-eight years after Mollie's death, and knowing his own life was closing—Newman decided to honor Mollie's memory. He commissioned a sculpture of his lady love to be placed in Skagway.

The inscription, written by the man who lost Mollie to the man who killed her, reads:

ALONE WITHOUT HELP
THIS COURAGEOUS GIRL
RAN A GRUB TENT
DURING THE GOLD RUSH
OF 1897–1898.
SHE FED AND LODGED
THE WILDEST
GOLD CRAZED MEN.
GENERATIONS
SHALL SURELY KNOW
THIS INSPIRING SPIRIT,
MURDERED OCT. 17,
1902

Jack Newman was unable to attend the dedication ceremony, but sent a message.

"I'm an old man and not longer suited to the scene, for Mollie is still young and will remain forever young," he wrote.

"Her spirit fingers still reach across the years and play on the slackened strings of my old heart and my heart still sings—MOLLIE!—my heart still sings, but in such sad undertone that none but God and I can hear. . . . "

Down in Seattle, Hannah Newman let her husband know that she was less than thrilled with Newman's tribute to his lost love.

"Where do I come in?" she asked.

Newman quickly arranged for a bronze profile of Hannah to be fastened on the exterior of what today is the Washington Athletic Club building, at Sixth Avenue and Union Street in downtown Seattle. The site was chosen because Hannah Newman's family had owned the land there since pioneer times.

Jack Newman died shortly after Mollie's bust was unveiled in Skagway. Newman had requested that he be buried in Skagway, beside Mollie's monument. Mrs. Newman had him buried in Seattle.

And today the "Angel of the White Pass Trail" still watches over children at play in old Skagway.

What a town!

CHAPTER 19

THE HAPPINESS MAKER

WAINWRIGHT—The children of Wainwright had been waiting on the shore of the icy Chukchi Sea since early morning.

"Moe's coming!" they shouted.

"Moe's coming!"

Moe—Captain Cecil W. (Moe) Cole, master of the vessel *North Star III.*

North Star III—fourth in the line of Bureau of Indian Affairs freighters that for more than fifty years served Alaska's native villages with annual supply runs of everything from heating oil to soda pop.

And packed in the ship's holds for each voyage were tons of candy for Alaska-native children that Moe and his wife, Luella, had collected from candy factories and friends in the Seattle area. Moe's greatest fun in life was to go ashore like a seagoing Santa and distribute the cargoes of sweets to rosy-cheeked Eskimo children. They called the big, gruff-talking skipper from Seattle the "Happiness Maker."

"I just happen to love kids," he said.

Moe's kids were waiting for him each season in remote settlements with strange-sounding names: Chignik, Akutan, Umnak, Unalaska, Nikolski, Atka,

Cecil W. (Moe) Cole, skipper of the North Star III, watches cargo operations from the vessel's flying bridge.

Togiak, Tununak, Tooksook Bay, Mekoryuk, Golovin, Stebbins, St. Michael, Unalakleet, Shaktoolik, Koyuk, Elim, Gambell, Savoonga, Diomede, Barrow, Point Lay, Point Hope, Kivalina, Kotzebue, Deering, Shishmaref—and now Wainwright.

I was aboard *North Star III* in 1972 to write about Captain Moe and his merry crew for the *Seattle Times*.

The 10,000-ton Victory ship from World War II was a smudge on the western horizon as the Wainwright children dashed from their homes. Close behind were their parents, who remembered receiving treats from Moe when they were youngsters.

"Moe's coming!"

Captain Moe was in the ship's galley, reading a batch of letters that village children had written for his birthday. The letters had been delivered to the ship as preparations were being made for offloading freight for Wainwright's 350 residents.

The captain's eyes were misty as he turned the pages.

"How about those kids?" he asked. "You'll see for yourself when we go ashore in a few minutes. They're the best."

"I love you, Moe," wrote a boy named Ryan. "Peace."

North Star III, a U.S. Bureau of Indian Affairs freighter, anchors in Kotzebue Sound to offload cargo for Kotzebue-area native villages on a day in 1972.

Howard Patkotak wrote: "How are you? I am fine. I hope you don't hit any icebergs. I love you very much."

"We have been expecting you," wrote Kathy Bodfish. "I wish you got lots of candy."

"Come quickly, Moe," urged Diane Vukapigak.

Moe pushed the letters aside and swigged his third cup of black-as-tar coffee.

"That's enough of that stuff for now," he growled. "We have work to do."

Wainwright's candy consignment was ready for Moe's visit. The skipper signaled a crane operator and climbed inside a big container, like a packing crate, to be winched over the side of *North Star III* to a waiting LCM landing craft. I followed a few minutes later.

Wainwright village, more than a mile away from the shallows where *North Star III* was anchored, was shining like a mirage in the morning sun. We started for the beach. The wind had an icy edge. Moe pulled his parka hood over his head and took inventory: gumdrops, peanut brittle, caramel corn, jelly beans, candy bars, etc.

The children began waving and shouting as Moe came into sight. Moe was waving back, so enthusiastically that when our boat plowed through the surf and rammed the gravel beach, he forgot to brace himself and took a painful fall.

He said something naughty that Santa probably never uttered.

But soon Moe was on his feet and wading through the cold water to be with the children.

"Get in line!" he yelled

Parents beamed in the background as their children swarmed around the candy man.

"I said, Get in line!" Moe shouted.

The giggling kids formed a single line and waited their turns as Moe waved to the grownups and reached for his bag of candy. Moe didn't just distribute candy: he had a wisecrack for each recipient that was guaranteed to bring a smile or a laugh.

"How's your husband?" he asked an eight-year-old girl.

"You're already too fat," he told a grinning boy, pretending to snatch away his candy.

"C'mon, get over here," he barked at a timid lad.

A village teacher whispered to Moe that one of the girls had applied lipstick in the visitor's honor. The youngster blushed and hid her pretty face as Moe approached.

Children in the Eskimo village of Wainwright queue to receive candy from Moe Cole as parents watch the happy scene.

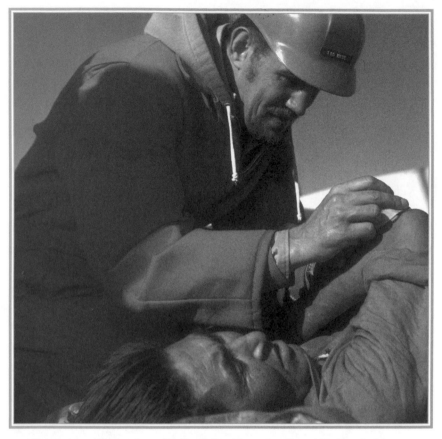

Ove Jensen, third mate on the North Star III, renders first aid to Roy Smith, injured during a freight-handling operation in Kotzebue Sound. Smith was a deckhand aboard a tugboat assisting in offloading freight from North Star III.

"Fine," Moe said. "Just don't tell my wife, Sweet Lips."

The children used every container they could find as Moe poured generous helpings of treats into paper bags, stocking caps, bread wrappers, and jackets with sleeves tied together.

Dempsey Bodfish, a lifelong Wainwright resident, smiled and told a friend:

"Look at that. I can remember Moe giving away candy here when I was that age. He's a good man."

It was a Pied Piper scene as Moe led a parade to the Wainwright school. The children followed, playing push-and-shove games with him all the way.

Hours later, when it was time to return to *North Star III,* Moe boarded the LCM and lighted a harmless firecracker that he had hidden for the occasion. He tossed it high in the air to explode. What a finale!

The children screamed for more. They waved until he was out of sight.

Suddenly, September or not, it began to snow, lightly, with feathery flakes drifting down onto the landing craft. Then, as suddenly as the snowfall had begun minutes before, a rainbow arched through the arctic sky, almost connecting the village with the *North Star III.*

✦ ✦ ✦

A FEW DAYS LATER, we anchored off Barrow—America's northernmost community, only 1,120 miles from the North Pole. No serious ice had been encountered on the approach to Barrow, but the threat remained.

This was the season of wild winds and heavy seas in the Arctic. Unpredictable pack ice could move in suddenly to seal off the top-of-the-world shipping route. It happened in 1970, when severe ice conditions prevented the ship from unloading at Barrow. More than two thousand tons of urgently needed supplies had to be offloaded far to the south and flown to Barrow

Now the *North Star III* crew was racing the weather again.

Jim Hughes, the school superintendent at Barrow, had declared a holiday in honor of the ship's arrival. It was an annual tradition so the school children could greet Captain Moe. For a while, however, it looked as if "Moe Day" might have had to be postponed.

Bitter weather blanketed Barrow with snow. Storm winds churned the Arctic Ocean on Barrow's doorstep to such fury that offloading of Barrow's freight had to be postponed.

The next day turned out sunny and calm. Moe hit the beach early in the morning—with three thousand pounds of candy. That's right, three thousand pounds, more than seven pounds for each of Barrow's four hundred children.

Well, "Moe Day" came but once a year.

Moe joked and worked for more than two hours to distribute the treats. Then the boys and girls cleaned up the litter and scattered for home.

"There will be no more candy until after dinner," one mother admonished.

Moe straightened up, surveyed the happy village, and said:

"It's a great life. You never go wrong doing things for kids."

The Arctic's summertime Santa headed back to the ship. There was more freight to be unloaded. The polar ice pack could drift in any moment and trap *North Star III.*

"See you next year—God willing!" Moe called as the landing craft turned toward its mother ship.

◆ ◆ ◆

CAPTAIN CECIL W. (MOE) COLE served on the Bureau of Indian Affairs freighter runs for most of the years between 1937 and his retirement in 1975.

There were four Seattle-based freighters for the BIA during that time— first, the *Boxer,* a 125-foot-long converted windjammer that ended its career as a banana barge in the Gulf of Mexico; then *North Star,* commandeered by the Navy in World War II for duty off Greenland and Iceland, later a fish packer in the sunny South Seas; *North Star II,* a small coastal freighter that served her final days in the Central Pacific before ramming a coral reef in Micronesia; and finally, *North Star III,* retired in 1984, never replaced by the federal government. Private shipping companies took over the run after the *North Star III* years.

"I didn't have much of a home life—grew up tough on the Seattle water-front," is how Moe described his childhood. He quit school after the eighth grade, fibbed about his age, and signed on the *Boxer* at age seventeen as a messboy.

"They made me a dishwasher," he said. "I've been trying to stay out of the galley ever since."

The next year, Moe joined the crew of the first *North Star* as an ordinary seaman—and soon after was bound for the Antarctic with Admiral Richard E. Byrd aboard *North Star.* There were two of those polar expeditions.

World War II brought suspension of the *North Star* operation. Cole went to work for the Army Transportation Corps on vessels sailing to Alaska. One of the wartime ships, named *North Coast,* was among the first to call at Adak Island in the Aleutians during the campaign to drive Japanese forces out of the islands.

By June 1945, with officer's papers earned through the Kildall Nautical School in Seattle, Cole was back aboard *North Star* as the second mate.

One day he decided to try shore work for a while so he could spend more time with his wife, Luella, and their sons, Bob and Jim. They moved to North Dakota (Luella's native state), where Moe found a job as a police officer in Fargo.

Moe Cole distributes candy from a stocking cap for Eskimo children in Wainwright village.

"That lasted about six months," he said. "I decided a cop's life wasn't for me. Too much sadness. Then I came back to Seattle and drove taxi for about a year."

In 1948, with prodding from his wife, Moe started over again on the original *North Star,* first as a junior third mate. By 1951 he was second mate on *North Star II,* by 1963 chief mate on *North Star III,* and in 1971 he was named master of *North Star III.*

"The sea is where I belong," he said.

Although he is remembered as the Arctic's beloved candy man, Cole also built a solid reputation as a wizard of ice conditions in the difficult waters of Alaska. Admiring crewmen said he could read the ice like a bushman follows game trails.

Moe Cole, a jovial bear of a man, began his candy distributions for Alaska kids in the 1930s. Back then he was buying the candy himself from wages of only sixty-four dollars a month.

"I was raised poor, so I knew how much candy meant to kids," he recalled. "We never had much candy at home. I hung around churches at Christmas time, figuring they would have candy."

In later years, Moe and Luella were able to obtain tons of donated candy. But a lot of their own money also went into the pot year after year.

"What the hell—you can't take it with you," the skipper said.

Also tucked into the *North Star III*'s crannies, along with the usual candy cargo, were Christmas presents for the children of Diomede village on Little Diomede Island, only two and a half miles across Bering Strait from Russian territory—dolls, nurse sets, model airplanes, toy trucks, etc.

The Diomede tradition began when Moe heard that Diomede kids didn't get much for Christmas. The next year one of his son's fraternity brothers raised money to help buy presents. Luella persuaded merchants around Seattle to donate toys and other gifts. And *North Star III*'s crew members added to the Diomede fund.

Wives of crew members joined Luella Cole to wrap the presents and address them individually to the children of Diomede. Moe had arranged to obtain the names through the village schoolteacher. There always was an extra carton of untagged toys, so no children would be left out by accident.

"You should see the kids cheer when we get to Diomede," Moe said. "That makes it all worthwhile."

THE HAPPINESS MAKER

✦ ✦ ✦

SEPTEMBER 1975. CAPTAIN MOE decided that it was time to retire.

"I wouldn't trade the life I've had with anyone," he told me during an interview in Seattle. "But it's time to call it quits."

Moe, then fifty-five, said he wanted to spend the rest of his years with his family and make up for some of the things he had missed during almost four decades of seafaring. Besides, his health was a concern. Asbestos from heavy insulation aboard the freighters had clogged his lungs.

A few days after our conversation, Moe went to a country fair in Monroe, near Seattle—the first fair he ever had attended. Then he took his grandson to a circus, the first circus he had seen since 1947. A few nights later he was home for the first birthday party with his family in about twenty-five years.

"I guess I missed a lot being away," he said. "But I'm going to miss those beautiful, wonderful kids up north."

News of Moe's retirement spread quickly through the North Country. I happened to be in Wainwright on another *Seattle Times* assignment when villagers cornered me.

"Are you sure Moe isn't coming back?" one youngster asked.

"No, he won't be back," I replied.

"I don't believe you—Moe always comes!" the boy said.

In December 1980, a call went out from Barrow: "We want Moe!"

It was to be a Christmas command performance.

A proclamation signed by Barrow's mayor, Nathaniel Olemaun, declared that December 19, 1980, was to be Captain Moe Appreciation Day. Students, teachers, parents—just about everyone in Barrow (population 3,500)—helped raise money for Moe's round-trip airfare between Seattle and Barrow. Moe has been away too long, they decided.

Moe's wife, Luella, took her husband shopping for a Santa suit and drove him to Seattle-Tacoma International Airport for the long flight to Barrow.

"He's so excited that he's getting to be impossible to live with," Luella said.

Moe, for once in his life, had trouble speaking when he was presented with a key to the city and then honored during a school assembly at Barrow High School.

"I'm scared," were his first words.

Never mind. Captain Moe always spoke a language of love with his kids in Eskimoland. No translations needed.

"All these years I've been away, and they're still thinking of me," he said. "Can you beat that?"

Moe reminisced about his candy deliveries. Sometimes, Moe said, he would announce his arrival with fireworks launched from a *North Star* landing barge.

"There were some big fireworks," he told his Barrow audience. "Some would go up in the sky, go boom, and come down with an American flag."

Moe remembered watching one fascinated youngster on the beach at Barrow.

"All the kid said was, 'Gee whiz!' every time I let go a rocket," he told the crowd. "I had about one hundred of those rockets that day and I must have gotten about one hundred 'Gee whizzes' for them.

"Golly, we had some great times."

✦ ✦ ✦

FEBRUARY 1989. CAPTAIN MOE was dying. His tired heart was giving out. Mabs and I visited him in a Seattle hospital.

"I have a request," he said with a mischievous smile. "Can you sneak me in a screwdriver [vodka and orange juice]? Put it in a Coke can and the nurses will be none the wiser. OK?"

Did I fill the order? Of course.

A few days later, on February 21, my friend, Captain Cecil W. (Moe) Cole, died at age sixty-eight. Luella said he had a smile on his face when he breathed his last.

There was a funeral at the Evergreen-Washelli Funeral Home in Seattle's north end. Standing room only. At the close of the service, an elderly Eskimo woman stepped forward in the chapel and embraced Moe's casket.

"Atata Moe," she whispered in her Eskimo dialect ("Grandfather Moe"). "Thank you."

Luella Cole followed in death six years later.

Village kids continued for years to search the northern horizons for Moe and his candy ship. But the Happiness Maker had made his final voyage.

CHAPTER 20

BEST FRIENDS

TEEKI

POINT HOPE—It was love at first sight.

I was walking through the churchyard of the little Eskimo village when I saw her—a snow-white husky puppy snuggled against her mother. They were huddled in a shallow crater melted into icy tundra by the mother's warm body.

It was a mild July day in the Alaskan Arctic, but the three-week-old puppy was shivering. I reached down, picked her up, and she burrowed into my jacket. The trembling ceased.

The Reverend Keith Lawton, Point Hope's Episcopal missionary, happened by just then and introduced himself. He looked at the puppy, half-hidden in my jacket, and smiled.

"She is one of ours," he said. "But I can tell that you love her. Now she is yours, if you wish."

I wished.

But how would I get her home to Seattle, more than 2,100 miles away? She wasn't even weaned.

"There's always a way," Lawton said, as if signing off a sermon.

"And she will need a name," he added.

The puppy peeked out of my jacket and yawned.

"I'll call her Teeki."

"Good name," the missionary said.

Teeki, short for Tikiraq, the Eskimo name for this ancient village on the shore of the Chukchi Sea.

It turned out that Teeki's parents, Mitzi and Lucky, were mainstays of Lawton's dog team for winter travels to villages in the Point Hope area. And it turned out that Teeki was the only survivor of her litter.

Now, if she were going on a long trip, Teeki had to learn to eat without her mother's help.

Jackie Lawton, the missionary's wife, suggested I try feeding the youngster with an eyedropper. That was good for a few swallows, but Teeki choked on canned milk each time I squeezed the rubber bulb of the eyedropper. I poured a puddle of milk into a saucer. Barely able to stand, Teeki tottered, fell, and tried to nurse the rim of the saucer.

An Eskimo woman showed me how to use a fingertip to dip milk into the puppy's mouth. Teeki licked the finger dry. Progress. Soon she was lapping milk from a bowl.

The next morning Teeki began the journey to her new home in Seattle. Air Force friends had offered to let us hitchhike as far as Anchorage on military aircraft. From Anchorage I called home.

"I'm bringing you a surprise," I told Mabs.

"What? Gold, ivory, furs?"

"It's a secret—see you tomorrow."

The next evening Teeki and I boarded a Pacific Northern Airlines jetliner for the last lap, Anchorage to Seattle. The dog was so tiny I couldn't bear to have her make the flight in the jet's luggage compartment. So I stowed her in the passenger cabin with me, hidden in a little cardboard box.

My squealing secret was literally out of the box soon after takeoff.

"That's a dog!" a stewardess screamed at me. "You can't have a dog up here."

Teeki whined for milk. I shouted back at the flight attendant: "What do you suggest? Should we open the door and throw her out?"

"I'm going to report you," she said.

This was one coldhearted woman. I had hoped that she would have a

Teeki, an Eskimo husky from Point Hope, meets our children in Seattle, in 1963. The kids (from left) are Virginia, Stanton Jr., and Kathryn. STANTON PATTY COLLECTION

look at my cuddly puppy, coo sweet things, and tell us to have a good flight. No way.

It was about five o'clock the next morning when Teeki and I entered the Patty home in Seattle and roused the family.

"So, this is the gold you were bringing me," Mabs said, nuzzling the puppy.

"She's beautiful."

Then our three children, Kay, Stan Jr., and Ginna, took turns holding Teeki and offering her treats. Teeki took command immediately, charming her way into the hearts of all. She let our older dog, Dino (for Denali), know that she intended to be boss. Dino, a laid-back mix of husky, chow, and a few other things, didn't seem to care.

But several days later our little Teeki became very ill. Distemper, was the diagnosis. It must have been distemper that had killed her littermates back in Point Hope.

We drove from veterinarian to veterinarian in Seattle, hoping that Teeki could be saved. Most of the doctors said there was no hope. But one, Tom Guilfoil, a vet who treated animals the way a fine pediatrician treats children, said he would try. It took almost three weeks of treatments, but Teeki recovered.

The airline let me off the hook with a scolding. Art Woodley, Pacific Northern's president, called me at the *Times* a few days after we reached Seattle.

"I heard you had a stowaway aboard one of our flights," Woodley said.

"It's true."

"Well, you are not to do it again," he said with a chuckle. "Oh, by the way, how is the dog?"

Teeki was with us for nine wonderful years. She even attended obedience school, and despite demerits for sitting lopsided during the drills, graduated with fair marks.

Most of all, Teeki enjoyed going places in the family car, with her rear-seat window rolled down as far as possible so she could poke her nose into the wind. We made many trips with cold wind and rain from that open window streaming over the backs of our necks.

"Will she bite?" strangers asked fearfully when we parked the car.

Teeki must have looked ferocious, like a white wolf, to persons unfamiliar with her sled-dog breed. But she was a loving pet that would wash anyone in range with her long, pink tongue. Children were her favorites.

Teeki also liked to sing. On cue, she would howl an arctic serenade whenever our children played the piano or sang high notes. At times, her pitch almost matched that of the music.

How about that? A husky with almost perfect pitch.

Dino, Teeki's henpecked companion, died in 1971, at age nine. And then, only eleven months later, Teeki became seriously ill. There had been permanent nerve damage from the distemper. Now her back legs were so weak she was unable to stand for more than a few moments. There was blood in her urine.

Monday, October 16, 1972, was a black day. Dr. Guilfoil said there was no hope for Teeki's recovery.

"Why don't you have a few minutes with her?" Guilfoil suggested.

Teeki's eyes begged to go home. She struggled to her feet and tried to push open the door to her pen. It was not to be. I nodded to Guilfoil, and he put our sweet snowball to sleep. I kissed Teeki one last time, slipped the collar from her neck, and hurried home.

It was a miserable afternoon. I was on deadline to write my weekly Alaska column for the *Seattle Times*. Teeki used to keep me company when I was writing in my little office in our basement. She would push my hands off the typewriter keys with her wet nose every few minutes to get attention. I didn't mind.

This time I had to write the column alone.

✦ ✦ ✦

RINA AND CZAR

THANK GOODNESS FOR Alaska friends.

Two weeks after Teeki's death, Mabs and I were invited to a party given by three couples with Alaska connections. It was a surprise party. The surprise was a four-month-old black-and-white husky from Nome.

"She needs a bath, and then she's all yours," said Bob Giersdorf, then an executive with Alaska Airlines.

Howard Farley, a musher friend in Nome, sent the dog as a gift after hearing about the death of our beloved Teeki. Farley, a founder of the Anchorage-to-Nome Iditarod Trail Sled Dog Race, always had a crop of would-be champions at his kennels.

"She's a daughter of Bozo, my lead dog," Farley said in a note that accompanied the puppy. "Her mother's name is Sheba." Alaska Airlines delivered the new puppy with flights from Nome and Anchorage to Seattle.

We named her Rina, short for Czarina—a nod to Alaska's Russian heritage. The name fit. Rina was the absolute ruler at our house.

Rina was our Christmas card for 1972. We posed her in a Christmas stocking. The photo made the *Seattle Times*.

"Merry Christmas from Alaska," was the caption.

There was another note from Howard Farley in Nome.

"I have a male dog for you, too. He's a beauty. You can pick him up when you are here in Nome for New Year's."

Yes, Nome for New Year's. It was a tradition for several adventurous couples. Nome in winter, on the coast of the frozen Bering Sea. Sled-dog mushing, ice fishing, and loafing. We would pack suitcases with winter gear and groceries for a New Year's Eve party at the Nugget Inn in Nome, and fly north from Seattle for the festivities.

The dog that Howard Farley had promised was penned in a little wooden doghouse with two of his sisters. His right ear had been torn in a scuffle with one of the girls. His eyes were as bright as amber jewels. His bushy tail wagged with excitement.

"He's ready to go home with you tomorrow," Howard said.

We decided to name him Czar.

Czar and Rina. A matched pair.

Czar was a gentle, loving combination of Siberian husky and malamute. Mabs still considers him her "all

Czar, a friendly malamute from Nome, helped my grandchildren learn to walk by allowing them to hold on to his shaggy back.

time" dog. Czar flew to Anchorage in an airline crate—this time in the plane's luggage compartment.

Ours was a happy home with Czar and Rina. Now there were grandchildren to help love the dogs from Alaska. The little ones learned to walk by holding to Czar's back. Czar, ever patient, seemed to know that was one of his jobs.

Czar also had a sweet tooth. Each afternoon he would purloin a gumdrop—never more than one—from a candy dish in our kitchen. We pretended not to notice.

Several months after our Nome visit, Rina and Czar presented us with a litter of five puppies. Howard Farley flew down to Seattle to select two for his team. The others went to live with friends.

Rina was a loner. She designated me as her best friend. Czar, a gregarious charmer, decided that Mabs needed his company.

I was in India, on assignment for the *Times* in October 1980, when Rina was diagnosed with incurable cancer. Mabs had the sad duty of telling me of Rina's death in a telephone call when I was on the way home. Rina was only eight years old.

Dear old Czar lived to be fourteen. We had a birthday party for Czar shortly before his death in March 1986. Friends sent cards and flowers. His big present was a cupcake topped with plenty of chocolate frosting.

A couple of years later, we carried the ashes of Rina and Czar home to Alaska. Our twelve-year-old granddaughter, Chrissy, was with us. She volunteered to pour the ashes into the Yukon River near the town of Eagle.

"Now they can go all the way home," Chrissy said.

✦ ✦ ✦

HEIDI AND LILI

GERMAN SHEPHERDS are great dogs, too.

After our three dogs from Alaska—Teeki, Rina, and Czar—we decided that it wasn't fair to impose city life on northern sled dogs. They require more space than a residential lot in Seattle. And they don't enjoy Seattle rain.

One Christmas, our eldest daughter, Kay Danielson, and her husband, Craig, presented us with a tail-wagging German shepherd. Her name was Heidi. Heidi was a loner, a one-family dog. She didn't much care for visitors, human or canine. In another setting, she might have been an ideal police dog.

Lili, a German shepherd, is remembered fondly by our family as an elegant lady.

"She belongs to you—or you belong to her," Mabs told me.

Heidi and I were inseparable. She lived for eleven years—first in Seattle, then in Vancouver, Washington, where we moved after I retired from the *Seattle Times.*

Heidi, ill with kidney failure, was put to sleep in September 1991.

Our house was quiet, too quiet, when I returned from the veterinary clinic with Heidi's leather collar.

"We're going to get another dog, aren't we?" Mabs asked.

"Maybe. We'll see."

Later that day, we found an advertisement for German shepherd puppies in the *Columbian,* Vancouver's daily newspaper. We drove to the address of the kennel and selected our next companion, a lively black-and-tan named Lili.

Lili was a pampered pet. When Mabs and I traveled, we boarded Lili at a country inn for dogs and cats. She usually was assigned a suite, with a doggy bedspread and a television set tuned to cartoons.

Lili didn't seem to have any bad habits. She never chewed on the furniture, never dug in the backyard. She didn't even bark when neighborhood dogs howled at police and fire sirens.

"She is an elegant lady," Mabs said.

Lili spent many days with me in my office when I started writing this book. She would nap on the carpet near my chair, and once in a while lift her head to see if it was time to quit work.

"Not yet, Lili. Then we'll play ball."

We lost Lili to cancer at age eleven. The veterinary clinic sent red carnations in her memory.

◆ ◆ ◆

SONIA

IT WASN'T LONG after Lili's death that we found a new best friend, named Sonia—a blend of our two favorite breeds, husky and German shepherd. Now we have it both ways.

Sonia looks like a full-blooded husky, with a bandit mask around her eyes. She is a high-energy challenge. Right now she is helping me to write the closing chapter of this book.

"Play ball?" her eyes ask when she gallops into my office with a yellow tennis ball in her mouth.

"You bet, Sonia—we 're almost at the end of the story."

Sonia and I get to know one another. This high-energy husky-shepherd puppy joined our family in 2002. MABS PATTY PHOTO

CHAPTER 21

A LUCKY KID

COAL CREEK—I have a lucky charm. It's a gold nugget as big as a birch leaf. It washed up in a gold pan more than sixty years ago when my father was prospecting a creek by the Yukon River.

"A real beauty," he said of the nugget.

Many years later, Dad gave the nugget to my wife, Mabs. She put it away with other keepsakes. But after my father's death in 1976, Mabs decided I should have it. She had the gold mounted on a slice of Alaska jade for me to wear on a string tie.

I never travel without it. And I never cease being grateful for a golden childhood in Alaska. No kid could have been luckier.

Fairbanks was home. But summers for me, from 1935 through 1941, were spent in mining camps on the Yukon River, just downstream from the town of Eagle.

Dad never said so, but I'm convinced that, just like stampeders on the trails to the Klondike, he had a serious case of gold fever. After his death, I found more than a dozen worthless stock certificates for various gold-mining ventures stuffed into his bank safe-deposit box. It was apparent that he had helped grubstake other miners with dreams of finding El Dorado.

Kathryn and Ernest Patty, my mother and father, in about 1955. STANTON PATTY
COLLECTION

I'm glad my father was that kind of dreamer. But it was strictly business the day he found the big gold nugget that I wear. He was on assignment to survey potential gold-mining operations one hundred miles or so northeast of Fairbanks.

If the ground turned out to be rich enough, then an American-Canadian syndicate would finance construction of a placer dredge or two to dig through the Yukon valleys. And the principals would hire Dad as their general manager.

The key financier was A. D. McRae, a wealthy businessman from Vancouver, British Columbia. Everyone called him General: he had been a major general with Canadian forces in World War I. The general always scared the dickens out of me when he visited the mining camps. He was a tall, arrow-straight man with a balding dome, a paunch, and a scowl that could frighten grizzlies.

But he couldn't intimidate my mother. She charmed him out of his spit-shined, high-top boots. He would replace the scowl with a gentle smile when she entered a room and looked his way.

In 1933, McRae wanted to get into the gold-mining industry and decided to examine some properties in Alaska. So, he traveled to the Alaska Agricultural College and School of Mines campus on the outskirts of Fairbanks to meet with my father, Ernest N. Patty, who then was the college's dean of mines.

"If I find a mine, I want you to operate it for me, Patty," McRae told Dad.

The next summer, with gold pan, packsack, and a .30-06 rifle, my father went hunting for the gold. Along the way he called on several longtime prospectors who had been working modest claims around Coal Creek and Woodchopper Creek since quitting the Klondike and other goldfields.

It wasn't easy to win the trust of these hermit miners. They were a secretive lot, living year-round in tiny log cabins scattered through the wilderness.

Maybe, I speculated, they had chosen this lonely life became of crimes or marriages gone bad. Maybe both, in some cases. But it's more likely that most of them drifted this direction simply because they craved solitude in a wild land where people didn't pry into a man's business.

"You are not to ask personal questions of these men," my father said. "They are entitled to their privacy."

Nobody knows more about these pioneer prospectors than Doug Beckstead, a National Park Service historian in Alaska. Beckstead is fascinated with the history of this mining district that in 1980 became part of the 2.5 million-acre Yukon-Charley Rivers National Preserve.

The prospectors and dredge crews who toiled here were a colorful lot, Beckstead says. He tells of Frank Bennett, who came into the country in 1889. Bennett had a tidy cabin on Mineral Creek, a little tributary of Woodchopper Creek.

"When you visited Frank, you took your shoes off and wore slipper-like shoepacs he kept by the door," Beckstead wrote in his mining history of Yukon-Charley.

Another old-timer was Martin Adamik, from Hungary, who learned to speak English by reading Shakespeare. He died here in the 1950s and is buried near his little cabin.

And there was Phil Berail, maybe the toughest man I ever met. Phil worked for my dad's mining company in summer as a hydraulic foreman, in winter as the camp watchman. He must have been impervious to pain. Beckstead says that on one occasion, Phil cut off a finger, wrapped his hand in a "dirty, old rag" to stem the blood flow, and went right back to work. Another time he broke an arm, fashioned a sling, and returned to the job.

There was a loner by the name of Frank Slaven, who operated a roadhouse down where Coal Creek meets the Yukon River. The National Park Service has preserved the old roadhouse where I spent several nights listening to rousing tales of the Yukon.

Frank talked to ravens—and the ravens seemed to be chattering back with news of the creeks.

I talk to ravens sometimes, too—and eagles and chickadees and dogs and wolves.

Some around here thought the Frank Slaven I knew might be Frank Slavin (different spelling), a heavyweight boxing champion from Australia. Not so, as far as I can determine. Beckstead agrees. Confusion continues because both Slaven of Coal Creek and Slavin, the pugilist, spent time in the Klondike.

I'd like to tell you one more story about the old-timers here—a story about Jack and Kate Welch. Both Beckstead and my father wanted them to be remembered.

The Welches ran the old roadhouse at Woodchopper from about 1929 to the mid-'30s. My father described Jack as a "big, rawboned man who had mastered the Yukon's rugged environment in a way few other men have done."

In winter, Welch carried the mail by dog team on the frozen Yukon River from Woodchopper to Eagle—a sixty-mile journey each way through bone-chilling blizzards. In spring, he would set a fish wheel in the river to catch salmon for himself and his dogs. Kate was the postmistress for Woodchopper.

During the annual breakup of river ice one spring, the Yukon went wild with crashing, swirling cakes of ice being tossed ashore like debris from a speeding bulldozer. A giant ice dam in neighboring Woodchopper Creek trapped the Welches in their cabin during a terrifying night.

"They never were the same after that," Dad said of the elderly couple.

"I'm losing my mind," Welch told his wife. "I'm better off dead. I'm going to shoot myself."

Kate pleaded with Jack, but he grabbed his rifle and went outdoors. A few minutes later, he was back. "I lost my nerve," he said.

An hour or so later, Welch went outdoors again. This time there was a rifle shot. Welch staggered into the cabin. He had shot himself in the side.

Kate helped him to bed, hid the rifle, and with the help of two canes hobbled through the night for two miles over a winter trail to get help. She managed to reach the cabin of George McGregor, their nearest neighbor. McGregor harnessed his dog team, lifted Kate into the sled, raced to the Welches' home, carried the wounded Welch to the sled, and mushed six miles to the Woodchopper mining camp. The winter watchman there sent a radio message to Fairbanks, and a few hours later both Jack and Kate were safely in a Fairbanks hospital.

The ordeal was too much for Kate. She died shortly after.

Jack refused to believe his wife was dead. He searched for her at the road-house and along the Yukon.

"She's hiding from me," he told workers at the gold camp.

Dad tried to tell Welch gently that Kate was gone. But Jack wouldn't listen.

Several years later, while compiling a book about his years in Alaska, my father wrote this ending to the love story of Jack and Kate Welch.

"Jack and his boat vanished. Weeks later, news started trickling back from small villages along the lower Yukon. People spoke of a mysterious white man sitting in a small boat just drifting down the river. Passing boats had hailed him, but he did not answer.

"The final word came from some Indians hunting on the Yukon delta. They had seen a white man floating out onto the Bering Sea. He was standing in the boat, shading his eyes against the late afternoon sun, looking out to sea."

✦ ✦ ✦

THE OLD ARGONAUTS—Frank Bennett, Martin Adamik, Frank Slaven, and the rest—pointed my father toward the gold here. Then Dad arranged for the McRae interests to option their claims and made sure the miners were paid fairly. Soon, huge dredges were rumbling down Coal Creek and neighboring Woodchopper Creek, harvesting Yukon gold.

Doug Beckstead has documented the story of the four-hundred-ton Coal Creek dredge, now in the care of the National Park Service.

It was built in San Francisco in 1935, dismantled, and packed for shipment to Alaska. The parts then were shipped to the old gold-rush town of Skagway in Southeastern Alaska, and there loaded aboard freight trains of the White Pass & Yukon Route bound for Whitehorse in Canada's Yukon

Territory. From Whitehorse, the dredge components were stacked aboard barges nudged by a Canadian sternwheeler downriver to the mouth of Coal Creek. Then the dredge, still in pieces, was hauled to the Coal Creek camp, about seven miles uphill from the Yukon River. There it was reassembled and began digging in the summer of 1936. A dredge for neighboring Woodchopper followed a similar route the following year.

I checked Beckstead's history book and found my name on the Woodchopper payroll. I must have been overpaid: I was having great fun, even if some of the grownups grumbled about "Patty's kid" getting in their way.

Getting to the mines each season was part of the adventure. One of my favorite memories was the day in 1935 when we headed for the Yukon in the gold company's new Dodge pickup. We had breakfast at the Model Cafe in downtown Fairbanks, then boarded the pickup that was parked across Second Avenue at the Nordale Hotel.

There were no such heroic calls as "Ho, for the Yukon River" as we three brothers crowded into the open bed of the truck. Dad sighted in on his brood and ordered: "No fighting back there! Do you understand?"

The Patty family prepares to depart Fairbanks for a Yukon River gold-mining camp in 1935. My mom and dad, Ernest and Kathryn, are standing by the Dodge pickup, while my brother Dale and I wait in the bed of the truck.
STANTON PATTY COLLECTION

Our journey took us more than 150 miles north on the all-gravel Steese Highway to the Yukon River at Circle City, Alaska —there, pickup truck and all, to board the sternwheeler *Yukon*. It was exciting to watch the red paddle-wheel spin and splash as we steamed upriver to Coal Creek.

When the *Yukon* reached Frank Slaven's roadhouse, we loaded into the maroon pickup and drove seven miles up a switchback road to the new Coal Creek camp. It was like a small community, with bunkhouses, a mess hall, a machine shop, and an office/commissary building stocked with goods ranging from Baby Ruth candy bars to Velvet pipe tobacco.

Our family had a small house on a ridge above the camp. No refrigerator was needed. My mother stored milk, eggs, and fresh vegetables in a pit under a trapdoor cut into the living-room floor. Cold air from permafrost below the house kept groceries chilled.

Drinking water was hauled from a spring down at the camp level—ice-cold water so sweet that none of today's boutique bottled waters could be better. But I hated carrying those heavy buckets home each time I climbed the trail.

By the time I was fourteen, almost fifteen, I begged to move into one of the bunkhouses with the mining crew.

"I'll think about it," Mom said.

Finally, she gave in, and I moved down the hill to quarters that later would remind me of Army barracks. My mother was less than thrilled when she learned that some of the miners were informing me about certain facts of life with racy stories. It was educational, to say the least.

Dad never said so, but I guessed that he figured that it was time for me to experience the rough-and-ready life. Three years later I would be leaving home to join the Army.

The first summers were all fun and little work. Most of my time was spent fishing for arctic grayling and hunting caribou and moose. We also tested our agility by walking and running along the pipelines that provided water power for the big hydraulic nozzles—like giant pressure washers—that stripped layers of dirt and vegetation to expose the gold-bearing gravels the dredges would devour.

That potential pay-streak was frozen gravel, hard as concrete. At first, the ground was thawed with "points" hammered into the earth. Points were heavy-gauge sections of inch-diameter pipe, like hollow spears, driven inch by inch with weights that fitted around the points.

The Coal Creek dredge digs for gold in the late 1930s. The dredge is preserved today as a feature of Yukon-Charley National Park. Stanton Patty collection

✦ ✦ ✦

It was something like hammer-and-anvil action in a blacksmith shop. Husky young men, many shirtless in the Yukon's warm summer sun, would lift the hammers, shaped something like barbells, and ram them downward to anvils locked onto the points. The point field rang with metal-on-metal thunderclaps as they toiled.

I never wanted that job.

At first the points used steam forced into them to thaw the frozen gravels, then water. Eventually, Dad worked out a system of solar thawing by peeling away the top layers and letting nature do the job.

Another of my wishes was granted by the summer of 1941. I wanted the job of piloting the D-2 Caterpillar tractor that towed a Keystone drill used to test the ground for the Coal Creek dredge. The drill worked like an old-fashioned butter churn, pounding its way into the ground. Then the drill crew would recover samples of the pulverized gravels and pan the slurry to estimate possible gold values. It was like mapping a money route for the dredge.

Early each morning, long before my shift began, I would wipe down the canary-yellow Cat and apply lubricants to its parts exactly as the operator's manual instructed. I fell in love with that D-2 Cat the way a high-school youngster pampers his hot-rod car.

Bottom-line time at the camps was what the miners called "clean-up." That's when they shut down a dredge, every two weeks or so, to collect the gold.

Our dredges worked this way: an endless chain of heavy-lipped, steel buckets dug the gravel and carried it into the innards of the dredge, to a perforated revolving screen where it was washed by high-pressure water jets. Most of the gravel passed through the holes in the screen to sluices where riffles caught the flakes of gold—and occasional nuggets. Rocks too big for the screen dropped onto a conveyor belt to be dumped from the stern of the dredge.

Beckstead says the Coal Creek dredge's clanging bucket line must have looked like "a chain of ice cream scoops, each capable of taking four cubic feet of gravel at a bite." Great description.

After the "clean-up," the Yukon alchemists went to work. They loaded the gold ore into a retort, a red-hot furnace, to separate the gold from impurities that banded with the gold in nature. End product: a crucible of molten gold ready to be poured into brick-shaped molds.

Buildings at the Coal Creek mining camp were mounted on skids so they could be moved by tractor as the gold dredge plowed the valley. My dad, Ernest Patty, who was general manager of the mining operation, stands at the lower right. STANTON PATTY COLLECTION

It was magic. I loved watching the process and hefting the heavy ingots of shiny gold. The gold bricks were shipped in mail sacks to the bullion depository at Fort Knox, Kentucky.

Later, as a GI at the close of World War II, I walked guard duty by the Fort Knox depository. We joked about how I helped protect the company treasure.

It's a long way from Coal Creek to Fort Knox. Funny how life takes you to unexpected places. But I'm glad I made that trip. Down in Kentucky, I found a wife for life—and now she wears my mother's bracelet of gold nuggets from Alaska.

✦ ✦ ✦

OCTOBER 25, 1947. The day I lost a brother.

By then, I was long gone from those lazy summers at Coal Creek and Woodchopper. I was newly married and taking journalism classes at the University of Washington in Seattle. My brother Ernest Jr., only twenty-seven years old, was the company pilot for the Coal Creek and Woodchopper operations. He also was superintendent of the two mines.

Ernie took off from Woodchopper for Fairbanks that day in his Grumman Widgeon. With him were three dredge employees. They never made it to Fairbanks. Apparently, Ernie was trying to turn back to Woodchopper because of sour weather when the plane, heavy with ice, crashed into a mountain. All four men were killed instantly.

Dad circled the wreckage with pilot Frank Pollack. In my father's book *North Country Challenge,* about his years in Alaska, he recalled a "feeling of peace" as he flew over the shattered Widgeon.

"It was almost as if Ernest Jr. were there in the cockpit with me, saying, 'Take it easy, Dad. Everything's all right.'

"Since that moment," Dad wrote, "I have never doubted the real answer to Job's question, 'If a man die, shall he live again?'"

Then Dad wrote about Yukon River trips the following summer with my mother, telling the readers a very personal story about the aftermath of Ernie's crash that he never had shared with me.

Twice that summer my mother and father loaded their gear into a little motorboat and traveled the two hundred miles downriver from Dawson City to Coal Creek. My mother, he said, would take a place in the bow with a sleeping bag and a pillow for a windbreak.

They had the Yukon to themselves. They watched caribou and moose swimming the river. One day they came abeam of a black bear paddling through a Yukon eddy, "close enough to see the fear in its eyes."

"We were alone with the river," Dad wrote, "seeing it as it had been when the early explorers found it, and all around us was the primeval wilderness, restful and healing."

I was cruising the same stretch of the Yukon a few seasons ago—from Dawson City to Eagle—aboard a little sightseeing vessel called *Yukon Queen*. And I was remembering the long-ago good times of my youth at Coal Creek and Woodchopper.

My brother Ernest Jr. poses in front of his Grumman Widgeon. Ernie and three others were killed in the crash of the plane in 1947. STANTON PATTY COLLECTION

Andy Bassich, the *Yukon Queen* skipper, shut down the engines and we drifted with the swirling current.

"Do you hear the quiet?" Andy asked.

The only sounds were the swishing of the river against the ship's hull and the trill of a songbird. Maybe it was a day like this on the river when my parents knew the healing power of the North Country. I'd like to think so.

Robert Service, the Yukon bard, said it best when he wrote about "the freshness, the freedom, the farness" of the North Country.

"O God! how I'm stuck on it all," he said.

Yukon Queen drifted awhile longer. I looked downriver, toward purple ramparts where bald eagles and peregrine falcons soar, daydreaming about family summers in the Yukon gold camps.

Journey's end.

I rubbed my good-luck nugget, and sucked a lung full of Alaskan air.

It was good to be home.

O God! How I'm stuck on it all.

EPILOGUE

BOB AND LORI GIERSDORF—fellow Alaskans, our dearest friends—died within a few weeks of each other as I was completing this collection of Alaska-Yukon yarns. I had hoped they would be around to read the book that for years they had been urging me to write. But it was not to be.

We four had traveled Alaska and the world together—following our dreams and getting into scrapes that would provide material enough for another opus. I'd call it *Two Guys with Very Understanding Wives.*

"Get on with your book," Bob said at our last meeting in the bar of a downtown Seattle hotel. We toasted our wives, Alaska, and our everlasting friendship.

But Bob was tired and lonely. He missed his Lori, who had passed on just a few days before.

When they buried Bob, his family placed Lori's ashes in his loving arms.

"Keep on dreaming," was the last thing Bob said to me.

It's a promise.

ABOUT THE AUTHOR

FAIRBANKS-BORN STANTON H. PATTY has been writing about Alaska and the Canadian Yukon for more than fifty years. Alaska was his beat when he was a reporter, and later assistant travel editor, with the *Seattle Times*. Other assignments for the *Times* ranged from covering the war in Vietnam in 1965 to reporting on international fisheries negotiations in Tokyo, Moscow, Geneva, Vancouver, B.C., and elsewhere. He took a leave of absence from the *Times* in 1968 to serve as the state of Alaska's first director of international fisheries. Patty retired from the *Times* in 1988, then became a busy free-lance travel writer/photographer. He and his wife, Mabs, reside in Vancouver, Washington, close to two of their eight grandchildren and their first great-grandchild. Patty has no plans to retire: "I'm having too much fun."

Mabs and I enjoy some quiet time in Denali National Park, in 2000. STANTON PATTY COLLECTION

INDEX